NOBODY'S PEOPLE

NOBODY'S PEOPLE

Hierarchy as Hope in a Society of Thieves

ANASTASIA PILIAVSKY

STANFORD UNIVERSITY PRESS
Stanford, California

STANFORD UNIVERSITY PRESS
Stanford, California

©2021 by the Board of Trustees of the Leland Stanford Junior University.
All rights reserved.

Printed in the United States of America on acid-free, archival-quality paper

Library of Congress Cataloging-in-Publication Data

Names: Piliavsky, Anastasia, 1981– author.

Title: Nobody's people : hierarchy as hope in a society of thieves / Anastasia Piliavsky.

Other titles: South Asia in motion.

Description: Stanford, California : Stanford University Press, 2020. | Series: South Asia in motion | Includes bibliographical references and index.

Identifiers: LCCN 2020025600 (print) | LCCN 2020025601 (ebook) | ISBN 9781503604643 (cloth) | ISBN 9781503614208 (paperback) | ISBN 9781503614215 (epub)

Subjects: LCSH: Kanjar (South Asian people)—India—Rajasthan—Social conditions. | Thieves—India—Rajasthan—Social conditions. | Social status—India—Rajasthan. | Rajasthan (India)—Rural conditions.

Classification: LCC DS432.K1923 P55 2020 (print) | LCC DS432.K1923 (ebook) | DDC 305.5/68809544—dc23

LC record available at https://lccn.loc.gov/2020025600

LC ebook record available at https://lccn.loc.gov/2020025601

Cover design: Angela Moody

Cover photo: A Kanjar-Bhat (left) from Gopalpura with two of his Gujar *jajmāns*. Photo by the author.

Typeset by Kevin Barrett Kane in 10.75/15 Brill

For my mother, Yelena

CONTENTS

ACKNOWLEDGMENTS

From start to finish, this book has taken a third of my life so far. A lot has happened since I moved to Mandawari in 2007, and I have accrued more debts than I can ever hope to repay. I have been the recipient of many people's generosity, which they lavished extravagantly, with no expectation of return.

Roeland De Wilde was there at the very beginning. Urging me to risk my reputation early and often, he introduced me to people who made it possible to do so with profit. Arvind and Shweta Singh, Brajesh Samarth and Kashika Singh, Shivdev Singh and Renu Rathore, Rajiv and Aparna Sahay, B. L. Sisodiya and his family, as well as the Sharmas, the Joshis, and the Billoos, took me into their homes and gave me invaluable comfort, encouragement, and practical help. Arvind Singh also helped with transcriptions and translations. The noble families of Begun, Bijaypur, and Bijoliya, and especially the late Rawat Sawai Hari Singh Begun and his son Ajay Raj Singh Begun, gave generously of their knowledge and hospitality. Mahendra Singh Mewar offered an oasis of intellectual company and much insight into the history of his kingdom. Baiji, Suresh, Indra, Bittu, and Tina Chattrapal gave me a second home in Begun and cared for me in times of illness, exhaustion, and melancholy, while sharing a wealth of knowledge and joy. Suresh also helped with the transcription and translation of numerous texts.

My greatest debt is to the many Kanjars who let me into their lives and trusted me with their secrets, on the condition that I write about *them*, with no anonymization. Most crucially, my work relied on the assistance of the Mandawari Karmawats, who took me into their homes and for many months shared their food and drink, merriment and debate. I hope they will treat any inaccuracies and misrepresentations with the generosity, patience, and good humor they displayed during my stay. Rameshwar Lal Kanjar, his wife Kalla, their sons Mahendra and Lakshman, and their daughter-in-law Shanta were my Kanjar hosts. As my guides into Kanjar society, friends, and intellectual company, they became my family in every way that gives weight to the word. My special gratitude also goes to Hari Ram Karmawat, Bholu Ram Jhanjhawat, and the late Kalu Ram Nat and their families, who provided tremendous help. Matthieu Chazal, Nakul Sierra, and Kaarthikeyan Kirubhakaran visited the village and shared much-needed fieldwork breaks.

My parents endured many months of anxious separation. Jonathan Norton weathered marriage to a student of anthropology, and all its requisite separations and intellectual angst, and I shall never forget (or forgive) his support. He risked his life in Rajasthan, and in Mandawari he will long be remembered for being as reckless as he was kind.

At early stages of writing, Nick Allen, Marcus Banks, Polly O'Hanlon, David Pratten, Bob Parkin, and Alice Taylor also read and commented generously on drafts, while Nick also humored many hours of my conversation. Jonathan Parry and Norbert Peabody read the manuscript closely and offered robust criticism. David Gellner read the entire manuscript, parts of it more than once, and kept my writing on schedule. David Watson in Cambridge drew the original maps, which were later adjusted by the team at Stanford. And it is the crack-of-dawn conversations with Alice Taylor, and the seminars we ran together, that carried me over the finish line.

Paul Dresch read draft after draft, both before and long after I submitted my thesis, enduring my intellectual and linguistic whimsies, and insisted that I stand by what I understood in the field, whatever the disciplinary and professional pressures. This book, and my intellectual life, whatever their worth, would not have been what they are without him. Long before that, David Eckel set my mind to India, whither Frank Korom shipped me off. What I have done there since was always in gratitude for their efforts.

At later stages, many people read drafts and engaged in fruitful conversation, most memorably Naor Ben-Yehoyada, Philippe Descola, Paul Dresch, John Dunn, Nicholas Evans, Taras Fedirko, Simon Goldhill, Sumit Guha, Paolo Heywood, Caroline Humphrey, Ward Keeler, Herbert Lewis, Geoffrey Lloyd, Alan Macfarlane, Maria Maglyovannaya, Dilip Menon, Lucia Michelutti, Lisa Mitchell, Parimal Patil, Vita Peacock, Pamela Price, Ramnarayan Rawat, Joel

Robbins, Arild Engelsen Ruud, Andrew Sanchez, Judith Scheele, Andrew Shryock, Marilyn Strathern, Akio Tanabe, Piers Vitebsky, and Kim Wagner.

Getting this book out into the world was hard work. It swims against powerful currents, and the force of their resistance often shook my nerve. Andrew Shryock's wisdom and wit kept me sane and helped me navigate the waters. Conversations with Joel Robbins gave me the intellectual courage I needed to complete the book, and Marilyn Strathern kept reminding me of the book's value. Finding intellectual camaraderie with Vita Peacock, Dilip Menon, and Ward Keeler has been a great joy. Maria Maglyovannaya's faith in me, and astute comments on drafts, always kept me buoyant. Throughout, Piers Vitebsky lent an understanding ear, a sharp editor's eye, and a shoulder to lean on. He read the manuscript more times and with more care than anyone else, possibly more than I myself, and I could not have completed the book without him by my side.

At Stanford I am grateful to Thomas Blom Hansen for taking a chance on this book, to Marcela Maxfield for seeing it through the rigors of the review process, to Susan Karani and Sunna Juhn for guiding it skillfully through production, and to Lys Weiss of Post Hoc Academic Publishing Services for taking excellent care of the text.

Work on the book was funded at various stages by a number of institutions. I first went to Mandawari with grants from the Departments of Anthropology and Religion at Boston University and from the Ada Draper Fund. My doctoral work was funded by the Rhodes Trust, the Wenner-Gren Foundation for Anthropological Research, and subsidiary grants from the Institute of Social and Cultural Anthropology and Wolfson College in Oxford. The book took its final shape in Cambridge, during fellowships I held at King's and Girton Colleges, the research projects funded by the European Research Council (grant no. 284080) and the British Social and Economic Council (grant no. ES/I036702/s1), and a Leverhulme Early Career Fellowship at the Cambridge Centre for Research in Arts, Social Sciences, and Humanities (CRASSH). Many ideas were born at King's, Girton, and CRASSH, whose communities offered the kind of intellectual nourishment that is unavailable in monodisciplinary settings. The final polish was funded by the "European Union's Horizon 2020 research and innovation program under grant agreement No. 853051" during an ERC-funded project on "India's Politics in its Vernaculars" at King's College London.

My most substantial personal and intellectual debt is to my husband, John Dunn, who has been reading drafts, lending moral support, and caring with me for Clara, whose debut made the book's completion that much more fun.

DRAMATIS PERSONAE

Old Shambhu	The oldest Kanjar in Mandawari, now dead, who was once the most fearsome local thief and who was semi-paralyzed after sustaining injuries in the 1991 pogrom
Ramesh	My Kanjar host and gang boss in Mandawari
Kalla	Ramesh's wife
Mahendra	Ramesh and Kalla's elder son
Lakshman	Ramesh and Kalla's younger son
Ram Sukh	Ramesh's well-to-do cross-cousin (from Kalla's clan)
Prem-ji	The Kanjar lawyer
Baiji	The matriarch of a royal drummer (Raj Damami) family
Suresh	Baiji's younger son
Indra	Suresh's wife
Rao Hari Singh	Hereditary Rajput chief of Begun
Maha	The Rao's elder son, who works as a tour guide in Udaipur
Ajay	The Rao's younger son, who now runs a hotel in the Begun citadel
Kalpesh	A young Kanjar bard
Devi Lal	An ancient Kanjar, once a famous thief
Mahendra Singh Mewar	The king of Mewar
Kailash-ji	A lawyer in Begun

NOTE ON TRANSLITERATION

I make use of Hindi, Rajasthani, Mewari, and Kanjari languages, which I used during my research, as well as some Sanskrit, Persian, and Urdu terms in current local use. All Indian terms, excluding personal and proper names, are italicized and follow the diacritical standard of Platts's *Dictionary of Classical Hindi and Urdu* (1886), with suffixes added (*lāthis, dharmic*) and "c" replaced with "ch" for readability. Where vocabularies overlap, I mark terms as belonging to the most broadly used language (a word that appears in Kanjari, Mewari, Rajasthani, and Hindi is marked as a Hindi term). Proper names are not italicized or marked with diacritics in the text. For Indian words that have passed into English, like chai, raja, or goonda, I use common Anglicized forms.

On 23 June 1991, in the last cool moments before sunrise, several thousand farmers encircled a hamlet, a *bastī* called Mandawari, in the North Indian state of Rajasthan. As the dawn swelled, its residents saw the outline of an armed mob, with the barrels of rifles etched against the crimson horizon. The mob formed a tight blockade that left no routes for escape. And so the residents grabbed what weapons they had to hand, shut their doors, and waited. An hour had passed by in silence when they heard the rumbling of tires on the stone path. Two police jeeps screeched to a halt, and out jumped a half-dozen officers. *We opened the doors*, remembered Old Shambhu, *and ran to them for help. We were terrified. Everyone ran, even the women.* The police inspector promised protection in return for the surrender of arms. *I told them*, said Old Shambhu, *the police are dogs. Don't trust them. They will cheat you.* And so they did. The officers rounded up every gun, cane, and pistol there was in the village, even slingshots that boys used for hunting rabbits and partridges, and threw them into the jeep. No more than a minute had passed since they drove away when Shambhu heard the blow of a whistle. This was the inspector's signal for attack.

The pogrom raged for several hours. The farmers bludgeoned children and men with clubs and mallets, jammed staffs up women's vaginas, set fire and blasted houses with dynamite. By noon, when news of the attack reached the district headquarters, five villagers had already died, several dozen were gravely wounded, and every house in the *bastī* had been razed to the ground. Help for survivors was slow in coming. For many, it came too late. Another five people died later in hospital, and Old Shambhu was left semi-paralyzed for the rest of his life.

News of "the incident" (*kāṇḍ*), as the attack came to be known, spread fast, and within a week India's then prime minister, Rajiv Gandhi, visited the *bastī* on his electoral tour of Rajasthan. A pageant of local dignitaries followed suit. Speeches were made in support of the "Dalits" (former "Untouchables"), and each victim's family received 100,000 rupees (approximately $1,500), enough to cremate and build cenotaphs for the dead. Local royals gave money out of pocket, a criminal case was filed in the high court, and twenty-one farmers were arrested on murder charges. But election time passed, the pogrom faded from memory, and life returned to normal. The farmers were released on bail, and in 2008, seventeen years later, at the time of my research, the case was still pending an appeal.

Nobody's People

The victims of the pogrom were a people called Kanjars from a caste of cattle rustlers and burglars in Rajasthan. Known locally as a "caste of thieves" (*chorõ kī jāt*),[1] Kanjars call themselves proudly robbers by hereditary family trade. Classified in British colonial law as a "criminal tribe" and treated accordingly, Kanjars themselves lay claim to an ancient robber pedigree. Most of them now cultivate fields, but burglary and cattle rustling remain their signature occupation. Such communities have long been important players in the political economy of South Asia. Employed as robber-retainers by landed chiefs, they worked as spies, escorts, watchmen, and hitmen who plundered the countryside to raise funds for and intimidate the rivals of patrons, whose armies they joined in times of rebellion and war. Today robbery—and robber castes like the Kanjar—are still deployed to settle disputes and redress grievances in the countryside. And so many Kanjars now make a living as robbers, watchmen, and go-betweens who mediate rivalries by intimidation and strategic theft.

Such robber castes have long been both feared and admired for the strength, courage, and wit it takes to rob. Occasionally, robber castes, like the South Indian Piramalai Kallars, did well for themselves, sometimes even becoming kings.[2] Many others, like Kanjars, however, ended up on the extreme social periphery. This is how, as Old Shambhu told me, this came to pass:

> *In the old days the Kanjars went together with rajas. Whatever rajas did, Kanjars did: hunting, raiding. But now they are nobody's people. Before they would go and steal from their masters' enemies. They went far. My father brought back goats from Neemach and gold and silver from Bhilwara. Once, he even brought a camel back from Gujarat. We had family everywhere. My*

mother's mother lives in Ahmedabad. There is a big Kanjar colony there, but they don't call themselves Kanjars. At that time, Kanjars had respect. They were the raja's people. No one would lay a finger on them. But now, see what happened. Where has the raja gone? He is in Delhi or hiding in his fort. Kanjars are nobody's people. So, what do they do? They will steal a few grams of silver, some poppy husk from the village next door. And then they give money to cops, so the cops don't file cases against them. But the cops just eat up the money. And then it's us, Kanjars, who get killed.

Ties of service that once bound Kanjars to local aristocrats, the Rajputs, unraveled during the Raj. British authorities, in their bid to disenfranchise the landed chiefs, labeled robber castes as "criminal tribes," or born delinquents, rounding them up into reformatory settlements.[3] By the time the British quit India, most landed chiefs could no longer afford robber castes (pp. 53–57, 136-38, 165). Most "criminal tribe" settlements were disbanded, and Kanjars found themselves on the loose: with no employment, no patrons, and an uneasy relationship with the police. If under Rajput tutelage Kanjars would steal far afield while protecting their patrons' dominions, the new police order had reversed all this. They began burgling locally, inside their jurisdiction, where they enjoyed some protection by the police, in exchange for a share of their spoils. What was once a relation of mutual protection with landed chiefs turned into mutual predation. Kanjars were now assaulting local landholders, who responded with increasingly frequent and vicious attacks (for more see chapter 3).[4]

What startled me when I spoke with the perpetrators of the pogrom was not the violence as such—few people would tolerate incessant burgling—or even that they admitted it openly, but their sense of entitlement to, and indeed pride in, the violence, and their justification of it. Several narrated their memories of the event with audible relish. One even brandished the cane he had used on the occasion, patting it menacingly on the palm of his hand with visible pride in his achievement. He did not understand why the pogrom should have attracted so much attention or why it should have drawn any official response. *They roam about like rats* [vo chūhe jaise ghūmate rahate], he spat, *going here and there. They take from one man, from another. You tell me: whose people are they? No*—he swiped the air sideways—*they have no lord* [mālik]. *They eat from everyone's hand* [har hāth se khāte]. *When it comes to*

Kanjars, you can be sure there is no truth, right, or justice [unke koī hak nahī hai]. *They are* bekār [*useless, dispensable*]. Lighting a cigarette, he thought to lighten the mood: *only people like you, English people* [foreigners], *sleep with them* [un ke sāth so jāte].

The Kanjars' constant assaults on their neighbors were intensely provocative. The adjacent village, whose residents led the pogrom, often suffered several thefts a week. A kid goat, a length of pipe, a bag of wheat; sometimes silver, gold, or the ever-so-precious poppy husk. Rumor had it that the last straw that set off the pogrom was a trail of poppy seeds spilt from a stolen sack that led to Old Shambhu's house. Theft may have been the pogrom's last-instance cause, but it was not its justification. The farmers felt *entitled* to murder Kanjars, not because Kanjars violated their property, but because farmers thought the Kanjars dispensable, mere vermin. The reason for this, as the farmer put it, was that Kanjars had no lord, no one to whom they belonged; they were nobody's people, strays, and, as such, had no intrinsic worth. In his own way, Old Shambhu's was the same story: the absence of masters as the reason for Kanjars' social desolation.

Kanjars were indeed the most marginal people—more so than sweepers and leather smiths, untouchable among untouchables[5]—not because they were ritually polluted, but because they were socially unattached. While sweepers (Bhangis) and leather smiths (Chamars) lived on the outskirts of towns and villages, Kanjars lived altogether outside, in separate settlements. This is precisely what first got me puzzling over the local calculus of social worth, which is to say hierarchy. If the lowest of the low were not the ritually most polluted, as I assumed previously, but the socially unattached, what did this say about the local logic of social value: about ideas by which people judged one another, gave and withheld respect, socially fell and rose?

Demotic Hopes

I first came to the Kanjar *bastī* in 2005, during the rains. I was brought there by a lawyer, a friend of a friend, whose family had been advocating Kanjar cases for generations and who had offered to introduce me to some of his clients there. Mandawari lies 6 kilometers as the crow flies west of Begun, a market town of about twenty thousand people (map 0.1). To reach the *bastī*, the lawyer drove the car along a smoothly paved road that ran through fields of wheat, poppy, and peanuts to the multicaste village of Mandawari, from which the Kanjar *bastī* takes its name. The asphalt ended here, and we continued on foot along a stony path across a stretch of land too parched to absorb rainwater that was now gushing fast over boulders, where the path once was. The advocate pointed to the remains of a police outpost (*chaukī*), a single broken wall jutting out amidst shrunken shrubbery. This was the settlement's outer edge (fig. 0.1).

The *chaukī* was erected right after the pogrom, ostensibly to protect the Kanjars, but in practice it was there to keep a watch over them. It was not long before the Kanjars smashed it to pieces. Here the path narrowed as it wound its way toward squat, low-roofed houses made of stacked brown slabs of stone. Further on stood a row of taller homes made of brick. This was the village center, from which we found ourselves separated by a pothole-turned-moat in the rains. It was also the end of the road for the lawyer and his patent-leather

FIGURE 0.1 The remains of a police outpost built outside the Mandawari Kanjar *bastī* following the pogrom. Photo by author.

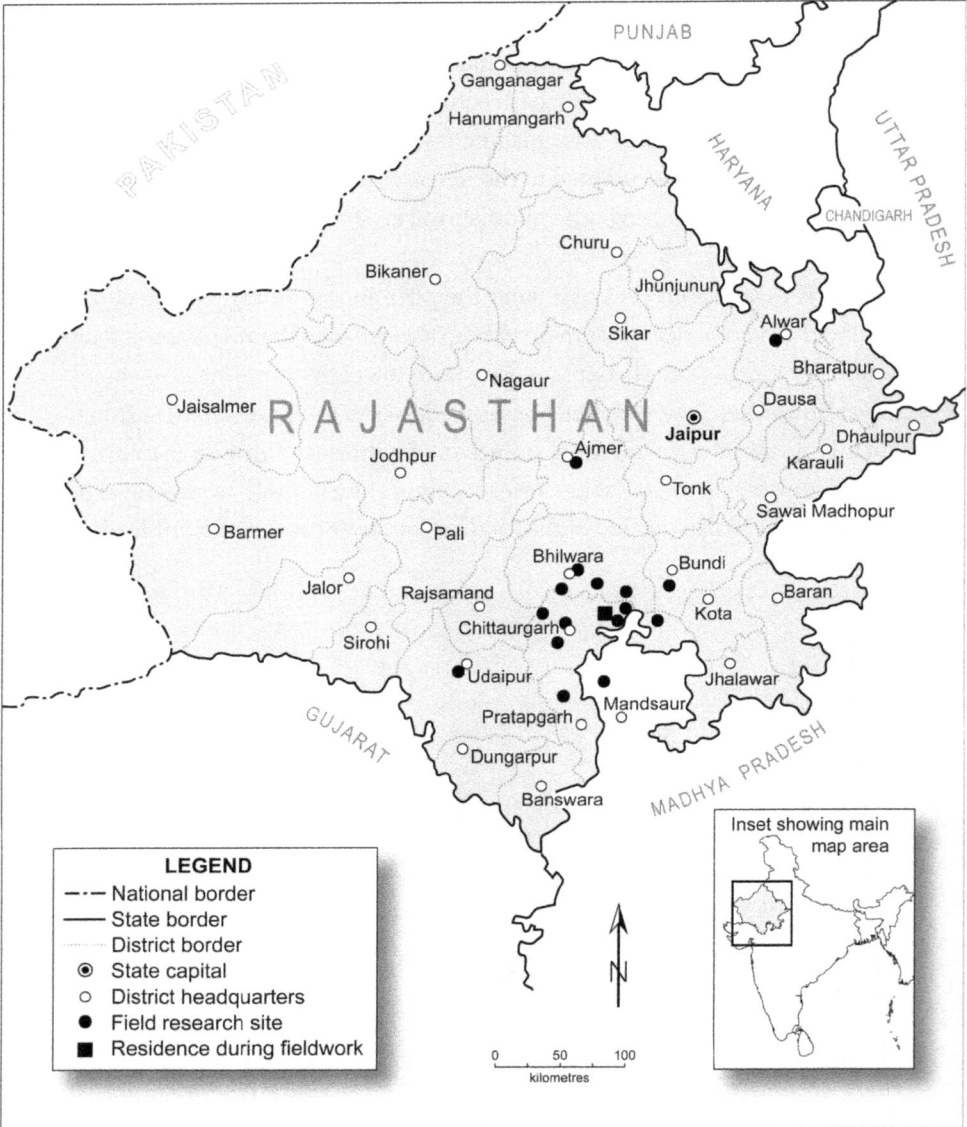

MAP 0.1 Field research sites. Mandawari, where I lived during research, is marked with a black square. Based on maps drawn by David Watson of the Department of Geography's Cartographic Unit, University of Cambridge.

shoes. I jumped in, knee deep, in my rubber slippers, to the cheers of a crowd now gathered to witness the scene. Two lunges and I was on a covered veranda, the very place that would later become my Kanjar home.[6]

There a stout, cheerful man in a shirt with rolled-up sleeves stepped forward, thrust a plastic chair in front of me, and said: *Speak, madam-ji!* This was Ramesh: a gang leader, an accomplished thief, an aspiring gardener, and one of the few men in the *bastī* who could speak and read Hindi.[7] While others stood by, bewildered, mulling over what the lawyer had brought—most had never seen a white "English" person, much less a white woman, before—Ramesh struck up a conversation. I told him that I wanted to write a book about Kanjar *culture and history*, and he replied: *Stay.* I agreed, and his wife Kalla poured me a glass of country liquor, or *madh*, warm from her still. I drank it "from above," as one does in the Indian countryside, without touching the glass with my lips, and again the crowd cheered. They had seen educated "madams" before (schoolteachers, nurses, activists), but they had never seen one drink *madh*. This sealed the deal, Ramesh told me later. *A drinking madam*, he laughed, *is always welcome with Kanjars.*

On my very first day in the *bastī*, Ramesh told me about the pogrom and about how things had changed since:

> *Back then, if we heard a car coming, the whole* bastī *would clear out and hide in the jungle. I lived in the jungle for weeks at a time. My son Lakshman carried food every day to the jungle. Kanjars were too frightened even to go to hospital. The babies were all born in the jungle. My appendicitis was cut out in the jungle, too. Five men held me down while the surgeon worked.*

Now Ramesh lived at home, where his wife could brew *madh* (an illegal business) in the open (fig. 0.2). His unplastered, one-story brick house had two rooms: one for storage and the other for his newlywed son. I moved into the storage room, which I shared with sacks of garlic and onion, while Ramesh and Kalla slept outside. The roughly stacked stairway led to the "upper floor" with but one half-built wall and no ceiling. Other houses around us were in a similar state of collapse; some had one floor, others two, most had one and a half. Some had no walls, others no doors or roofs, and many had stairs that led up to the open sky. To my eye, these were snapshots of penury and desolation. The *bastī* looked like a war zone.

FIGURE 0.2 Ramesh (right) hosting on his veranda. Photo by author.

What Ramesh saw around him, however, was progress (map o.2). When we clambered onto the roof of his house to smoke beedee cigarettes in the evenings, he would point to this or that neighbor's home improvements and explain that each was built from the proceeds of a successful burglary. Kanjars had fields, too, but most of them were small and harvests were much less reliable than night raids. Since the pogrom, when national attention turned to Mandawari, making local authorities more cautious about arresting "Dalits" (former untouchables), Ramesh had managed to build the stairway and a porch with a water tank underneath. He even bought a horse and planted an orchard behind his house, where he showed me rows of struggling saplings of guava and lemon trees. His house, he explained, was not half-collapsed, it was half-built—not a ruin, but an image of aspiration.

Police officers, NGO workers, government servants, and other well-meaning locals could not say enough about the Kanjars' immunity to "uplift." Kanjars, they said, refused to "improve" (*sudhāranā*): to abandon their drinking, meat

eating, and thieving habits; to send their children to school; to bathe; and to
work in the fields. As far as the well-wishers were concerned, for Kanjars a
bright future lay in their learning to be like good townsfolk, like themselves:
well washed and oiled, schooled and teetotal, with respectable jobs. NGO activists and retired policemen would organize meetings for the "improvement of
Kanjar society" (*kanjar samāj sudhāranā*), where they pressed this progressive
vision on their sparse, deathly bored audiences. Ramesh snubbed these meetings, as did most others in the *bastī*. Only children and young women would
go. This was a chance to dress up, go out, and spend a day chatting and drinking tea with friends. Ramesh found the NGO wallahs' vision of progress from
"filth and illiteracy" to a schooled and groomed life insulting. Pouring scorn
on the gospel of teetotal vegetarianism, he found the very idea that he should
emulate polite townsfolk abhorrent and absurd. *Who am I,* he would spit in
disgust, *a bloody shopkeeper* [baṇiyā] *that I should eat grass?* Nor did he wish

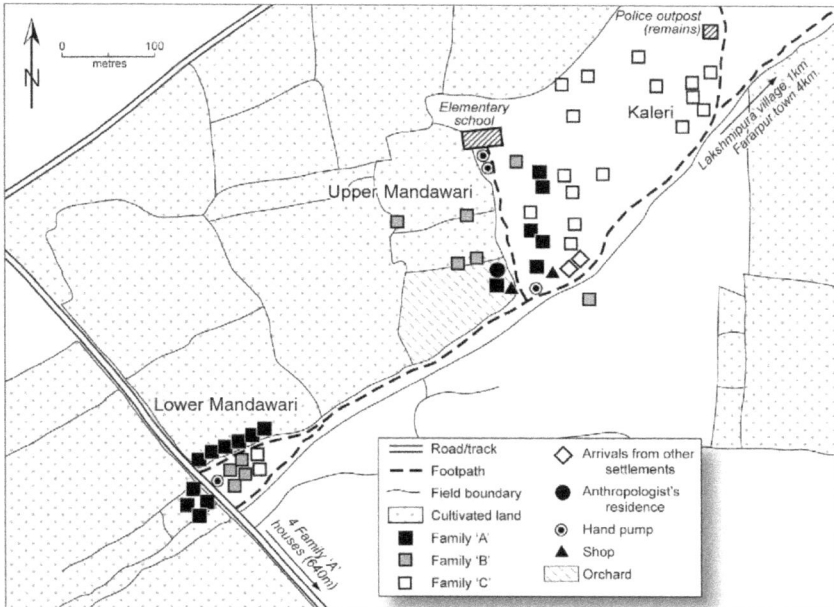

MAP 0.2   Map of Mandawari, where I lived during research. Based on maps drawn
by David Watson of the Department of Geography's Cartographic Unit, University
of Cambridge.

to send his sons to school: *School rots children's minds* [skūl bacchŏ kā dimāg bigarṭā], he would say, *just look: they sit around repeating* kā-gā-khā-ghā [*the ABCs*] *all day long and then they don't want to do any work. They get this idea that you can sit around doing nothing all day.*

His vision of a good life was different. At night, when there was current in the electrical wires that Kanjars tapped, he would watch gangster Bollywood flicks with his sons and neighbors, cheering on the big, bad, mustachioed mafia dons. These were his heroes. Some things that Ramesh yearned for appeared, at first glance, like the trappings of a provincial, middle-class dream—a pukka house and a motorcycle, a Hero Honda Super Splendor, perhaps even a small car—but what he wanted them *for* was decidedly un-middle-class. A tall house would do well as a watchtower for keeping an eye on the goings-on around the *basṭī*, a motorcycle would be handy for negotiating stony paths in the pitch dark of nocturnal raids, and a car would take him in style to the weekly court hearings. Ramesh wanted a boozy, buccaneering, freewheeling life with plenty of meat and liquor for dinner, not the schooled, comfortable life of the townsfolk, at which he sneered. He wanted a gloriously *Kanjar life*. And he wanted the recognition of a Kanjar: a magnificent thief, a gangster, a big man.

This book, which started out in an effort to understand why my Kanjar hosts found themselves on such an extreme social periphery and how they tried to improve their lot, grew into an attempt to grasp the basic terms in which local people, Kanjars and others, imagined dignified, respected lives: the values basic to their social ambitions, whatever these ambitions may in fact have been.

A large South Asianist literature now details a range of formally organized aspirational projects: social recognition and political protest movements, mass religious conversion, identity activism, the work of NGOs. These projects are shaped by the ideology of human, citizen, and democratic rights, by the language of state and international law, by middle-class "hegemonic aspirations" (Fernandes & Heller 2006). But most people I grew close to in Rajasthan were not members of social or political movements, nor had they read the Indian constitution or public law, and they were only distantly acquainted with the language of NGOs and IGOs. Their hopes were, as all hopes are, tightly woven into the local fabric of social value—into the complex of assumptions that they had grown up with; ideas that organized their relations with friends, neighbors, and family, with leaders and gods; ideas that shaped how they judged one another; ideas through which they gave or withheld respect; ideas that framed their hopes and their disappointments. It is within these ideas—these systems of value—that any attainment or "good," be it a rustled goat or a university degree, had to be embedded to have any meaning. These values found expression in a wide range of idioms, all of which were nonetheless grounded in some basic, widely shared principles. These were not explicit statements of ideological commitment or the "values" touted by politicians ("Hinduness," "Dalitness," "family values"), but tacit assumptions and intuitions by which people live. My Indian hosts and interlocutors had not traded their own visions of life for ones inscribed in the Indian constitution by its (anglophone) founding fathers, or for agendas of international organizations or NGOs, or for urban middle-class aspirations. They had not come to regard their own way of seeing and being in the world as an obstacle to living well. On the contrary, and unsurprisingly, it was their structure of hope.

And so, this book is about a lot of India. For, however vigorous the country's social and political movements, however intense the discussions among its progressive intellectuals, the vast majority of people who live in India are not social reformers, political activists, "progressives," or employees of NGOs. Despite the growth of Indian cities, most people—nearly 70 percent—still live in villages, where life still revolves around homes, fields, temples, families, market squares, and village platforms, not multiplex cinemas, Facebook accounts, or offices of NGOs. This life is one to which students of South Asian society have grown increasingly tone-deaf in recent decades, having tuned in to the India that is urban, mediated, activist, and middle-class.[8] This is especially true of writings on aspiration, over which, if one is to judge by the academic literature, rich people and professional activists hold a near complete monopoly.

In the single most cited essay on aspiration in South Asia, Arjun Appadurai writes that "the capacity to aspire" is "a specific cultural capacity" (2004: 67), to which the rich have privileged access: while "the relatively rich and powerful invariably have a more fully developed capacity to aspire," the poor have a "more brittle horizon of aspirations" (68–69). Their own culture offers the poor two options: "compliance [with] the norms and beliefs that support their own degradation," or their rejection "by violent protest or total apathy" (69). The poor do have "a sense of irony, which allows them to maintain some dignity in the worst conditions of oppression and inequality" (65), but "the posture of 'voice'" and "empowerment" can be gotten only from activists, who unlock the gates of hope with "keywords" of Euro-American development, such as "plans," "commitments," or "precedent setting" (77–78). His example is an internationally funded, Mumbai-based NGO, which actively "cultivates the capacity to aspire among its members" (73). Condescension is as loud here as it is among the do-gooders in Rajasthan, whom Ramesh so resents: the Mumbai NGO "cultivates voice among the poor," it "allows the poor to discuss and debate," and through it "these poor families were enabled to see" (83, 77). "Every effort should be made," concludes Appadurai, "to encourage exercises in local teaching and learning which increases the ability of poor people to navigate the cultural map in which aspirations are located and to cultivate an explicit understanding of the links between specific wants or goals" (83). For without such instructions, "the poor" remain, quite literally, hopeless.

Few put the point quite so bluntly as that. But the aspirations that poor nonactivists are allowed in academic analysis are often attenuated at best. Jonathan Anjaria, for example, writes that the aspirations of hawkers in Mumbai "are humble, and relate more to the realities of everyday experience on the street than to a larger transformative political agenda" (2012: 70). Veena Das (2007) insists that Indian poor people's hopes are smothered by "skepticism"; while Bhrigupati Singh altogether wonders: "Is aspiration necessarily 'good'?" (2015: 116). The question only makes sense if we see "aspiration" as a narrow set of class-specific desires, the technical sense often ascribed to the word in current South Asianist writings.[9] But surely it is no bad thing to hope for a better life, the ordinary-language sense of "aspire"? Surely, all humans can hope and strive for better lives. Ramesh was certainly skeptical (like most human beings, he had reservations and doubts, and he was not easily convinced), and he commanded a wicked sense of irony, but there was nothing humble or brittle about his hopes.

Depictions of hopeless, suffering subjects that are so common in current anthropology (Robbins 2013a) echo the discourse of misery promulgated by

NGOs, reflecting less the reality of people's lives than the growing reliance of anthropologists on professional activists, who often act as gatekeepers, especially in harsh research locations (poor villages, urban slums). The force field of NGOs is indeed difficult to escape.[10] NGO workers welcome the newly arrived anthropologist and offer contacts, research assistance, educated company, perhaps even a motorcycle, and lodgings that may be the only place around with running water and a mattress on the bed. Every time I have set out on research in a village or a slum, I encountered NGO hospitality and have had to work hard to escape its lure.

The norms I describe in this book are not confined to the conservative, old-fashioned backwaters of India, a common stereotype of Rajasthan. While Rajasthan's image as the bastion of feudal traditionalism is touted by the tourist industry, the state is much more unremarkable than that, historically, culturally, and politically. In fact, it is in many respects as typical as any region in India can be of the whole. It was never a stronghold of royal anticolonialism: the kings of Rajputana, as Rajasthan was called during the Raj, collaborated readily with the British (a glimpse of this history appears in chapter 3), with whom they never entered into armed conflict, unlike royals in other parts of India. Nor was it a bastion of anti-Independence: several of its kingdoms, including Mewar, were among the first to join the Indian union, with only one (Jodhpur) refusing to accede (again, typical of the country at large). Nor was Rajasthan ever a still pond of docile feudalism. As I discuss in chapter 3, it was the site of one of the biggest pre-Independence peasant uprisings, and today it has enough Dalit activism, NGOs, and women's and tribal assertion movements to dispel the image of conservative premodernity (e.g., Hardiman 1987; Unnithan-Kumar 1997; Weisgrau 1997; Moody 2015; B. Singh 2015). Unlike Jharkhand, Andhra Pradesh, Bengal, or Kerala, Rajasthan has never been ruled by a regional party. Notwithstanding the stereotype, it is difficult to find anything in Rajasthan's social and political history, or its current life, that makes it at all peculiar.

The idea of state-sponsored "social uplift" through reservations in education or state employment was foreign not only to Kanjars, but also to many other lower-caste, lower-class people. This was in part because in Rajasthan (as in many other Indian states) belonging to a Scheduled Caste has little practical value.[11] For Kanjars specifically, formal education and government employment were part of the outside world, which they rejected. While living with Kanjars, I bumped into the category of "reservations" (*āraksan*), to which Scheduled Castes are entitled, but once, when I met the only Kanjar in southern Rajasthan with a university degree.[12] Prem-ji had gone to school and then to university, where he was a star student, on government scholarships for Scheduled Castes. He then got a master's degree in law, moved to a nearby market town, and set up a small legal practice in the session court. Before I met him, I had thought that here was, finally, a case of drastic social mobility. But I was wrong. Prem-ji's one-floor, unplastered house was on the edge of a slum on the town's outer periphery. He had an education that most villagers, not only Kanjars, could only dream of, and he had a "middle-class job." But he was still a Kanjar, and the very neighbors who would advocate "Kanjar uplift" kept well away from him and his family. Worse still, he had also become a pariah among Kanjars, who saw his life as a betrayal. They turned him out, threatening him whenever he came to visit his natal village. Eventually, his father asked him to stop visiting him at all, as the neighbors would beat him up after each one of Prem-ji's visits. A mild-mannered, taciturn, and sharply intelligent man, Prem-ji was socially isolated, and miserable. He could not visit his father, and his wife was threatening him with divorce. He was also terrified for his two young daughters' futures. *How will they ever get married? Where will they live?* Reservations, education, and a respectable job had landed him in a social void. Without valued relations, state uplift was not only meaningless, it spelled social doom.

In Pursuit of Hierarchy

Talk of "social uplift," ubiquitous in India's activist and middle-class circles, is echoed in the social scientists' narrative of "social mobility," a progressive movement toward a set of presumptive aims that can be rendered statistically: more years of education, better hygiene, more gender equality, lower dowries, fewer child marriages.[13] Social scientists have long imagined mobility as a process of emulating one's superiors in an attempt to become their equals, or to gain an equal footing on the rungs of the "social ladder" (see Bourdieu 1984 [1979]: 125). In India's sociology, this idea was most famously formulated by M. N. Srinivas, who argued that lower castes pursued higher status by imitating the Brahmans' high Hindu (Sanskritic) lifestyle (their dietary and sartorial codes, marital and ritual practices, education, manners) in a process he called "Sanskritization" (1952a; 1956). The idea was that one could rise socially by imitating or becoming in significant respects *equivalent* to one's social superiors.

There is little evidence that anyone has ever actually managed to get themselves mistaken for Brahmans. The accumulation of attributes of the dominant in itself had little effect. And Srinivas himself knew as much, remarking that the adoption of Sanskritic practices was actually the *outcome* of social mobility rather than its cause, something that people did only once they had already attained higher status by other means (1956; 1959). And yet the trope of emulation, or the pursuit of equivalence, has persisted in studies of social mobility, whether these are now conducted in terms of caste, modernization, or class. It runs through studies of Adivasi (tribal) and Dalit (former untouchable) movements. These studies reject Srinivas's acceptance of hierarchy as a system that the undercastes did not reject as such, in favor of a full-fledged egalitarianism as the necessary foundation of claims to freedom, dignity, and respect. If Srinivas had the lower castes clambering up the caste ladder, the new generation of social scientists have them tearing it down in pursuit of universal equality.[14]

But Ramesh had no interest in equality. He did not want to be like anyone else, upper-caste or caste mate. His heroes, to the extent that he had them at all, were Bollywood baddies. Otherwise, he was violently opposed to being treated on an equal footing with anyone. He did not, for instance, want the police to treat him as they treat others. There was no talk of human or citizen rights; instead, he wanted *special* treatment: for officers to take fair cuts of his profit and leave him to burgle in peace. He wanted to be above others, not like them: to command respect and the recognition of a grander, more powerful man. He wanted to be a "boss," a "don," a "danger man" (some of the few words he knew in English), with a bigger gang, a larger house, more parties, more money for entertaining more guests. As he often said, *I want to have many men eating from my hand.*

His vision of a good life relied on social attachments, which were, as he saw it, fundamental to honor and respect (*ijjat*). Where Old Shambhu lamented that Kanjars were *nobody's people*, Ramesh turned this around and often

repeated proudly that Kanjars were *nobody's slaves* [kisī ke gulām nahī hai].
If slavery was dire compulsion, rightful service (*sevā*) to a patron was, on the
contrary, an intensely desirable state. Ramesh did not only wish to *be* a big man
with his own underlings. He also wanted to *have* big men (or big women) he
could attach himself to, people who would protect and provide for him. And
so he was always on the lookout for patrons: among landlords, policemen,
and rich townsfolk. He even tried to find one in me. This was a search not
only for employment, but also for lasting relations, bonds. Ramesh was not
alone in his preoccupation with patronage. Talk of patrons was everywhere.
People of all classes and castes spoke incessantly about patrons they had,
patrons they lost, and patrons whose favor they yet hoped to win; they spoke
of political and divine patrons, excellent and failed patrons, and they boasted
about their own clienteles. Caste, village, and family histories were punctuated with accounts of patronage. While local elites showed off the fields and
houses that their families had been granted by royal patrons, Kanjars blamed
their social misfortune on the dissipation of patronal bonds. Patronage was
the basic measure of status and respectability, of social worth. Its idealized
form framed expressions of social hope and its failures in actual life were the
source of bitter disappointment.

The language of patronage is hierarchical. It is ontologically and normatively nonequal, taking asymmetry to be the basis of social life, and also a
social good. Patronal relations, normatively imagined, even if infrequently
instantiated in their ideal form, encompass the hierarchical values of asymmetry, attachment, and care, which are central to local valuations of social life.
These hierarchical values, which earlier generations of anthropologists have
written so much about, have not faded from people's imaginations. They are,
on the contrary, everywhere: in the language and choreography of deference,
in talk of "big/small [*baṛe/chhoṭe*]" people, and a rich lexicon of honorifics,
master-servanthood (not slavery) and patron-clienthood. These norms clash
with the liberal values of equivalence and personal autonomy, but locally they
are seen not as an obstacle to social ambition, but on the contrary as its chief
cultural resource. Like other normative ideas, the hierarchical ideal is all too
often betrayed. Then people do complain bitterly about disparities of wealth
and power as inequities —they complain about inequality. They complain

about it, however, not as a corruption of egalitarian norm, but, on the contrary, as the collapse of hierarchy: of virtuous social asymmetry.

Hierarchical value is not all there is—no value is—and egalitarian ideas are and have long been in circulation. The language of rights, citizenship, and brotherhood is certainly part of the vernacular political lexicon (e.g., Béteille 1986; Hansen 2001: 72–73; Kohli 2001). And various horizontal communities organized, at least notionally, through one or another kind of equivalence (caste associations united by a shared political purpose, caste conglomerates united by occupational identity [such as Chamars or Yadavs], or Naxalite and Hindu nationalist organizations united by a common ideology) are now undoubtedly prominent features of the Indian political landscape.[15] However, demands for recognition, the staking of claims, and contests over state benefits are still most often framed in hierarchical—not egalitarian—terms, through appeals to communal *distinctiveness* (being most backward, downtrodden, poor, a Dalit) and *special entitlements* (including reservations as part of the positive *discrimination* policy), not equal human or citizen rights. This has been as true of the transgender (Hijra) protests as of various instances of Dalit claim-making and the Gujar-Meena clashes in Rajasthan. While Dalit intellectuals have been advocating egalitarianism since the early twentieth century (Rawat 2011), today when Scheduled Castes or Dalits make demands on the state, they tend to do so through hierarchical principles, through appeals to the state as a generous patron, a sort of big man writ large (e.g., Subrahmanian 2009; Witsoe 2013). This fact has not been lost on India's political thinkers, from Ambedkar to Pratap Bhanu Mehta, who have lamented the fact that the Indian masses, good though they are at staking claims, fail to do so through egalitarian principles (Mehta 2011).[16] Other commentators have allowed the possibility that India's vertical, patronal politics may contain redistributive, perhaps even democratizing, possibilities (Chatterjee 1998; 2004; Jaffrelot 2007; Breeding 2011), but they refuse to see this as the citizens' own normative preference, as anything other than deviation from the egalitarian order of state law. The urban poor, writes Partha Chatterjee, engage "strategically" in patronal politics because their "habitation or livelihood lies on the other side of legality" (2004: 56).

But for most of my interlocutors, the language of equality (and citizenship and rights) was a distant echo whose normative appeal was far from obvious, or about whose value they were deeply ambivalent.[17] To Ramesh, the very word "equality" (*barābarī* or *sammantā*) rang foreign. He said he had only heard it used when he visited Gujarat some time before, among shopkeepers who would say *barābar* ("even") when they struck a deal. My attempts to discuss notions of citizenship, or human or Dalit rights, usually met with confusion or uninterest, or I was simply told that *these things have no meaning* [is chījõ mẽ koi matalab nahĩ hai].[18] They were things politicians and NGO wallahs talked about on TV or at rallies, things that bureaucrats said when they were being purposefully abstruse. This was "government talk [*sarakārī bolī*]," official waffle that bore, as far as they were concerned, little relation to their lives.

It was only grudgingly that I realized the centrality of hierarchical values to my hosts' life, and it took me years to acknowledge that I could not write an honest ethnography unless I came to terms with hierarchy as *a value, a norm.* For neither descriptions of caste hierarchy as a system of purity and pollution nor the equation of hierarchy with inequality captured what hierarchical values meant for the people I lived with, or why they saw in hierarchy a social good. My realization was grudging not least because I was raised in the Soviet Union by devoutly egalitarian Marxists, not least because I had been warned by my seniors that, for a young South Asianist, hierarchical values were the kiss of death: the very word stank of the bad old days of frigid structuralism, essentialism, elitism, imperialism, generalization, patrimonialism, and Louis Dumont (India's chief theorist of hierarchy, now banished by scholars of South Asia as the poster child of all these sins). I have since experienced the prudence of my colleagues' warning: time and again my attempts to discuss the value that my hosts see in hierarchy have filled seminar rooms with disapproval thick enough to cut with a knife. What was I up to, politically and morally? Or, as one reviewer put it, the endeavor "reeks of imperial and Brahmanical paternalism," and is "ethically and politically unfit for print."

These experiences only convinced me of the need to think with—not against—hierarchical value. For moral anxiety creates intellectual blind spots, and the blind spot that now surrounds hierarchy in the study of India is as conspicuous as it is vast. No one disagrees that in India, however strong the winds of Euro-American modernity, whatever new values are now in circulation, however spirited its democracy, hierarchy remains an important social norm. And yet no theoretical discussion now surrounds hierarchy, no debate on what it actually means to the country's people, why it persists, what makes it legitimate or even desirable for all kinds of people, including those "down below." The only thing that one can acceptably do with hierarchy nowadays is denounce it as inequality.

But for my hosts, inequality and hierarchy stood poles apart. They were not pining for inequality, with which hierarchy is so often confused. Nor did they wish to have less, be thought of as less, or be treated as "low [*nīch*]" people, a derogatory state. Nor did they lust after being exploited by the powerful and the rich, and none of my friends in Rajasthan, including the Kanjars, took abuse lying down. The pages of this book are full of insubordination, contestation, and even violent retaliation against failed or abusive patrons. Yet their solutions to the problems of their lives were often not egalitarian. They did not see equality as the necessary condition of dignity, justice, and flourishing, of social respect and the freedom to better their lives. They took it as given that people were born and raised to different wealth, status, and power. But they did not see these disparities as a problem in principle. In themselves, disparities were neither good nor bad—what made them good or bad was the *use* they were put to in relations with others. The crucial consideration was whether those with more did more *for others*, whether they honored their privilege by assuming responsibility for those with less. The more wealth a patron had, the better: as wealthy as possible, but only on this condition. The alignment of social standing with social responsibility is, as I shall be showing throughout this book, the crux of hierarchical value.

If in egalitarian judgment, inequality is itself a social ill—an iniquity—and the cure lies in its eradication; in hierarchical judgment, inequality is a problem only when it does not entail obligation, and the solution lies in getting those with more to give and do more for others. Wealth, power, and status are worthless—or, more to the point, wrong—when unencumbered by responsibility. A rich or a powerful or an elevated person is magnificent if they are caring and generous, and despicable if cruel and miserly. When my friends complained about a wealthy landholder, it was not because they compared his fortunes to theirs and begrudged him his wealth, but because they accused him of failing to share with them, to look after them in a way incumbent on him as their superior. The problem, for them, was social rather than arithmetical, a failure of obligation rather than of equivalence. Justice did not lie in commensuration or the comparison of self to others, and the sense of injustice was less of envy than disappointment. The solution lay not in the zero-sum logic of distributive justice, but in the cultivation of *relational attitudes*—loyalty, generosity, care—attitudes that make up a good, mutually beholden life.

Anger at inequality, envy, and the corollary anxieties about the "evil eye [*najar*]" were of course everywhere. As were property disputes and accusations of hoarding. But the cleavages of envy, *najar*, and litigation fell precisely either where relations were not hierarchical in the first place, or where hierarchy fell apart. Rivalry is fierce among Kanjar families, which, as we shall see, are not arranged hierarchically, just as it was among the ambiguously ranked Patidars in Gujarat described by Pocock (1973) or the brotherhoods in northern Rajasthan described by Gupta (1997). It also arose when former or would-be patrons failed in their duties to their subordinates to such an extent as to remove all expectations and hope, which is to say, when the spirit of hierarchy collapsed. It was then that people would start to compare and complain that others had more (more money, more jobs, more political connections or whatnot); they started thinking commensuratively, through imagined equivalences, and the problem was diagnosed as inequality rather than irresponsibility, as a failure of equality instead of a failure of relations. Such egalitarian verdicts, however—complaints about inequality as the corruption of ideal equality—were not assertions of moral order, but, conversely, statements of moral mayhem: they signaled the collapse of responsible social life.

Hierarchy versus Inequality, or Thinking with and against Dumont

This book is about this inegalitarian normative ethos grounded in mutual obligations and care rather than in the justice of equivalence. It is about considerations of responsibility structured by difference rather than of commensuration. It is, in other words, about hierarchy.

The elision of "hierarchy" with "inequality," their treatment as synonyms, which is now so common in the social sciences, makes it impossible to discuss, or even perceive, inegalitarian norms. The word "hierarchy" is an imperfect gloss for these norms (see p. 16), but the contrast between hierarchy and in-equality creates a space where these norms can be thinkable in their own terms, or indeed at all. For talk of all social asymmetry as "inequality" mistreats hierarchical value for egalitarian vice, mistaking an ethic of responsibility for an irresponsible social outcome. But as Talcott Parsons remarked long ago (1970), pronouncements of "inequality" are of course value judgments—there can only be racial inequality among people who place value in color of skin or wealth inequality among people who value wealth. By taking "inequality" to be a self-evident fact rather than a value judgment, analysts mistake *ideas* about social positioning for a visible, palpable arrangement *of rank, an order of* "stratification," a social "pyramid." They mistake, in Saussure's terms, *langue* for *parole* (Saussure 2011 [1916]): the structuring principles of a system for their myriad enacted manifestations.[19]

Insofar as I am trying to understand the *langue*, or social life's orienting principles, which I see as the only way to make social life legible, I am with Dumont. I am not with Dumont the South Asianist, with whom I share neither the vision of Indian caste hierarchy, nor the contrast between "tradi-tional India" and the "modern West," nor yet the contrast between hierarchy and individualism, which I shall argue go together rather well. But I am with Dumont as a social theorist who insisted that to study social life is to study the values through which people appraise, judge, and act. I am also with him because he remains the anthropologist who mounted the most sustained conceptual critique of what he termed "Western ideology," or what we would nowadays call "liberalism," a critique he mounted over the course of his entire career in a quartet of books: *Homo Hierarchicus* (1966; 1980), *Homo Aequalis* (1977), *Essays on Individualism* (1986), and *German Ideology* (1991), only the first of which is usually familiar to scholars of South Asia, who in rejecting Dumont, and with him excising hierarchy from their ana-lytical vocabularies, have thrown the baby of his work on value out with the bathwater of his theory of caste. This is a pity, not least because hierarchy persists as an important feature of Indian social imaginations. Not least because the baby, rescued and raised by anthropologists of other parts of the world, has inspired some of the most exciting current anthropological work—on morality and religious conversion, nationalism and democracy, globalization and cultural change, gender and sexuality, labor relations and the politics of European academe.[20]

I am also with Dumont because I share in his three convictions about the nature of social life, and its analysis. First, that humans are essentially judgmental creatures. Our evaluative judgments are not additional to the way we perceive the world, but are intrinsic to our perceptions. We can perceive the act of pouring oil onto a flame as a libation only if we are aware of the ritual value of the event. If we perceive it through commercial value, the very same act will appear as the disposal of costly foodstuff. Just as we cannot understand utterances in a language without understanding the meaning of words and its grammar, we cannot understand how people act without understanding the values that motivate and constrain how they act.

His second conviction was that hierarchy is basic to all purposeful action. "Man does not only think, he acts," wrote Dumont, "he has not only ideas, but values" (1980: 20). And "wherever there is value, there is hierarchy" (1981: 21), which is to say that whenever we appraise and judge, we give precedence to one idea over another, creating a hierarchy of mental objects. Hierarchy is, in other words, basic to how people judge, decide, and, insofar as they act at all purposefully, act. And it can be a powerful engine of change. While in his writings on South Asia Dumont often painted normatively stable pictures, his broader comparative project was about historical change: namely, the rise of cultural liberalism in modern Euro-America (see especially Dumont 1976; on this see Ortner 1984; Duarte 2017: 652). Several anthropologists have thought with him about large-scale change as a consequence of shifts in structures of value.[21] In this book I am attempting something different: to think about the microdynamics of change as an outcome of actions motivated and shaped not by a shift in values, but by already existing, and sometimes intensely persistent, values that orient ways in which people try to change in their lives.

Dumont's third conviction is that social analysis must be dialectical, a dialogue between values espoused by the analyst and ones that she is attempting to understand. This is why Dumont opens his opus on India, *Homo Hierarchicus*, with a quote from Tocqueville on the United States; this is why he spent the last three decades of his life writing about Europe. The contrast between self and other, which Dumont often invoked, and for which he paid dearly as social scientists wrote off analysis of cultural differences as "othering," was heuristic, a way of making sense both of the object of one's analysis and of oneself. The sense of analysis as a dialogue with the people you are trying to understand, and the normative humility that it requires—not the sanctimonies of "reflexivity" or "positionality"—is central to Dumont's work.

The trouble with Dumont's comparison of India and the West is that while insisting on hierarchy as a *structure of value* fundamental to social life, he thought that hierarchy as a *structure of social relations* had been displaced in "the modern West" by egalo-individualist norms. But in Euro-America hierarchical relations—whether between parents and children, teachers and students, bosses and workers, or doctors and patients—*are* in fact deeply valued, even as we often deny the fact (Haynes & Hickel 2016; Angle 2017). The contrast, I suggest, is not between two fundamentally opposed systems of value. Rather, it is between the hierarchical norms that are as central to life in Euro-America as they are to life in India, on the one hand, and the egalitarian normative doctrine that now dominates metropolitan imagination, on the other, making it hard to recognize the presence and power of hierarchy in our own lives.[22] I hope that the readers of this book will glean something not only about rural Rajasthan, but also about their own lives, wherever these may be. Seeing this will demand of many readers the moral effort of suspending their egalitarian loyalties in the hope that, should they be willing to spare the effort, they will find its fruits intellectually rewarding, and fun.

NOBODY'S PEOPLE

Chapter 1

HIERARCHY AS HOPE

HIERARCHY IS INDIA'S BIGGEST SCANDAL. For the self-consciously modern, globe-trotting, rich, English-medium-educated citizens of the world's largest democracy, it is embarrassing to be members of the most famously hierarchical society on earth. The denizens of chic city enclaves will tell you that hierarchy is India's dead weight, the burden of backward, illiterate villagers, and they will flatly deny having any part in it, laughing, should you inquire about their caste, which they will say is the lore of yore. This denial of hierarchy is often visibly at odds with how the deniers themselves interact with servants, colleagues, and family, with the strikingly vertical choreography of their everyday lives. Those who enter the academic profession will join the chorus of critics who decry hierarchy as systemic oppression, writing about "degrading hierarchies" (Appadurai 2004: 65) that leave no room for the dignity of human will. The indignities of Indian "hierarchy"—caste-ism and clientelism; paternalism and dynastic politics; the plight of women, Dalits, and various other "subalterns"—fill the pages of novels and monographs, glossy magazines and academic journals alike. What appears even more objectionable than hierarchy itself is its patently widespread cultural endorsement, including among people "down below." In this archaic and seemingly motionless order of subjugation, how can anyone form their life's purposes? How can most of those whom it imprisons conceive of, let alone pursue, a good life? How can there be ambition and flourishing? Where is there room for hope?

And yet India throbs with ambition. Its village councils, voting booths, exam halls, and session courts brim with hopeful pursuits. From the advance of the burgeoning middle class to the political upsurge of lower castes and the rise of Narendra Modi from poverty to the prime minister's seat, India holds out one story after another of startling social ascent. Social ambition is not only headline fodder, but something that Indian citizens genuinely value a great deal, something that even a casual visitor will feel all around. One thing that has always struck me about people I have met in India, regardless of their position in life, is the voracious vigor of their ambitions. Nobody, not even the most downtrodden, slumps into a sullen acceptance of their fate. Nomads and farmers, civil servants and residents of city slums all talk incessantly about ways in which they intend to improve their lives, often through elaborate, sometimes improbable, schemes.

Meanwhile, hierarchy flourishes in every corner of Indian life: at home and at work, on the streets and in classrooms, in hospitals, government offices, political rallies, and courts of law. It shapes how people carry themselves, what they wear and eat, how they speak, whom they marry, where they work, and how they vote. In formal and familiar settings, at village hearths and in New Delhi drawing rooms, hierarchy is the ordinary grammar of life. It shapes relations between individuals as much as those within and among groups, relations within and beyond castes, not only between them.

So what is it like to live an ambitiously hierarchical life? This book gives an account of hierarchy as a source of active social imagination, as a normative idiom and a set of social principles through which the people I have known in India advance their lives. Taking readers on an ethnographic journey to the North Indian countryside, it shows how hierarchy frames, motivates, and enables my Indian hosts' and interlocutors' ambitions, and why they look to it as a vehicle of their hopeful pursuits. It shows how and why hierarchy operates as a cultural resource for the making and unmaking of persons, why people appeal to it to assert their worth and pursue better lives, how it assists their movement through the social ranks—and why its absence can lead to social obliteration.

To perceive dynamism in hierarchy asks most of this book's readers to reconsider what they think "hierarchy" is—a word that evokes images of oppressive stasis, what Dipankar Gupta called "a passive layering of crust upon crust" (2005: 21). The reader will need to reflect on the beliefs that make them averse to the idea: that personal autonomy is the root of all purposeful action, and that equality is this autonomy's necessary precondition. To the egalitarian, "emancipatory" (Ferguson 2013) mind, hierarchy appears as a structure of diminishing freedom and opportunity, as an intrinsically oppressive system, a social permafrost. While endowing superiors with power, resources, and privilege, it reduces the subordinates' capacity to judge, decide, and act, humiliating them and crushing their humanity.

The beliefs in autonomy and equality are foundational to how metropolitan thinkers now see the world; they are pivotal to their conceptions of dignity, justice, and flourishing, indeed to what it means to be human at all. In anthropology, however much its practitioners try to distance themselves from Euro-American sensibilities, these beliefs have shaped the choice of analytical concepts, the kinds of topic anthropologists prefer to study, the sorts of argument they tend to make, and the types of theory that they find most alluring. They have also made hierarchy into a pariah concept, blocking from view what ethnographic evidence puts plainly in sight: the fact that people the world over place positive value on hierarchy, not only in supposedly traditional hierarchical societies, but also in "modern, egalitarian" ones.[1]

Nobody's People is an effort to put hierarchy back in its place, as an intellectual resource vital not only for comprehending India, but also for undertaking the broader comparative study of social life. In showing why my friends in Rajasthan see value in hierarchy, I invite readers to reflect on what thinking with hierarchy—not against it—may reveal about their own lives. I shall further suggest that the logic of hierarchy is not only amenable to ambitious living, but forms the very essence of it, and that this is not only true in rural Rajasthan, where people openly celebrate hierarchy, but also among strident advocates of equality, wherever and whoever they may be. I suggest that hierarchy, rather than being a particular social form, is a fundamental aspect of any cultural environment where people see ambition and personal achievement as the necessary constituents of a good life. Challenging the hoary contrast between "holism" and "individualism," I suggest that the people I write about here are as individualist as they are hierarchical, and that being both implies no logical or moral conflict.

Whatever Happened to Our Favorite Quarrel?

In a lecture Dumont gave to the British Academy in 1980, he complained that he failed "to sell the profession the idea of hierarchy" (1981: 209). Even in 1980, at the height of hierarchy's career in social theory, when Dumont's *magnum opus*, the expanded English-language edition of *Homo Hierarchicus*, went into print, its earlier editions (1966; 1970) having already attracted a large global readership, the task of convincing social scientists that hierarchy may be a value, in analysis or even in ethnographic fact, was decidedly forlorn.[2]

There is much to disagree with in Dumont's work (see my prologue, and below in this chapter). But in summarily dismissing his work, anthropologists have not only rejected his theory of caste hierarchy, but have also abandoned all theoretical interest in hierarchy. If hierarchy was once South Asianists' favorite quarrel, which generated many exciting theoretical insights that the region's scholars were known for, today it has altogether vanished from their debates. While caste still animates theoretical discussions (for example, Gupta 2004; S. Guha 2016), hierarchy has lost all polemical purchase (but see Gupta's reflections 2000; 2004).

Let me be clear: this book is not about caste. For caste is not hierarchy, and hierarchy is not caste. As a general category of Indian collective life, "caste" is amorphous and has been invoked in all kinds of discussions, ranging from colonial social classification to village relations and democratic mobilization. The question of hierarchy, or normative inequality, is a different matter. It is a question of relational logic, which may or may not involve communities we call "castes." If an earlier generation of anthropologists assumed that caste and hierarchy were inexorably entwined—that caste was essentially hierarchical, and hierarchy in India was necessarily "caste hierarchy"—more recent work has pulled caste and hierarchy apart (for a recent overview, see Vaid 2014). Writings on the "substantialization" (Dumont 1980: chap. 11) of caste or its "ethnicization" (Barnett 1977: 158–59) have shown that castes are not necessarily arranged hierarchically (for an overview, see Manor 2010), while work on political patronage (Piliavsky 2014) and family life (Trawick 1990) has described hierarchical principles operating deep inside and far beyond castes. In this book, since I am interested in hierarchy rather than caste, I am engaging with works on caste only when they are relevant to the questions raised in my study—that is, with studies that address hierarchy in the analytical rather than the activist mode.

Discussions of caste now focus on identity politics, intercaste competition, or the leveling of caste by development and the democratic process.[3] It is as if the forces of democratic modernity took the pyramid of caste hierarchy apart, setting in motion a society that had been inert previously and by tradition. The eviction of hierarchy as anything other than inequality from regional anthropology has been so decisive that two new compendia of "key terms" in South Asian studies have no entries for the word (Jeffrey & Harriss 2014; Dharampal-Frick et al. 2015), and one of them, tellingly, redirects readers from "hierarchy" to an extensive entry on "inequality" (Dharampal-Frick et al. 2015). Wide-ranging recent collections of essays on hierarchy include pieces on Vietnam, Hawaii, Mongolia, and the Ottoman empire, but not one on India (Rio & Smedal 2009; Haynes & Hickel 2016). In 1988, when Gloria Goodwin Raheja published her seminal intervention in the debate on Indian hierarchy (of which more later), Valentine Daniel thought that "her findings [were] bound to have the effect of kicking that keystone that has prevented a long-overdue avalanche. The landscape will be different" (from the back cover). The landscape has certainly changed, but not as Daniel had hoped. No avalanche followed, not even a rumbling. It was more as if the snow simply melted away.

It is not that India's anthropologists have lost all interest in hierarchy. On the contrary: it comes up in their writings again and again. But their interest in it is no longer theoretical. So how and why did Indian social science, once the chief laboratory for hierarchical theory, lose all interest in it, despite such rich intellectual antecedents and hierarchy's patent persistence in Indian life? At fault was a mix of (1) the latter-day politics of regional studies; (2) anthropology's new normative commitments; and (3) Dumont's picture of caste hierarchy itself. I shall discuss each in turn.

The Politics of Regional Studies

In 1980, when the second edition of *Homo Hierarchicus* went into print, India's social sciences were undergoing a major transformation and becoming suffused with political advocacy. If an earlier generation of anthropologists focused on endogenous patterns of action and thought, on "ethnosociology" (analysis through local categories), cosmologies, systems of value, forms of personhood, and relational norms, by the 1980s analytical interests aligned increasingly with the project of Indian nation-making. As in the discourse of the republic's founding fathers, so in the social sciences, India's political modernity, development, anticolonialism, and the "uplift" of the lower classes became the prevailing concerns. The outlawing of caste hierarchy and untouchability, the abolition of royal titles and the inclusion of anti-discriminatory provisions in the Indian Constitution were each echoed in writings on the "ethnicization" of caste, the rise of nontitular political elites, and the plight, resistance, and upward mobility of the Dalits. Criticisms of colonialism saturated the social sciences, and development became such a major focus of research that much regional anthropology now more closely resembles development studies than sociology.[4]

The study of local conceptual and value schemes gave way to reflections on inequality (its origins, variety, and perpetuation, as well as resistance to it), which emerged as the chief focus of South Asianist scholarship (and social science at large). This new literature described how Indian citizens struggled for and achieved (or failed to achieve) social, political, and economic equality, the presumptively universal aspiration and the precondition of justice and participation in modernity. "As an ideal and a value," wrote André Béteille,

> equality has acquired a certain appeal in every part of the modern world . . .
> if there is an overall design in the [Indian] Constitution, that design may
> be said to put equality in the place of hierarchy and the individual in the
> place of caste. Hierarchical values are repudiated, and the commitment to
> equality is strongly asserted. (1986: 121, 123)[5]

If in 1986 Béteille was uncertain about what "the Constitution actually signifies for the different sections of Indian society" (1986: 123), today few social scientists doubt that every Indian covets its pledge. This egalo-normative standard now runs through Indianist writings as different as histories of labor and class, studies of gender and women's rights, peasant revolts, citizenship, neoliberalism, democracy and globalization, making odd bedfellows of Marxists and feminists, nationalists and postorientalists, democrats and advocates of human rights.

There were, of course, good reasons for regional scholars to start paying attention to formal politics, caste mobilization, Dalit movements, and the work of NGOs, in which the earlier generation of "village ethnographers" had little interest. But for all its promise and good intentions, this new social science brought with it an influx of advocacy that made it increasingly difficult to distinguish analysis of a phenomenon from its endorsement. Any account of values tends to be read as a commendation, and suspicion creeps in that the author may be promoting the unattractive aspects of lives in which these values are espoused: economic, political, and social abuses; misogyny; racism. From this point of view, the idea of hierarchy as a social good comes to stand for one or both of two cardinal academic sins: orientalism and elitism. And anyone entertaining it is complicit either in "othering" one's interlocutors or in endorsing their oppression. The Marxist version of this view is straightforwardly dogmatic: "Any social hierarchy . . . is perpetrated and perpetuated by elites and is struggled against, as circumstances permit, by those they oppress. This is true in India as everywhere else" (Berreman 1971: 17). Postorientalist objections differ more in style than substance. "Hierarchy," wrote Appadurai in a widely cited assault on Dumont, is "an elegy and a deeply Western trope for a whole way of thinking about India, in which it represents the extremes of the human capability to fetishize inequality" (1986: 745). And elsewhere:

> Hierarchy is one of an anthology of images in and through which anthropologists have frozen the contribution of specific cultures to our understanding of the human condition . . . [it is] a language of incarceration . . . that confines the natives of India. (Appadurai 1988: 36–37, 40)

Anthropology's Flatlands

Hierarchy disappeared not only from the study of India. From the 1960s, it began to vanish right across anthropology. The origins of its demise lay in postwar politics—the fall of the European empires and the rise of the American. As political advocacy came to dominate social sciences, inequality emerged as the principal problem of social analysis, as did the concomitant questions of power, domination, and resistance (see Lewis 1998 on this). As Joel Robbins observed,

> Various sorts of Marxism, feminism and cultural studies, along with the
> specific theories of Bourdieu, Bakhtin, Foucault, Gramsci, Hall, Saïd etc.,
> have ... motivated anthropologists to be on the lookout for [inequality] in
> all domains of social life. (1994: 23)

Hierarchical forms like rank, kingship, or chieftaincy and hierarchical norms
like holism, asymmetry, or (inter-)dependence, which earlier generations of
anthropologists have written so much about, fell by the wayside.

Meanwhile, the ideal of equality proceeded to entrench itself in the minds
of many as a kind of natural, protocultural fact (on this see Lewis 1998 and
Gregory 2014). If in the 1960s and 1970s neo-Marxists and feminists openly
championed equality as a universal norm, by the 1980s egalitarian norm was so
integral to the social scientists' unconscious that they no longer felt the need
to advocate it explicitly. As Peacock (2015) observed, from then on, analytical
egalitarianism gained ground in social theory less by open advocacy and more
by the proliferation of flat model metaphors: networks, rhizomes, fractals, ho-
lograms.[6] While two-dimensional imagery filled the pages of journals, lecture
halls resounded with calls to "flatten" the social: from Deleuze and Guattari's
summons to *A Thousand Plateaus* (1980) to Latour's instructions on "how to
keep the social flat" (2005: 165–72).

More fundamentally, the flattening of social theory was propelled by a
broader turn within social sciences away from structuralism and its associated intellectual practices. This turn assumed various forms, but its shared
premise was the rejection of what was *thinkable* in human life in favor of what
was *visible or experiential*—a turn, in other words, to empiricism. Since then,
this new social science has run the gamut of theoretical trends: from analyses
oriented by the idea of "practice" to transactions, actions, and various forms of
processualism, object-oriented ontology, discourses on immanence and embodiment, agency and materiality, infrastructure and so on. The many avatars
of this new empiricism, different as their sources and purposes may have been,
shared the basic conviction that what we can see, feel, or touch—our "direct
experience," not people's perceptions and judgments—is what constitutes
social life. In the end, as David Pocock wrote, "the realm of ideas was reduced
to epiphenomenal status" (1988: 204).[7]

One popular recent variant of this approach, Actor-Network Theory (ANT),
altogether expels values and categories, which Durkheim boldly termed "social

facts" (1895), from its analysis. Bruno Latour, the leading theorist of ANT and the most frequently cited contemporary "anthropologist" (he actually trained as a theologian) bids us abandon our interlocutors' motivations and purposes, their principles and norms, indeed, the very categories through which they think, in favor of what he calls "actual entities:" "actual interactions" and "actual occasions" that can be "directly observed."[8] If you "follow the actors themselves," writes Latour, and remain "as literalist, as positivist" as possible, you will "descend from the abstract ideas to the real and material local world" (2005: 170, 169). You will find yourself inside a perfectly "flat ontology," undifferentiated by considerations of worth. "By sticking obstinately to the notion of a flatland," he further asks, "are we not registering now in our account a view of the social rarely seen before?" (2005: 220).

Well, not entirely. Five decades earlier a very different social theorist, Fredrik Barth, advanced an analytical style, known as "transactionalism," with a striking affinity to Latour's. Barth argued that "society" was constituted not by what people thought, but by moment-to-moment interactions between self-advancing individuals (Barth 1959). It was a mistake, he argued, to think that people structured their lives through shared ideas, because in reality life consisted of actors, their actions, and the "social networks" they formed (Barth 1992).[9] At first blush, Barth and Latour bear little resemblance: the first was an old-fashioned postfunctionalist and the latter an avant-garde, post-postmodern *philosophe*. If Barth described autonomous, rational entrepreneurs, Latour writes about dehumanized "nodes" on "agentive grids." If Barth imbued his actors with sundry motives and attitudes, Latour strips his of either. And yet for both, the core analytical concept is the "network" of ontologically equivalent actors. Their networks have no hubs, centers, or leaders, no axes, and no unifying structuring principle apart from their actors' equivalence. Like connects to like—cellphones to cellphones, train stations to train stations, and individuals to individuals—by virtue of being the same.

The appeal of the network as a model of sociality lies in its promise of "greater naturalism," in its capacity to give access to life through what appears like direct, culturally unmediated experience, to get to life "as it really is" (Barth 1992). The model may make sense, at first glance, to a checkers player, but a chess player will protest that pieces play different "roles," that one cannot learn to play chess by noting simply that pawns and kings are both pieces or by recording the trajectory of their moves across the board. To learn the game is to learn the roles of the pieces and the rules of their engagement. How much more is this true of human life. We do not live among abstract "actors" or "agents," but among friends, colleagues, and relatives, among neighbors and fellow-citizens—*people* who play different roles in each other's lives and have different obligations toward one another. Social relations rest on shared (if not uncontested) understandings of these obligations and roles (Goffman 1956). Without such shared understandings we could not possibly tell Gilbert Ryle's winks apart from blinks (Geertz 1973) or understand what a handshake or a kiss or a promise is. What can possibly be learned from thinking of them all as "interactions"? We could not understand why we cuddle pet rats while killing pest rats. They may be the same species, but, for all intents and purposes, they are different animals. Or, as Edwin Ardener wrote, the careful recording of the movement of chairs, rate of footfall, tilt of the floor, or squeaks in linoleum in a room (the kind of "literalist" analysis that Latour advocates) tells us nothing about what is actually going on until we learn that this is a dinner party (1989: 48–50). Without meaning, social science loses its basic heuristic (and ethical) bearings. As John Dunn (1978) once put it, it is not only dim, but also rude to describe anyone's conduct without asking them what they themselves think they are doing.

Flat models, however, exert an irresistible charm over egalitarian audiences by casting egalitarian value as a freestanding fact: "life as it really is." Flat models are, of course, anything but value-neutral. Their affinity with egalitarian individualism—the cosmology of essentially equivalent, free-floating actors—allows the analysts' own, culturally specific normative intuitions to infiltrate social theory in the guise of impartial analysis. "The real and material local world" is in fact a mirror reflecting the analyst's own normative vision. This is precisely why Durkheim, his students, and later Dumont insisted that moral facts are the foundation of human reality: things can never be experienced directly, since every perception, even the most "basic," rests on a category in our minds (Durkheim & Mauss 1963 [1903]); and every category is also necessarily value-laden—we can hardly tell right from left without passing a value judgment (Hertz 1960). Any claim to the study of human life through "direct experience" is thus an analytical and moral trap, which presents the analyst's own cultural evaluative judgments as hard, universal facts. Pets and pests become mere "animals," and the intricate architecture of social roles is replaced by actors transacting (like business people) with identical others in pursuit of their own, equally knowable, and identical (profit-aimed) "interests." Instead of studies of other people, social scientists end up with a parade of self-portraits in fancy dress.

While the egalo-normative stance was consolidated in anthropology after structuralism, anthropologists have always been particularly susceptible to it. At its very inception, anthropology commanded attention both within and beyond academia as a vindication of the idea of primeval egalitarianism, of the movement of human society from "simple, egalitarian societies" to complex, hierarchical ones. In his pioneering study of the Iroquois League, Lewis Henry Morgan (1881), a founding father of American anthropology, described its members as being "equal in privileges and in personal rights" and thus as inhabiting a natural "communism in living," an idea that inspired Engels's theory of "primitive communism" (1902 [1884]). Franz Boas also famously insisted on "primal equality" (e.g., 1911). In the context of nineteenth-century evolutionism, the assertion that the "primitive" people whom anthropologists studied were not only fully modern, but also exemplary, was groundbreaking. But it also entrenched equality as anthropology's jurisdiction.[10]

As experts in "simple egalitarian societies"—tribal, hunter-gatherer, acephalous, band-level, segmentary, or various kinship societies—through much of the twentieth century, anthropologists purveyed many kinds of horizontal models of sociality.[11] Think of the classics read by every undergraduate student of anthropology: Malinowski's *Argonauts of the Western Pacific* (1922), Mauss's *Essay on the Gift* (2002[1925]), Evans-Pritchard's *The Nuer* (1940), Lévi-Strauss's *Elementary Structures of Kinship* (1969 [1949]), or Sahlins's "The Original Affluent Society" (1972). Models of *kula* reciprocity in the Trobriand Islands, much as segmentation in Nuerland, presuppose equivalence as the basic condition of sociality (even if in ethnographic fact, exchange in them is always asymmetrical, with persons and objects invariably ranked). In *African Political Systems* (1940), a founding text of political anthropology, Meyer Fortes and E. E. Evans-Pritchard are explicit enough about the egalitarian remit of (political) anthropology. If state societies are hierarchical, stateless societies—those meant for the anthropologist—have "no sharp divisions of rank, status, and wealth," they are "homogenous, egalitarian, and segmentary" (Fortes & Evans-Pritchard 1940: 5, 9). This program is especially striking (indeed self-contradictory), given how much Africanists have written about chiefs, hierarchy, and kings, including in *Political Systems* itself.[12]

Against this background, anthropologists have projected a long slideshow of "acephalous" and "egalitarian" models onto societies that were in fact neither acephalous nor egalitarian.[13] As anyone who has read Malinowski's and Evans-Pritchard's ethnographies knows, both Trobriand and Nuer societies had elaborate aristocratic orders and a sharp division between nobles and commoners as their chief structural feature (many Nuer were in fact Dinka clients or slaves; see Sneath 2018). In the tribal Middle East, known for classical theories of segmentation and reciprocity, social imagination turns out to be "strikingly hierarchical" (Shryock 1997: 227): "nothing corresponds to the image of a needle weaving to and fro . . . Wealth in goods or in children comes vertically, as it were, from God . . . not from horizontal transactions" (Dresch 1998: 114). "Even the so-called 'egalitarian' or 'acephalous' societies, including hunters such as the Inuit or Australian Aboriginals, are in structure and practice cosmic polities, ordered and governed by divinities, ancestors, species-masters. . . . There are kingly beings in heaven where there are no chiefs on earth" (Sahlins 2017: 24). Where equality *is* widely in evidence, mostly among small groups of hunters and gatherers, far from being a "proto-cultural condition" (Sather 2006: 73), it is usually an *achievement* (e.g., Clastres 1977; Cashdan 1980; Woodburn 1982; Robbins 1994), hard won from hierarchy as the basic condition of life (Boehm 2009).

And yet anthropologists continue to teach their students the old story of the Original Equal Society, culling horizontal models of reciprocal exchange, bonds of shared blood, unconscious structures, psychic unity or shared experience, collective consciousness or mentalities, or shared ownership from ethnographies of profoundly hierarchical life (on this, see Sahlins 1983: 32). Think of the social sciences' most basic concepts: "class," "community," "culture," "tribe." They all presuppose bonds through one or another equivalence. Think of "identity" ubiquitous in the social sciences: "the quality or condition of being the same in substance, composition, nature, properties, or in particular qualities under consideration; [to] absolute or essential sameness" (*OED ad loc.*). Or think of the spread of "ethnicity" in anglophone academic and popular vocabularies, which has flattened the language of collective life: tribes are now "ethnic minorities," and castes are "ethnic groups" (e.g., Eriksen 2002: 8–9; Chandra 2004).

This flattening is part of broader changes in anthropology, which has grown positively allergic to difference in recent decades (Sahlins 1999a).

Even the anthropology of "radical difference," "otherness," or "alterity," which has been challenging the creed of identity-based solidarity, has not shed presumptions of basic equivalence. Societies, which Viveiros de Castro has termed "disjunctive" (2001) and which are based on difference rather than identity, people are still equals, conjoined by an equality of difference rather than an equality of sameness, but by equality nonetheless. This logic is commensurative (for more on this, see below and in chapters 6 and 7). Each person is equally other, stranger or enemy, in what Harry Walker has aptly called "equality without equivalence" (2020).[14] It is all as in the old AT&T advertisement: "What makes us all the same is that we are all different" (Robbins 1994: 30). This view leaves no conceptual room for differences of degree, only for differences of kind, no room for differences between differences, no room for discursive differences that arise and fade within social intercourse, only ontological differences that are essential and fixed (for a critique, see Humphrey 2012).

This egalo-normative commitment in the social sciences has meant that huge energies have gone into thinking through inequality as a *problem*— its sources and consequences, and resistance to it—but virtually none into analysis of egalitarian value,[15] and nothing like the sustained critique of individualism.[16] In this, anthropologists have kept close company with Western philosophers, who tend to treat equality as "an obvious and generally accepted truth" (Dworkin 1977: 272; also Waldron 2002: 3; Iglesias 2001: 114–15).[17] If one expects philosophers to stick by the norms of their own societies, the failure of anthropologists to tackle the subject is more surprising. For who, if not anthropologists, is to question features of their own cultural folklore, like the idea of "basic equality"? But even Dumont, who understood better than most that equality is a value and egalitarianism an ideology, did not subject it to sustained historical analysis or critique. While offering an elaborate discussion of individualism in *Homo Hierarchicus*, Dumont made only cursory remarks on Rousseau's and Tocqueville's views of equality (Dumont 1980: 17), thinking egalitarianism a mere corollary of individualism, which "follows immediately from the conception of man as an individual" (1980: 11).[18] His *Homo Aequalis* (1977) promised a genealogy of Euro-American egalitarianism, but ended up as a treatise on individualism, a category that stretches over thirty-one lines in the index, from which "equality" and "egalitarianism" are altogether absent.[19] His later essays on "modern ideology" are again about individualism (1986).

The Pyramid in the Room

And yet, against this flat horizon, Dumont's hierarchical pyramid rises tall. His is by far the most cogent and enduring vision of inegalitarian moral ordering in social theory, with which anyone who wishes to think about hierarchy must still reckon.[20] His account runs, roughly, like this. Hierarchy is not social stratification, not an unequal ordering of society, but a structure of values. Every culture is oriented toward, or in Dumont's language "encompassed" by, a paramount value, in relation to which people make evaluative judgments and reckon social worth. In every culture, hierarchy is "the *principle by which the elements of a whole are ranked in relation to the whole*" (Dumont 1980: 66, emphasis in original). This is to say that people's different value judgments are always ultimately oriented toward something they value most, a value that encompasses their cultural order, making it an ideologically coherent "whole." In cultures where people most value the individual—the post-Christian, Western cultures—people orient their lives toward individual happiness; and where they most cherish "society taken as a whole" (Dumont 1980: 232), they forsake personal ambitions for "the global order" (9). On the level of value, wrote Dumont, all cultures are arranged hierarchically because evaluative judgment, which is at the center of "culture," is a process of ranking things. And yet only what he called "holist" cultures reproduce the hierarchical structure of value in social form. For this, India offers the perfect illustration. Here the worth of every group and individual is determined in relation to the ideological whole by the degree of ritual purity that each is thought to possess. Social worth can be found "in the conformity of each element to the role assigned to it in the whole of Being as such" (Dumont 1980: 334). The Brahman-priests who handle the purest (divine) things, and thus embody the value of purity, are at the top, represent the whole, and so "encompass" the rest of the social order; people who deal with the pollution of organic life (barbers, midwives, or butchers), are, conversely, at the bottom.

There are many chinks, large and small, in Dumont's edifice, and they have already been fingered by a large army of critics.[21] But whatever his theory's nuances and infelicities, two central and closely related ideas give it a clear overall shape. The first is the idea of a *social whole*, and the second is Dumont's vision of the *nature and location of value*. Both are heirs to a time-honored tradition in Europe. The specter of a social totality has long haunted Western social theory: wholes imagined as self-sustaining organisms or systems of complementary parts, wholes bound by common identity, wholes that are ideological, structural, or organizational have been the building blocks of both Western social theory (see S. James 1984) and Euro-American common sense.[22] Like the other wholes before his, Dumont's is a stable, self-organized, and self-sustaining unity. But it has one distinctive feature: it is shaped by a single transcendent idea, a point that Dumont illustrates with the story of Adam and Eve:

> Adam—or "man," in our language—is two things in one: the representative of the species mankind and the prototype of the male individuals of this species . . . You may well declare the two sexes equal, but the more you manage to make them equal, the more you will destroy the unity between them (in the couple or the family), because *the principle of this unity is outside them.* (1980: 240, emphasis in original)[23]

This is the crux of Dumont's analysis. The source of order is singular, transcendent, absolute, and eternal. People are located in the world through the degree to which they possess the attributes of this source, of this paramount value, be it purity, wealth, nobility, or whatever else. What Dumont meant by "value" were the treasured attributes that people (collectively or individually) can possess, and which I shall call *possessive values*.

While crafting hierarchy out of Indian material, Dumont used an (unacknowledged) old European blueprint. His immediate inspiration came from Hegel, but the idea goes back to medieval theology and further still to the antique origins of Christianity. Its most enduring formulation was the concept of the Great Chain of Being (Lovejoy 1936), an idea first articulated in ancient Greece and later adopted by medieval thinkers.[24] Every one (and every thing) in the chain, from rocks and pets to kings and archangels, was arranged along a ladder of rank that reached up to its ultimate source in God. Every creature, substance, and entity was ranked along this single scale of value, depending on how close each was to God and how much of His defining attribute (Spirit) each possessed. Kings had more Spirit than peasants, gold more than lead, cats more than slugs, and so on.

The idea of a unitary *scala naturae* was first developed by Aristotle, who ranked all living creatures by the degree of vitality they possessed; for Christian thinkers God replaced Aristotle's vitality as they refashioned this value ladder into one whose every rung "represented a divine institution, an element of the organism of Creation emanating from the will of God ... the value assigned to each order would depend not on its utility, but on its sanctity—that is to say, its proximity to the highest place" (Huizinga 1955 [1919]: 57–58). The idea was institutionalized in the Christian church and later reverberated through the writings of Europe's godly thinkers from Aquinas, Dante, and Ficino to Leibniz, Hegel, and Husserl.[25] Later still, it was entertained by Rousseau, Tocqueville, and Durkheim before Dumont.[26]

The word "hierarchy," which means literally "divine or sacred rule," was part of this theology, which depicted the universe as a stable edifice graded by proximity to God.[27] This perfect, eternal positional order has been depicted as a pyramid ever since, from Didacus Valades's sixteenth-century drawing of the Great Chain of Being to the American dollar bill, with its masonic pyramid and the luminous eye of God as the hovering copestone. Dumont would no doubt take issue with this characterization, lest hierarchy as an order of value be mistaken for a chain of command, a structure of power or inequality, or social stratification, from which he was at pains to distinguish it.[28] And yet the pyramid captures all the rudiments of Dumont's theory of hierarchy: the dual principle of ranking and encompassment (on this, see Graeber 1997), the monism, and the top-down order of possessive value. This hierarchy is certainly a religious vision, as Dumont insisted, but is it an Indian one? Where are the pluralism, the pragmatism, the cacophonic vitality of Indian life? Where are the 33 million gods competing for their devotees' loyalties? While writing at length about the Christian origins of individualism (1986; 1980; 1994), Dumont himself left behind some hefty artifacts of Christian faith: a church-like monolith that bears little resemblance to most of what we know about life in India, or indeed anywhere else.[29]

Dumont's was a *theological hierarchy*, a classificatory map of an all-encompassing universe, a "cosmology" of the sort that has long haunted the post-Christian social sciences. But the idea of such a static totality is incompatible with much of what we know about hierarchical societies, whether in medieval England or in contemporary Rajasthan. Far from being millponds of docile harmony, hierarchical societies have always effervesced with conflict and discontent. The hierarchical polities of medieval Europe were certainly no less tumultuous than the democracies of today, if anything more so. For the *demotic hierarchies*, or ideas about norms of relating, have little to do with the visions of harmony that theologians (whether Brahman or Catholic) ascribe to ranked orders, pinning the flutter of butterflies to the cork boards of their cosmologies.

It is little surprise, then, that while anthropologists of Christianity continue to invest in Dumont (e.g., Robbins 2004; Mosko 2010; Haynes 2017b), South Asianists have sold off their shares in him. Much more profligate was their disinvestment from hierarchy as an object and category of analysis, their refusal to think about it, not only with Dumont, but at all. Not least because hierarchical value remains an important aspect of Indian life. Not least because the abandonment of the discussion has meant that Dumont's model of Indian society, ranked by degrees of ritual purity, has quietly persisted in academic and popular accounts alike. For, despite its protracted disavowal by India's historians and anthropologists, the purity-pollution value complex still implicitly dominates accounts of "traditional" Indian hierarchy. It is still the go-to model in introductory courses and explanations offered to layfolk, when they ask what caste is (a point made by Jodhka [2012: 12]). It is still the model that the most recent synoptic theorization of caste sets out to disprove (S. Guha 2016).

While a large army of critics denounced Dumont's theory on empirical grounds, *conceptually* it has remained remarkably intact. Critics have shown that not everybody in India sees Brahmans as the highest caste; that alternative scales of value place chiefs or rich merchants on top; that values other than purity have been at work (courage, power, wealth, urbanity); and that hierarchy has its coercive side.[30] They have also shown that hierarchical thinking, of the kind Dumont described, holds no monopoly over Indian moral imaginations, which have ample room for individualist and egalitarian values, too. And yet, even Dumont's most serious conceptual opponents, such as McKim Marriott or the "neo-Hocartians" (on whom more shortly), still share his rudimentary analytical structure: a social whole encompassed by a preeminent caste (whether Brahman, Kshatriya, or any other "dominant caste," or combination of these), which embodies a paramount, possessive value—a value attributed to and possessed by people and entities (purity, power, auspiciousness, or any combination of these and others).[31]

There are also materialist or (broadly) Marxist readings of hierarchy, but these pose no analytical challenge to Dumont, as they see value as a closed question, one that is not and cannot be opened, for it would challenge the basic premises of their analysis.[32] The materialist theory of caste works on the egalitarian premise that disparities of resources and power are the basic causes of social injustice. A magisterial contribution to this tradition of thinking has been made by Sumit Guha (2016) in his account of caste across the centuries. Showing definitively that ritual purity is but one idiom of status on the Subcontinent, Guha argues that the hierarchy of castes has always been grounded in disparities of wealth and power. Any "cultural values" (Brahmanical or otherwise) glossed over the social "reality" (2016: 109) of land ownership and the exploitation of labor, or served as symbolic resources deployed strategically (à la Bourdieu 1984 [1979]) in pursuit of power and wealth, the protocultural, universal ends of life. Historically, various corporate groups asserted power over clusters of villages, from which they collected taxes, or entered into subsidiary alliances with kings, on whose authority they collected them. Guha's is important work. Deploying a vast array of historical evidence, he shows that in India social positioning—or "caste"—was never a calm or a consensual process, but always dynamic, competitive, and open to negotiation. He further shows that rank was never reckoned only in the Brahmanical idiom (see also S. Bayly 1989); that it was entangled in finance and politics; and that Europeans, on arrival in South Asia, joined in the South Asian game of rank reckoning. But without explicit attention to values, one is left to guess at what these rules actually were. Guha is "deeply skeptical of attempts to trace socio-economic institutions to fundamental values" (Guha 2016: 116). And yet, in order to give an account of motivations in the order that he describes, he finds himself appealing to values, which, following Barth (1965), he takes to be the pursuits of "interested" individuals. While dismissing "efforts to find a single, unified rationale for the internal workings and external relations of each of India's thousands of castes" (2016: 1), Guha's own account implies a highly unified rationale oriented toward wealth and power. But what were wealth and power *for*? the freedom to have power over others? so as to amass wealth? in order to further exploit others? for the sake of amassing more wealth? The analysis brings us, full circle, back to Dumont and the problem of value.

Hierarchy sans Holism

Dismantling the pyramid will take two analytical moves: to sever the link between hierarchy and holism, and to rethink the location and nature of hierarchical value.[33] It is one thing to insist on holism as an apperceptional mode and an intellectual method: to treat all social forms as products of broader relational complexes. This is just good anthropology. It is quite another to imagine a bounded collective entity as either an orienting value or an enclosure for people's lives (see Dresch 1998; Pirie & Scheele 2014: 16–21). There is a world of difference between heuristic holism and ontological holism, between holistic thinking and thinking in terms of collective wholes. There are, no doubt, hierarchical models, like Catholic cosmology or the Brahmanical *varṇa* theory, which invoke bounded totalities.[34] But my friends and hosts in India did not think in wholes. Surely, they cared about communities—families, castes, villages, the nation—but they were no more susceptible to the idea of an all-encompassing whole than my egalitarian friends back in Britain. And perhaps rather less so. Recall Tocqueville on the totalizing passion of American egalitarians:

> As conditions are equalized in a people, individuals appear smaller and society seems greater, or rather, each citizen, having become like all the others, is lost in the crowd, and one no longer perceives [anything] but the vast and magnificent image of the people itself. (2000 [1835]: 641)

Or think of the idea of the nation-state, which is both perfectly egalitarian and perfectly holist, an idea that puts the lie to the alignment of hierarchy with holism and egalitarianism with individualism.[35]

What concerned my Indian interlocutors instead of social wholes were social *relations*, a fact already attested voluminously in the ethnographic record. India's anthropologists, whatever their theoretical stance, have described at length the fastidious, even obsessive, attention to relational norms in India's cultural imaginations. They have shown that here people care a great deal, and can explain to foreigners in fine detail, who can give what to whom, and how; who can and cannot marry whom, and how; which foods, words, gestures, and substances can pass between people, and in which order of precedence.[36] What makes all these rules very difficult for an anthropologist to grasp or even remember is that they apply to people not generically, but relative to the positions and roles in which people find themselves. As a person goes about their life, shifting from being a son or daughter to being a brother or sister, a husband or wife, a student, a guest, or a researcher, they are measured by different moral criteria. Obligations and expectations constantly shift. As people in many cultures recognize explicitly (e.g., Read 1955; Iteanu 1990), there are no generic humans or abstract moral codes, only particular roles and expectations appropriate to them. Morally, persons exist only within relations. It is relations, not abstract tenets, that anchor their evaluative judgments, an idea enshrined in the old South Asian concept of *dharma*, or the person- and role-particular moral code, an idea that reverberates through ancient literature (Olivelle 2009) and current ethics alike (Pandian & Ali 2010).

And yet, oddly enough, in the study of India, relations themselves have never figured as *locations of value*. As pillars of an already existing order of value, yes, but not as the moral coordinates of people's lives in their own right. Dumont himself wrote extensively about the minutiae of relational norms in India: rules of labor and marriage relations, contact and commensality, inter- and intracaste transactions, the exchange in gifts and services, and so on. He knew that these norms maintained the separation and ranking of castes, kept intercaste pollution in check, and so secured the Brahmans' superlative purity. He saw that the relative purity of castes was not assigned solely by occupation and birth, but was also negotiated in interactions. And yet, in his account of "preeminent value" relations fell out of sight. They were mere "interactions" with no intrinsic moral content, which, as Dumont rightly noted himself, "cannot replace the overall ideological orientation" (1980: 91).

Other theorists have placed more analytical weight on relations. Long before Dumont, Hocart wrote of gift-giving as the backbone of South Asia's social and political life (1927; 1950). Communities in the region, he argued, revolved around kings or chiefs, who were not only power holders, but also guardians of their cosmos, and so of their life. South Asian polities, argued Hocart, took shape through life-giving sacrifice, in which the king was the "chief actor who supplied the offerings and bore the expense" (Hocart 1970 [1936]: 35; also Dumézil 1973). While the king's continued generosity upheld this sacrificial order, his subjects acted as "priests," who performed various services that kept the king, and with him the cosmos, pure. My own argument takes a lot from

Hocart, who took relations seriously, had no time for the obstructive boundary between politics and religion (or ideology), and even hinted at the idea of a hierarchical individual, which I shall develop here. And yet, even he saw relations as ancillary to the order that he imagined as structured by the possessive value of purity as the moral foundation of South Asian life. In Hocart's world, as in Dumont's, value was the property of people and entities—the king, his subjects, the polity, the cosmos—not of relations.

Hocart inspired Dumont's sharpest critics, who argued that chiefs rather than priests were paramount in South Asia,[37] that hierarchy was as political as it was religious,[38] and that what gave caste its shape was power and not only purity.[39] The richest ethnographic account in this "neo-Hocartian" mode was Gloria Goodwin Raheja's (1988b) study of a North Indian village, in which she argued that life revolved around a landholding patron caste. The patrons gave gifts to others in exchange for ritual services, gifts through which they transferred their inauspiciousness, thus morally "poisoning" their recipients (also Parry 1994). Patrons reigned supreme not because they were the purest born, but because they continually shed "inauspiciousness" onto others.[40]

While Dumont thought that caste rank was a function of birth and occupational purity, the neo-Hocartians saw rank as a product of gift-service relations. But for them, as for Dumont, relations still ultimately served various possessive value aims, whether ritual purity, dominance, power, or auspiciousness. Just as the Brahmans' purity anchored caste hierarchy for Dumont, so did the king's purification anchor Dirks's polity, and the patrons' auspiciousness served as the pivot of Raheja's village life. The analytical compass still pointed to possessive values rather than relational ones.

McKim Marriott was the only anthropologist who moved some distance toward a truly relational theory of hierarchical value in South Asia. Deploying ethnographic material from across the subcontinent, he showed that here rank was not a measure of purity, but instead "castes were ranked according to the structure of interaction among them" (1959: 96). Marriott saw just what Hocart saw (although he never cited him): a system of gifts and services as the foundation of caste. Marriott's basic calculus of rank was quite simple: each transaction involved an asymmetric exchange between people who gave and people who served, and givers were superior to recipients,[41] with the most prolific donors floating up to the social top and perennial servants sinking to the bottom.[42] Rank was not set in stone, and, at least in theory, people could work their way up by exercising generosity and expanding their servant clienteles. Intercaste relations were dynamic, competitive, described by Marriott as a "tournament," where each caste vied for supremacy, trying to "score" by aggressive giving (1968: 154).[43]

Although Marriott wrote that relations were the "master conception on which village thinking about caste constantly focused" (1968: 145), in the end, he too turned away from his own argument: the relational frenzy and alchemy of mutual co-creation that he documented so carefully ended up serving value aims that were external to them. He was never entirely clear about what exactly these aims might be, or rather, he changed his mind about them: at one point he insisted that the caste tournament was a pursuit of dominance or supremacy (1976: 123, 127); elsewhere that "transactions are oriented ultimately ... towards ... power understood as vital energy" (1976: 137); and somewhere else still that the transactional strategies deployed by different castes were determined by their "inborn codes" (1976: 123). Or he simply reverted to Dumont's vision in which "Brahmans take the highest place through their own divinity" (1976: 129; also 1959).[44] For all his insistence on the evaluative significance of relations, and the rich ethnographic support he marshalled to make his claim, ultimately for Marriott relations were in the service of possessive values, values that were properties of persons rather than of relations.

Elementary Norms of Hierarchical Life

During fieldwork, I was adopted by a family in Begun, a family from a caste of drummers, who took me in when I fell ill with pneumonia and needed a refuge from the rigors of life in the Kanjar *bastī*. They became my adopted family, and they took it upon themselves to instruct me in local ways. My chief mentor was Baiji, the family matriarch, who taught me how to speak, dress, and eat like a Rajasthani. I was a bad student: I drank, smoked, lived apart from my husband, and drove a motorcycle around town "like a boy." None of this was appropriate for a young, married woman. But as Baiji taught me her "culture" (*sanskruti sikhānā*), I also did my best to explain my own ways to her, and in time she came to appreciate that women from the "English caste" choose their own husbands, travel abroad alone, or even get divorced, if they wish. But there was one aspect of my marital life that she just could not grasp. When my then husband visited me in Begun, Baiji became deeply perplexed by the way she saw us relate to each other. We went about town together, cooked and ate together, laughed, chatted, and fought like equals. Baiji's husband had been dead for some time, but his photo hung high on the wall, and every morning Baiji adorned his icon with garlands of fresh marigolds. His memory was so sacred that she would not so much as utter his name. And here I was, asking my husband to serve me cups of tea. Her son, Suresh, explained to her that in England husbands and wives live together as equals, "as friends" (*dost jaise*).

That she could not understand. How could such a vital relationship be equal? Friends, she said, come and go (*dost āte-jāte rahate*), but there is only one husband. No wonder, she remarked, the English get divorced every other day, adding pointedly: *in Rajasthan we treat our husbands like gods* [ghar walõ ko devatā mānate], *we serve them* [unake sevā karte]. Now that she was the head of the household, Baiji made all major and most minor decisions in it, and her family obeyed, just as she had once obeyed her husband. Even though her son was the breadwinner, it was Baiji who kept in her tin the money he earned. This was her prerogative, but also her responsibility (*jimmedāri*), for it was she who was the family bread giver (*anndātā*), its matron, its head, even if she herself did not earn the money. Baiji's family was warm and tight-knit, and I loved spending time with them, but nobody in it was equal.[45] Every part of daily life, from getting out of bed to eating, bathing, dressing, going out, and going back to bed, followed a strict order of precedence. Every evening Baiji burned incense before her husband's icon, and every morning her children and grandchildren touched her feet while she dispensed to them her blessings. Eventually, when I joined in their routine, she welled up with tears, tapped me on the head, and said lovingly: *Now you really* are *my daughter.*

In Baiji's world, rank correlated directly, not inversely, with care and intimacy.[46] This is how I was taken into her home: as a member of the family, a daughter with a particular role and rank. Baiji found it inconceivable that a husband, who ought to provide and care for his wife, could be her equal, or indeed that he should be. *Of course your husband is bigger than you, he has more strength* (takat), she once said in response to my feminist musings on marital equality, *How else could he feed you?* Friends cannot possibly care for you the way your parents or husband or elder siblings do. They may have responsibilities *to* you, but they are not responsible *for* you, in the way that parents are meant to be for their children or the way husbands are meant to be for their wives (for more on this, see pp. 43–44). And isn't care what one wants from a marriage? Which is why "serving" (*sevā karnā*) one's husband was not a sign of humiliation, but constitutive of a loving relation. And so Baiji, in teaching me how to be a good wife, kept repeating: This is how we serve our husband: we massage his legs, we cook, we clean. This is what a wife *is*. Euro-Americans going on a date look for parity, whether in their tastes in music, shared political views, or common family backgrounds; they may delight in each other's differences, but it is things they discover to have in common that will suggest to them that a "relationship" is in the cards (Gullestad 1986). To Baiji, this logic made little sense. Surely, someone who can protect and provide for you cannot be your equal, making inequality basic to the most important ties in one's life: between husbands and wives, parents and children, gods and devotees, ancestors and descendants.

Egalitarian logic, of whatever hue, treats the *properties that people possess*—whether wealth, common humanity, skin color, dignity, rights, privilege, opportunity, or whatever else—as the basis of judgment. Equal people, it tells us, ought to "possess . . . a like degree of a (specified or implied) *quality or attribute*; [be] on the same level in rank, dignity, power, ability, achievement, or excellence; [have] the same rights or privileges" (*OED, ad loc.,* emphasis added). As Gerald Cohen put it, egalitarians take it for granted "that there is something which justice requires people to have equal amounts of" (1989: 906). This is not to say that egalitarians do not care for social relations. Moral philosophers who have argued for "relational equality" note that meaningful equality can be found only in equal mutual treatment and respect, not in the equal distribution of resources or the leveling of living conditions or personal attributes (Anderson 1999; Scheffler 2010). Relational equality has also been discussed at length by anthropologists of Melanesia, where people are rendered equal, not distributively, but "through the exchange of equivalent things . . . by making the partners to the relationship equivalent in their 'gifts'" (Robbins 1994: 39–40; 2004). But even this process rests on commensuration: the equivalence of gifts, and thus of their givers. Equality may require exchange, but it is ultimately what people *have* that makes them equal.

By contrast, Baiji's judgment of what constitutes a good marriage and what makes people within it flourish (or at least avoid divorce) begins with relational considerations. Her moral reckoning does not simply reject equivalence. It makes all considerations of parity or correspondence—any kind of commensuration—altogether irrelevant. What matters instead is who is responsible to whom, for what, and how. To understand how this works, consider the archetypal hierarchical bond in your own life, whoever and wherever you are: the parent-child relation. No doubt, should you start comparing parents and children, you will find all kinds of similarities and differences, but such a comparison makes no sense of the relationship. What makes someone a parent is the fact that they are responsible (morally, legally, financially) for their children. The obligations that constitute this relation are never equivalent; their balance may shift over time, as parents and children assume greater or lesser degrees and kinds of responsibility, but it will never be precisely level.

Hierarchical thinking places value in the *content and properties of relations*. The primary criteria of judgment are relational qualities (loyalty, care, generosity) and relational states (attachment, belonging, incorporation), not virtues like valor or purity. If loyalty and generosity can be thought of as "virtues" at all, they are *transitive virtues*—cultivated and reckoned in relation to others rather than as properties of the self. Care is a property not of the self, but of relations, and it becomes manifest only within and through relations. Possessive virtues or "character," like strength, courage, or probity, do matter, but only insofar as they are deployed to relational ends. Strength and wealth elevate people socially only when these are deployed in the care of others. To use Dumont's language, relational value encompasses possessive value. In different parts of India people have tended to valorize one or another virtue (or set of virtues) associated with a preeminently positioned community. In rural Rajasthan what people celebrate, instead of Brahmanical purity, are the valor and strength associated with Rajputs, who have long been the preeminent patron-donors. In Tamil Nadu, it is Brahmans who have often played that role, hence the honor given to ritual purity. In Begun, people may agree that Kanjars have the courage and strength that is celebrated in Rajputs, but this recognition alone does not afford them respect. What matters is their "strayness," their unattachment, their lack of proper social ties. As Guha (2016) has shown, across India and throughout its history various caste attributes, of which purity is but one, only marked a social precedence that was in fact reckoned with respect to relations.[47]

The encompassment of possessive value by relational value is what Robbins (2004) has called "relationalism," a sensibility that locates value in social relations and accords them the highest moral honor. What is less clear in Robbins's work is what difference having relations as the locus of value makes to the overall structure of value. I shall argue that the privileging of relations as the location of value radically changes the structure of value as well as the structure of relations that are organized by it. The relational calculus of human worth is not a linear accumulation of value. People do not acquire social worth simply by engaging in more relations, in a way that one might accrue virtues. They are judged, instead, with respect to a set of multiple, positionally determined values. As we shall see, sometimes it is good to have many relations and sometimes it is best to have only one. Kanjars, bereft as they are of vital relations, may appear like the Papuan "rubbish men" who have no relations (Burridge 1975). But for Kanjars the trouble is actually that they have far too many relations—but of the wrong kind. They engage promiscuously in a disheveled array of relations instead of securing fixed, steady bonds, which, as we shall see, are essential for good social standing.

If possessive values can change diametrically and at times very fast (as in cases of religious conversion), relational principles are much more resistant to change and can cause the greatest grief when forced into abandonment or too rapid change (e.g., Vitebsky 2017). Think of the rise of egalitarianism in seventeenth-century Western Europe. The most radical and controversial egalitarian assertion was made not by philosophers who advocated "basic human equality"—an idea that was already central to early Christianity and Roman law (Hoekstra 2013)—but by Quakers and Levellers who were advancing new relational norms. It was not their insistence that people were "fellow creatures" that scandalized their contemporaries, but their egalitarian handshake: the "uncouth, strange, and Immodest" practice of "feeling and grabling" (Bejan 2011: 414).

In India, the durability of relational principles does not mean that, in trying to follow them scrupulously, people are in any way immobilized. On the contrary, because relational principles enjoin people to *act* in particular ways, they leave room for creativity, improvisation, and change. In fact, these principles are the basic notation of local social dynamism. The vitality of the structure is not a matter of value reversal or simple value flip-flopping, as posited by Dumont (1980: 225, 244; also Houseman 2015 [1984]; Robbins & Siikala 2014), but of adhering to principles that in themselves presuppose creativity and change.

The Life-Giving Bond

In Northern India these principles take concrete form in a relational formula that spans social spheres and contexts, shaping relations between parents and children, gods and devotees, teachers and students, political leaders and followers, hosts and guests, among many others. This relational formula— patronage—encapsulates and puts into practice the basic principles of hierarchy. It is hierarchy's elementary social form. It involves people who give and people who serve, and has already been documented meticulously by scholars of South Asia. From the courts of premodern kingdoms to household relations, devotional practices, political representation, and village relations, we know that people right across the subcontinent have long built their most important social bonds out of the asymmetrical pairing of obligations to give and to serve (see Piliavsky 2014b for an overview). Some patronage bonds are given by kinship: parents are their children's patrons; husbands, the patrons of their wives; and elders, of their juniors. Others are inherited at birth (relations with a caste's traditional patrons, for instance); yet others are forged over the course of life. Since in ordinary English usage we think of "patronage" as an instrumental relation with sponsors, customers, or financiers, rather than as a bond of intimacy and care, it may seem odd to think of parents as "patrons." But in India what I call patronage is conceived in much more vital terms, as a tie of concern and personal obligation, which involves practical support as the embodiment of care and love. That is why in rural North India people often address employers, patron-gods, and political patrons as "parents" (*mā-ī-bāp, bav-ji*) and describe themselves as their "children" (*aulād*).[48]

That givers are superior is a maxim as ancient as South Asian history itself (an observation pivotal to Mauss's [2002(1925)] famous analysis of gift-giving). The earliest known texts in the region focus on munificence as the defining duty of above-standing men (yes, in this context mostly men): early temple

inscriptions praise royal largesse and document royal gifts, ancient legal treatises enjoin leaders to generosity, and liturgical literature describes royal rituals
as complex systems of gifting.[49] Crystallized over millennia in the institution of
kingship, the duty and privilege to give (*dānādhārma*) has long defined political
authority in South Asia (Richards 1978; Stein 1980; Dirks 1987; Olivelle 2009). It
has been at the heart of religious and domestic life (Appadurai & Breckenridge
1976; Clark-Decès 2014), and it is alive and well today in public and domestic
contexts, in homesteads and on politicians' platforms. It is alive, for example,
in the practice of hospitality, which is lavished eagerly, but received with reluctance, for by accepting gifts offered by hosts, guests accept a subordinate
position (see chapter 8).[50] There is nothing demeaning about subordination
as such. On the contrary, as we shall see, it is a privilege that many seek. But
it is something that people seek only from particular people, those to whom
they attach themselves and from whose attachments they draw honor.[51] It is
not so with neighbors or in-laws, with whom rank differences are an ever-
fraught, unsettled business, and so they avoid visiting one another, dodging
the demeaning effects of hospitality. Here the gift really is "poison," as Raheja
(1988b) and Parry (1994) thought. Once, when I brought some presents for my
Brahman hosts, I was told point-blank: *you can't give—it is the big people among
us who give* [hamāre baṛe dete]. Kanjars, in contrast, had no trouble with my
generosity, in fact they were very much after it; I was rich, white, and educated,
and, for all they knew, maybe I even worked for "the government" (*sarkār*). So
they hoped for my patronage, for my provision and protection from the police,
which, as we shall see, I provided, unawares.

What Indian patrons must show, and what they are judged on, first and
foremost, is their capacity to "feed" (*khilānā*), that is, to provide and care for
their people. This is why people celebrate them with honorifics like *anndātā*
(bread giver) or *ann dev* (god of grain). "Feeding" is often quite literally what
patrons do. Eating and feeding lie at the heart of local devotional practices,
household exchange, weddings, and other places where patronal bonds are
forged. Feasts are as central to the life of modern-day royal courts (Balzani 2003;
Ikegame 2013) as they are to village patronage and electoral politics (Piliavsky
2014c; Wouters 2015; chapter 8 here). Feeding is not merely symbolic, but an
enactment of the moral essence of giving (as we shall see in chapter 6). This
process has been familiar to anthropologists for a long time. As Mauss (2002

[1925]) had argued, giving is a foundationally consubstantive act: to give is to share oneself with others and, as an act of consubstantiation, feeding makes this fact maximally concrete.[52]

To be a patron is to disseminate oneself to one's recipient-servants by "feeding"; to have a patron is to absorb or "eat" their personal substance (chapter 6). This personal substance—the set of mental, physical, and moral dispositions that Marriott and Inden (1973; 1977) referred to as "bio-moral substance"—is known across Northern India as *khanadān*, which people say means literally "the gift of food" (*khānā dān*).[53] *Khāndān* (usually glossed simply as "family") is not "identity" or a person's inherent property, but rather character acquired in social intercourse and, more precisely, through vertical relations with those who "feed." *Khāndān* is what Indian children receive at initiation, during communion with their patron-deity when they enter the social world, when they become a person (see chapter 6). It is not only castes and families that are united by patronal communion. Every social unit, every community, be it a caste association, a political party, a student union, or a sports club, requires a patron-deity of its own in order to exist (De Neve 2000; Piliavsky 2015b; chapter 6 here).

This idea of exogenesis, the derivation of self from other, is integral to hierarchical morality. Perhaps most obviously this idea is embodied in the widespread institution of stranger-kingship, where a sovereign outsider gives life to his polity (Sahlins 1981; 1985: 73–103; 2008; Sahlins & Graeber 2017). Most elementally, the idea is that everyone must come from somebody else, persons can only come from other persons (human or divine). This is what we may think of as a theory of anthropogenesis. In Northern India, it is expressed in the idiom of substantive co-creation, in the idiom of "eating" from or of your superiors. This is why the parent-child relation, the concrete, universal manifestation of hierarchical exogenesis, is the archetypal hierarchical bond. The source figure, what Sahlins calls "metaperson"—a parent, a patron, a god—is preeminent not because they represent or exemplify a paramount value, but because they are the source of their subordinates' being. In this sense, relations with parents and patrons, descent and masterhood, kinship and kingship are the same in principle.

Social worth does not come from encompassment by an impersonal value, but is a measure of proximity to the source. All value, in other words, is personal. This is why, as we shall see, having a single patron is so crucial in local calculations of rank. This normative preoccupation with existential sources, what Peter Bellwood (2006) called "founder ideology," has been discussed extensively by anthropologists of Austronesia in their writings on "precedence" (e.g., J. Fox 1988; 1994; 2009; Fox & Sather 1996; Vischer 2009). But it is also present implicitly in the vast anthropological literature on descent, and more explicitly in a wide range of studies of rank and status (perhaps most notably in Sahlins [1958] and Geertz [1980]). Hocart wrote about an "order of precedence" as the basis of social differentiation (1970 [1936]: 37) and Dumont himself, when not advocating encompassment, thought of hierarchy *as* precedence: "hierarchy, or rather the existence of an order of precedence, a status ranking, usually compels recognition" (1980: 75). The idea of precedence presupposes neither a social whole nor holistic encompassment. Instead, it posits an ordered series, or a concatenation of asymmetric relations across the spectrum of social life. Instead of ascribing an overall shape, a whole, to human societies, it describes a *relational logic* that guides people's actions and steers life as a "process of coming into existence" (Fox 1994: 34).

The long-held belief among social scientists that castes are professional guilds ranked by degrees of occupational purity has obscured the descent-like structure of caste, in which each is conceptualized in relation to others as a *service community*, united by a shared trade conceived as a service to a master, and envisioned as its descendants. Thus Hocart: "The European thinks of the barber and the washerman as men who ply a trade inherited from their forefathers; but that is not the native point of view" (1970 [1936]: 115; also 1950). Castes, he writes, are communities *that perform particular (ritual) tasks for a specific master.* Indeed, as Marriott noted, in India "an occupation is a kind of behavior rendered as a service by one caste for another" (1959: 98). There are no generic priests or drummers, only priests or drummers for someone in particular. And the drummers for goatherds and the drummers for aristocrats are socially as distant as goatherds and aristocrats themselves. They dress and eat differently (following their patrons' ways of dressing and eating; see chapter 7), they go by different caste names, and they certainly neither eat with each other nor intermarry. For all intents and purposes, they are members of different castes.[54]

The importance of exclusive and durable patronal attachments in reckoning rank is evident (if seldom discussed explicitly) in studies of traditional village exchange relations, known as *jajmānī* or *birat* (chapters 3 and 7). At the foothills of the Himalayas, studied by Berreman, the highest ranking castes were the family priests who had exclusive and durable ties of service to single patron families; and lower ranking castes had looser and more generalized patronage (1972: 57–58). Parry likewise observed that in Himachal Pradesh barber priests (*purohits*) who were bound to patrons by exclusive service ties ranked above other craftsmen (*kamīns*) with looser, more generalized service bonds, who, in turn, ranked above unattached "beggars" (*māṅgāts*) with no certain service attachments in villages at all (1979: 59–71). In South India, too, Fukuzawa showed that holders of hereditary, land-tied service rights (*watandārī*) ranked above servants with temporary (*uparī*) labor rights (1972: 34). The same has also been shown by ethnographers to be true of Rajasthan's craftsmen, entertainers, and bards. Those of them who enjoy hereditary service bonds rank above those employed on a short-term, contractual (*āyat*) basis (Kothari 1994: 206). And those who work for a single patron (*jajmān*) or a patron family rank above those who serve several villages, who in turn rank above those engaged in "patronage shared by all" (*siroli birat*), or service to a scattered array of patron castes (Snodgrass 2006).

Everybody needs a patron, for to be is to belong. As Ramesh neatly put it, *every man belongs to someone, every man has a master* [*sab ādmī kisī ke to hote, har ādmī kā mālik hai*].[55] Every community has its own divine patrons (chapter 6). Human masters, however, are much harder to come by (chapter 7). And we shall see the problems of those for whom this is not so. If patron gods locate people within their families, clans, and castes, it is human patrons who anchor people in wider society by giving them the recognition of people who belong. It is these vital bonds that Kanjars so painfully lack. They do work for different local employers—for whom they spy, police, burgle, and negotiate disputes—but this work happens offstage, it is not recognized publicly, and it does not help them escape the infamy of stray, masterless men (chapter 4).

And a masterless person is hardly a person at all. If patrons are the source of personhood, then people who "eat from everyone's hand [*sabhī ke hāth se khāte*]," people like the Kanjars, have no coherent or definite origin, substance, or self. They lack integrity, which here is not a moral metaphor, but an actual lack of a coherent social self. In their neighbors' eyes, unattached vagrant people (*ghumnewāle*) are as loose as their relations, existentially as much as morally, and so they lack social worth. This is the deep conceptual source of Kanjar exclusion, and of the Mandawari pogrom. As stray or masterless people, Kanjars are existentially indeterminate and so morally obsolete.

We do not need to travel to extreme social peripheries to see the importance of patronal attachment at play. Take, for instance, the Brahmans. Conventional wisdom, and Dumont, tell us that Brahmans are the highest caste. But ethnographers have shown that Brahmans have occupied all kinds of status positions, from high to low to middling. We know that while Brahmans who acted as family priests (*purohits*) were socially very elevated (see Parry 1979: 59), Brahmans who were village priests ranked somewhere in the middle, alongside potters and gardeners (Mayer 1960: 71), and Brahmans who acted as funerary priests ranked among the lowest castes (Parry 1994). Degrees of purity and pollution cannot possibly explain this difference because all three kinds of Brahmans claimed proximity to the divine sources of purity and also performed polluting rites. What instead explains their status differences are the degrees of their attachment to patrons. While family priests enjoyed exclusive, hereditary rights of serving a single aristocratic family, village priests served a less regular community of village patrons, and funerary priests on the banks of the Ganges would work for all and sundry who came to cremate their dead. What counted was not purity, but the fixity and exclusivity of hierarchical attachments. Those with steady service bonds to one patron did well for themselves, and those with a motley array of patrons would do abysmally.[56] What further enhanced the status of the kings' family priests was not their purity, but their role as the keepers of royal patron gods, who were essential for the king's authority.[57]

If all gifts carried with them moral "poison," as Raheja (1988b) and Parry (1989) argued, every service community would be equally despoiled.[58] But gifts are a hazard only when they are exchanged haphazardly. When they come from one's own patron, they carry with them the most cherished thing—life itself. As Hocart observed, kingship—that is, patronage writ large—was essentially part "not of a system of government, but of an organization to promote life, fertility, prosperity" (1970 [1936]: 3). This is a point that Sahlins (2017) has

recently extended into an argument for kingship—or polity based on generosity—as the basic structure of social life. The dual point about the generativ-
ity of gifts and the social precedence of those who give is embedded in the
English word "generosity," a cognate of "generate," "gender," and "genus."[59] The
neo-Hocartians overlooked this crucial point: that the king is not only a vessel
of purity, but himself the real, substantive source of life. In other words, the
patron as *pater*. Generosity was the universal pillar of kingship because it was
literally and ritually, materially and cosmologically, a life-giving bond. This is
not an "idealist" or a "culturalist" model. Generosity needs resources, making
"economic" considerations central to any patronal order. And it is precisely the
conflict between the normativity of largesse and the practicalities of acquiring
its means that places moral tension at the heart of all patronal orders, with
patrons ever vulnerable to charges of venality (chapter 8). This is what David
Gilmartin has called the "paradox of patronage" (2014).

Hierarchical Individuals

The gift of life flows both ways. If patrons transmit their *khanadān* to servants, it is servants who make their patrons into big men (or women). When
patrons "feed" their servants, they share, and thus expand, their selves by
incorporating their donees. By giving, they absorb their gifts' recipients, becoming (or trying to become) bigger people, socially enhanced. As a Rajput
friend of mine put it: *Men who give are big men—that's how we see it—the
more a person gives, the bigger he becomes. That is why in Rajasthan people
believe that Rajputs are the biggest caste.*

If belonging to patrons is the basic condition of being, it is being a patron
that allows people to become truly grand, and ultimately the grandest thing
of all—an individual (see below). Because one is what one does in relation to
others, by fulfilling one's obligations, one can make and remake oneself. One
moves onward and upward not by releasing oneself from bonds, but by entering into them judiciously. These norms can certainly restrict, but in able hands
they are levers—indeed, the very conditions—of socially creative opportunity.
As in the South Africa described by Ferguson, hierarchical dependence was
never "a problem or a debility—on the contrary, it was the principal mechanism for achieving social personhood" (2013: 226). There are, of course, limits
to self-advancement. The other party must cooperate, and the relationship

must be publicly recognized. This is precisely where the Kanjars' attempts at mobility often falter (chapters 3, 6, and 8). For both the prospects and perils of hierarchy are relational, contingent on efforts of everyone who is involved. And (as anywhere else in the world) most attempts at upward movement are unsteady, incremental, and slow. As people go through life, they become older siblings, parents, or heads of family: bigger people with more dependents and respect, but also with greater responsibility. The ambitious can try to fast-forward their social advancement by assuming more responsibility for others, by taking charge of provision, protection, and care (see Piliavsky & Sbriccoli 2016). In this world, where everyone is at once patron and servant—even royals are servants of patron gods—positions constantly shift, and there is nothing like a discernible social whole or a steady arrangement or shape to society. Instead there are shared *principles* that steer how people judge, decide, and act, that motivate people's pursuits, and locate them socially.

Conceptually, this world is highly coherent, with a few simple ideas shared over great stretches of space and time. Conceptual coherence does not mean social cohesion or "solidarity," with people slotting effortlessly into set positions inside a bounded whole. Nor does it amount to agreement, harmony or stasis. The world I describe is in constant flux. Everyone is at once servant and patron to many, roles they continually acquire and lose. What constitutes a "gift" and a "service" is rarely uncontested (see chapter 7), relative positions are continually renegotiated and reinscribed, and relations (and fortunes) are incessantly made and unmade. People change their positions not by a primitive accumulation of possessive value, but by changing their position relative to others. Some movements may unfold before an ethnographer's eyes, but most take much longer and become visible only in the *longue durée*, as we trace the slow rise and fall of communities (as I shall do in chapter 5). In North India, these relational principles have persisted remarkably across time, social levels, and circumstances, enjoying moral purchase across differences of caste, religion, and class,[60] and across community-specific possessive values, irrespective of whether a group specially cherishes ritual purity, strength, auspiciousness, valor, education, wealth, or whatever else. For a long time, this has been the basic vocabulary of the ambitious poetics of social life. If the copycat model of Sanskritization never actually helped anyone rise in the ranks, what has done so is the cultivation of patronage. The best documented instance of this is what historians have termed "Rajputization" (or Kshatriyaization), a process by which India's tribal groups have attained Rajput, or royal, status (e.g., S. Sinha 1962; Pocock 1955; Singer 1964; Kulke 1976; R. Sinha 1992). This process can be mistaken for a Rajput-focused variant of Sanskritization:[61] a cultivation of Rajput instead of Brahmanical attributes by the lower castes. In fact, the process has a very different logic; the difference is subtle, but crucial.[62] Rajputizing communities were not Rajput copycats, but in fact *became* Rajputs by capturing resources and land that allowed them to lavish largesse on newly acquired subjects, and so attain Rajput standing. Tribal chiefs in Western India became entitled to Rajput *attributes* (royal regalia, a royal history, and eventually even Rajput wives) only once they established themselves as patrons capable of supporting a sufficiently large communities of subjects. This process has long been the backbone of South Asia polities (e.g., Gordon 1994; Skaria 1999), ever in flux, ever the achievement of enterprising individuals. Here hierarchical norms were the chief mechanism of individual self-advancement and ambitious individuals, who actively deployed and maintained these norms.

As in the eighteenth-century polities, so today, hierarchy is not opposed to individual action, achievement, and responsibility. All these have great importance in the India I have come to know. In fact, I shall suggest that here hierarchy constitutes and enables individuality. If we abandon the conviction that hierarchy must be a ranked totality or a collectivist ideology, and conceptualize it instead as a *relational logic*, we will see that hierarchy and individuality go together easily and indeed rather well. As Mattison Mines (1988; 1994) perceived some time ago, in India people take great interest in individuals: in the details of their characters and biographies, their achievements and failures, personal motivations, reputations, and so on.[63] Whenever people recount history, discuss political events, or reflect on family problems, they focus on prominent individuals, on what they are like and what they have done. Here the idea of the individual is important not only for appreciating individual lives, but as a structural constituent of social and historical order. Indeed, as I shall show throughout this book, the individual is intrinsic to hierarchy: both as the endpoint of hierarchically organized social ambition and as hierarchy's pivotal structuring principle.

Let me explain. The hierarchical individual stands in contrast to the Euro-American egalitarian individual, whom Dumont invoked when he contrasted holism with individualism. In Euro-America's (post-)Christian, post-Enlightenment ideology (if not necessarily in Euro-American everyday moral reckoning), each person is born an individual. Individuality is an inherent condition, ungraded and unqualified. But in rural North India people are not *born* individuals, they *become individuated* through a protracted, cumulative, and frequently arduous process that may take a lifetime, or more. Here individuality is not a given state, but a hard-won achievement. This idea is inscribed in the Brahmanical theory of life stages, or *āśramas*, which prescribes rigid rules for the early stages of life (a student's, a householder's), but releases the old for solitary contemplation and finally for the ultimate individuation of retirement (*sanyās*) from social life. Such a retiree, the Hindu renouncer, whom Dumont imagined as holism's solitary antithesis, is not the exception to the hierarchical order of life, but its pinnacle. The process of individuation is readily visible in everyday life. If in Europe and the United States it is the young who tend to radicalism and displays of individuality, in rural North India it is older folk who brim with idiosyncrasy while the young conform meticulously to established norms. It is also usually older, grander, or more distinguished people who are feted as individuals: gods, gurus, elders, film stars, business magnates, political leaders.

A hierarchical individual is someone who has achieved something. Unlike the autonomous post-Christian individual—a person separate from and equal to others—the hierarchical individual is by definition attached and unequal to them. If this egalitarian individuality is rooted in *difference*, hierarchical individuality is based on *distinction*.[64] A distinguished person is not more valuable in an abstract sense, but stands in a particular relationship to the others and is distinctly valuable *to and for them*. The former is a matter of separation *from others*, the latter of being distinguished *among others*. Like Weber's "charisma," individuality is not the property of a person, but a structural effect of the relations in which the individual is enmeshed.

If the egalitarian individual is an atom in a flat network, the hierarchical individual is a grandee; not an island, but a mountain peak. One can distinguish oneself in all manner of ways—spiritually, professionally, financially, politically—but one is recognized as an individual only when one does something magnificent *for others*, when one assumes responsibility for them. When Rajasthani grandees (royals, businessmen, headmen, politicians) give an account of their splendor—that is, of their individuality—they will always tell you about the many people, processes, and institutions that are in their charge. They will define their individuality by the extent of their social involvement. They will list things that they have done for their community, institutions that they have founded, or decision-making processes in which they have authority. The same is true in Tamil Nadu, where big men likewise define their individuality by the extent of their social involvement (see M. Mines 1994: 14). When others discuss distinguished people, they describe things that those people have done for them: funds they have made available, families they have supported, or security they have provided for others. The more significant their actions, the more vividly personal is the mythology that surrounds them. In local narratives, the grandest patrons—kings, gurus, or chief ministers of states—are the most incandescently individuated, and their magnificent qualities are celebrated on millions of posters and in innumerable legends of their deeds. They are not just individuals, but super-individuals.

People describe the uniqueness of grandees not as a matter of their being different from others, but of being *their* guru, political leader, husband, or mother. The icons of patrons that hang on the walls of ashrams, political party headquarters, or living rooms depict people who are revered not for being singular geniuses, but for being heads of religious sects, political parties, or households. If egalitarian individuals are autonomous figures, hierarchical individuals are deeply implicated in others, by virtue of both their responsibility toward them and the existential bonds that I discussed above. These bonds are the basis of social distinction and personal distinctiveness, which go hand in hand. To become a distinctive person—an individual—is to be socially *distinguished*. Dumont, who thought the individual a creature of egalitarian ideology—and hierarchy's value antithesis—had to place Hindu ascetics, whom he rightly saw as intensely individuated, outside ordinary Indian society. But, in the eyes of Hindu devotees, Hindu renunciants (*sanyāsīs*) are not external to social life, they are its final stage (*ashramā*), its pinnacle. Renunciation (*sanyās*) is not the abandonment of social life, but its exalted culmination.

Which is why in common parlance renunciants are often called Mahārāj—not "holy man" or "ascetic," but "great ruler" or "king."

As the source of people's collective selves, of their *khanadān*, the patron is the local communities' keystone. Because communities are defined by incorporative ties to their patrons, they are anthropomorphic in principle: their histories are often told as the stories of their patrons' achievements and failures, and their character as the character of their patrons. Educated Rajputs explain, for example, that their patron deities' iconography is a map of their *khanadān*. *The icon of our goddess,* explained Mahendra Singh, the king of Mewar, *is like a map of our character. We retrace this map in our minds every day when we do our morning prayers.* We shall hear Kanjars saying, and acting out, a strikingly similar view in chapter 6. And this is of course what Sahlins (1983), following Chadwick (1926), described as "heroic" sociality, bound not by horizontal links or any kind of equivalence or identity, but by vertical bonds with "metapersons" (Sahlins 2017) as the structural anchors of social life.

Far from being a system of stasis, hierarchy presupposes and enables people's capacity to will, judge, and act. It is thus the framework of freedom—not freedom from social bonds, but freedom as the capacity to act effectively in the world—and, as such, it is the necessary condition of hope.

Chapter 2

THE LORDS OF BEGUN

FROM THE HIGH OPEN TERRACE of his family citadel, Rao Hari Singh, the hereditary lord of Begun, commanded a sweeping view of the town and its environs. From this place, the highest in the landscape (bar the telecom tower), he pointed down a steep narrow staircase through a filigreed archway to a large square courtyard below. In this Peacock Court (*mayūr chauk*), built in the formal Mughal style, guests arriving in Begun would tether their horses and elephants. Now we could see my motorcycle, which I had left in the courtyard and which was surrounded by a muster of peahens pecking at the parched square patches of earth where the rose garden once bloomed. The Rao pointed to the stacked marble domes—there are seven Hindu and two Jain temples in the citadel—and to the rounded domes of the satellite mansions (*havelīs*). This is where the Raos' chief treasurer, temple priests, and the majordomo, as well as the visiting vassals, would stay. All around us, just below eye level, rose the mold-blackened ramparts and bastions where gates cut through the citadel's two vast walls. *And this is the "Kanjar mansion,"* chuckled the Rao. *It's the old prison, where we housed the likes of them before 1947.*

The citadel, parts of which date back to the 1430s, stretches over 30 acres of land on the western bank of the River Brahmani, which cuts a seasonal path across a fertile valley known for its rich wheat and poppy harvests (fig. 2.1). To the south and west of the valley rise the rolling Aravalli Mountains and to the east lies the Chambal River valley, which has long housed famous dacoit (bandit) gangs. Surveying the sun-battered plain that stretched out before us, the Rao pointed out a huddle of tents: *these are the traveling blacksmiths, Gadoliya Lohars. They come around here every year. Have you ever seen them at work? Their women working those mallets—a hard-working lot—very fine, very fine . . .* Farther on, just beyond the river, beneath a line of large *mahua* trees was a small village. *These are our water chestnut pickers*, the Rao explained. *My grandfather Megh Singh-ji settled them there.* Farther still, barely visible in the haze that hung low on the horizon, were the outlines of some tent-like structures made of sandstone that shone pink in the setting sun. These were the cenotaphs (*māsatiyā*) of the Rao's ancestors, the dead lords of Begun. This was also where in 1822 Rajasthan's great historian and British political agent, James Tod, pitched a camp, in which he spent a long period of convalescence after a fall off an elephant's back.

Having taken in all this splendor and history, we turned west to face the molten disk of the sun setting briskly over the town. A worn tape of a Muslim call to prayer crackled in the near distance, and a kite fluttered in the sky.[1] *Marvelous, marvelous*, the Rao murmured, adjusting his shawl in the evening chill. *Such great natural beauty. You have chosen your research location very wisely. You must be enjoying it much.* I sipped my preprandial whiskey, leaned over the parapet, and took in the clamor of dogs, horns, and hawkers drifting up over the chaos of rooftops and electrical wires below. *Yes, this is indeed the most enjoyable research location*, I said, and the Rao returned a vague, distracted smile: *So, this is our sleepy little town—welcome! Come, let's have dinner.*

Over goat masala, a secret family recipe that he had prepared himself specially for the occasion, the Rao gave me a rundown of his family history. Hari Singh is the twenty-fourth Rao of Begun, one of India's largest fiefdoms (*thikānā*), a sizeable "little kingdom" (Cohn 1959), which once encompassed five hundred revenue villages.[2] It was founded in 1430, when Mewar's crown prince, Chunda, abdicated the throne and received in return the largest grant (*jagīr*) of fertile land in the easternmost part of the kingdom. He was also made chief among Mewar's sixteen premier nobles (*umrāos*), with the title of Rāwat Sawāi, literally "lord-and-a-quarter." Chunda's descendants, the Chundawat clan, have ruled Begun ever since. If Begun was Mewar's premier fiefdom,

FIGURE 2.1 The Rao's palace in Begun. Photo by Serge Poliakov.

Mewar was India's premier Rajput state. Ruled for the past thirteen centuries by the world's oldest continuous dynasty, it was the only Rajput state that never succumbed to invaders, its kings and queens always preferring death to defeat. An emblem of Rajput valor and sacrifice, Mewar is the home of legendary Rajput heroes: the beautiful thirteenth-century Queen Padmini, a sort of "Helen of India," who immolated herself to avoid capture by the Delhi Sultan; and Rana Pratap, who refused to surrender to Akbar in the sixteenth century. The room where we now sat formed a perfect backdrop to this illustrious history. Decorated from ceiling to floor with mosaics and frescoes, clad with thousands of tiny mirrors and pieces of colored glass tessellated into vines, peacocks, and flowers that framed the small colored windows, the room glowed with sapphire and ruby and emerald light that moved across it, kaleidoscope-like, giving it the feel of a disco hall, a medieval church, or a brothel.

The Family Polity
This was one of the few rooms in the palace that remained almost exactly as the Rao remembered it from his childhood, a time of luxury in the last days of

the Raj. Growing up in the 1940s, he had eight personal attendants to himself:
men who dressed him and bathed him, men who cleaned him and cooked
for him, men who drove him to and from school. At that time, the palace had
five hundred household staff: personal attendants of the Rao and each one of
his family members; chefs and drivers, horse keepers and elephant keepers,
guards for each of the citadel's eight gates, people who looked after cattle,
prison guards, cleaners, accountants, a housekeeper, a master of ceremonies,
a treasurer, and a major-domo. A small army of priests looked after the temples in the citadel, with the family patron god Dwarkadish alone being attended by twenty-five priests. Each dish that was served to the chief's family
was prepared by a separate chef who specialized in its preparation. The department of entertainment employed dozens of dancers and musicians, and
the department of concubines housed about fifty women (*bhagtāns, tawāifs,*
and *randis*) who entertained the Rao with music, singing, dancing, and sex.
An army of watchmen and spies kept the Rao abreast of the goings-on in
the fiefdom, and a substantial military force stood by, ready to join him in
times of war, rebellion, and feud, and on hunting expeditions. This is where
Kanjars, too, found employment. The chief's family also employed hundreds
of local families, who performed for them all kinds of services: delivering
milk, fruit, and flowers to the palace; tending to the Rao's babies and gardens;
playing drums during celebrations; cutting hair; stitching garments; making
jewelry; carving stone; making ropes, pots, and furniture; writing family history; and singing poems of praise. *All these were our people, our family,* the
Rao said. *We have always treated them like our own family. Like our children.
It has always been like that. That's why, when I go out in the bazaar, the locals
shout "bav-ji! bav-ji* [*Father, father*]*!"* To demonstrate the intensity of their reverence, he folded his hands before his forehead in a high *pranām: that's the
kind of respect that the locals have for me, for who I am.*

What the Rao was referring to, in rather exalted terms, was the idea that
a polity was a family (*parivār*), which is also how many old people in Begun
spoke about the *ancien régime*—the "rule of kings" (*rajyõ kā rāj*)—which they
recollected with fond nostalgia. Less like a contemporary Euro-American family bound by blood and more like the ancient Roman *familia,* which included
not only kin but also servants, domestics, and slaves, this polity-family included

the Rao's relatives by descent and marriage as well as his family by ties of loyalty and service.[3] What made this a "family" was the fact that they were all loyal to the Rao, who was responsible for them, as a father is for his children.

The idea of kingship as parenthood and of polity as a family has a long pedigree in South Asia, where it appears throughout ancient and medieval writings. Kings are described repeatedly as fathers and, as such, held responsible for their subjects: for their intellectual, moral, and physical well-being, for protecting and caring for them (R. Singh 1996: 10–12). "All men," reads one of Ashoka's edicts, "are my children and just as I desire for my children that they obtain every kind of welfare and happiness in this and the next world, so do I desire for all men" (Bhandarkar & Bhandarkar 2000: 63). This idea has long shaped the practice of kingship on the subcontinent, where kings have been held personally responsible for defending their domains, protecting the moral order (*dharma*) by sponsoring worship, maintaining justice (*nyay*) by adjudication, and keeping prosperity in their realm with continuous largesse (e.g., Richards 1978; Stein 1980; Shulman 1985; Dirks 1987). As Price (1989) noted in her seminal article, the paternal duties still substantially shape the political leader's role, something that has since been attested ethnographically across the country's length and breadth (e.g., Sundar 2007: 228; Price & Ruud 2010; Piliavsky 2014; chapter 8 of this book).

The Rao was not merely responsible *to* his servants, as contractual employers are to their employees, but also responsible *for* them, in the way that parents are for their children. The relation of responsibility was grounded in a normative logic of loving care, not contractual accountability. And this is why the old townsfolk still refer to the Rao as *bav-ji*, "respected father." This parental, comprehensive responsibility was most evident in the Raos' relations with their household staff and especially with the bondspeople, such as the queen's ladies-in-waiting (*dāijās*) or the watchmen (*hajūrīs*) who joined the household as chattels in the queen's dowry and who were fully in the Rao's keeping. He had to feed and clothe them, fund their education, and even arrange and pay for their marriages. The rest of his servants were not as fully in the Rao's keeping, but the idea of comprehensive, parental responsibility for their lives defined how they related to him: what they expected from him, the kinds of demands they made, why they accepted or challenged his authority, why they grew disappointed with him, or staged protests. And it defined what the Rao in fact did: his sponsorship of temples, his adjudication of disputes, and the many "gifts" that he lavished on the local residents. Baiji's house, like most others in central Begun, came into her family's ownership as a royal gift given to her father-in-law for providing musical training to the Rao's concubines. The Rao was not only the biggest employer, but also the chief "justice" of the domain, and he was the one who gave people land. His people depended on him, materially as much as morally. This is what made him their "father": the source and protector of life, of social, material, and moral well-being and procreation.

This went both ways. The Rao's life, too, was in the hands of his servants or workers (*kamīn jāt* or *kām karne wāle*), who took care of every one of its practical and ritual aspects, from delivering and nursing his babies to bathing and dressing him to stacking and lighting his funeral pyre. People from each servant caste were both professional specialists who provided vital services (there were priests, barbers, drummers, gardeners, and others) and ritual specialists who were in charge of the ritual cycle of the Rao's life.[4] Without the barber, the potter, the drummer, the gardener, the priest, and other servants, he could not have a proper birth, wedding, or funeral, for even weeping in mourning over his death was done by servants rather than relatives.[5] And without correctly enacted life-cycle rituals, the Rao's life had no proper shape or course. In fact, without them, he could not so much as be (properly) born or die.

This exchange created a family that was more than metaphoric. It generated true family bonds, which is to say, bonds of shared existence, what Sahlins neatly termed the "mutuality of being" (2011). What is distinctive about this familial feeling is that people recognize explicitly that family bonds are not given by birth or blood, but are the outcome of social intercourse. This is why people say that the collective substance, the *khāndān* shared by members of such a family, means literally the "gift of food" (*khānā-dān*). Exchange is explicitly an act of procreation. And those who partake in it become, literally, family, an idea made plain in the language of parents (*mā-ī-bāp*), children (*aulād*), and family (*parivār*) used to describe those involved in such family-polities. The sense of familial intimacy does not mean that families are oases of harmonious calm. It is not only obvious, as Shryock remarked, *pace* Sahlins, that kin relations are often suffused with "conflict, abuse, abandonment, exploitation, and outright hatred" (2013: 272), but also that family intimacy is precisely what makes for the intensity of conflict within them. The more people depend on one another, the more they expect, the more is at stake, and so the more drastically things can go wrong, and the more bitter are their grievances.

The *Jajmānī* Principles

Across Northern India, the familial logic of such relations is most commonly known as *birat*, and in other parts of the country as *balutā* or *rājā-prājā* relations. In anthropological literature, it has been described in greatest detail in the voluminous, if now outmoded, literature on village patronage, known as the "*jajmānī* system."[6] The practical details of such relations have, naturally, varied across regions, scales, contexts, and time, but their foundational principles have remained, *mutatis mutandis*, steadfast across large stretches of space and time (for a recent overview, see Clark-Decès 2018). The classic model described a system of exchange that centered on a caste of landowning patrons (*jajmān*s), to whom the others owed professional and ritual services, in return for which they received payment gifts, always including food, with the *jajmān* iconically dividing the grain heap on the threshing floor among his servants.[7] This literature was later denounced for fetishizing a timeless pan-Indian village community (Good 1982; Fuller 1989; Caldwell 1991), and the term *jajmānī* fell out of use as a relic of positivist, village-bound ethnography blind to struggle, movement, and change.

The caricatured "village republic," after Henry Maine (1861), locked into an eternal cycle of ritualized transactions, with every actor listlessly following the script, bears little resemblance to life in India, now or ever, in villages or anywhere else.[8] This caricature, however, was more the creation of critics than of the ethnographers themselves, who gave a rich sense of variation, struggle, and change in *jajmānī* relations. William Wiser, who first described these relations in a North Indian village (1936), and who later became the chief target of criticism, devoted no less than one-third of his book to variability, conflict, and changes within the system, detailing the many problems, tensions, and disagreements in the system, which he insisted was not a fixed script, but a "set of rules and conventions" (Wiser 1936: 10) that framed mutual expectations, the demands people pressed on one another, the claims they made, their sense of authority, and their acceptance or rejection of it.[9] Wiser's insights fell prey to empiricism. The *ideas* that he discerned—the rules of the game, which allow us to understand how it is played and indeed to grasp its very point—were mistaken for the moves players made, and so were dismissed as incoherent because different players did different things at different times, or broke the rules. While discarding the presumptive transactional "system," anthropologists lost sight of the *relational principles, which are* exemplified by *jajmānī* exchange, but which also shape relations far beyond economic and ritual transactions between village castes (a point made by Karanth 1987).

Accounts of *jajmānī* relations hold out four vital lessons about hierarchical norms, as they are entertained in India.[10]

1. *In India, hierarchy is not a specifically Hindu value-matrix of purity and pollution. Jajmānī* relations involve Muslims, Christians, Jains and tribal peoples, and, crucially, rank is not determined by ritual purity.[11] The highest-standing people in any given location—the *jajmān* patrons—were not Brahman priests, but the biggest landowners, whom Srinivas called the "dominant castes" (1959). If Brahmans happened to be the *jajmāns*, this was not because they were priests, but because they were landlords. But *jajmāns* can also be Jat cultivators or Gujar herders (e.g., Raheja 1989), and then Brahmans are merely one of their servants "treated on an equal footing with the other castes" (Majumdar et al. 1955: 211). While Brahmans themselves will no doubt tell you that purity, to which they claim a monopoly, is the paramount value, *jajmānī* studies showed that it is in fact the capacity to provide, protect, and care that places people on top. Although anthropologists have argued that giving was a way to purify oneself by shedding ritual pollution or inauspiciousness, this has been disputed, as few, if any, recipients of patronal gifts see them as polluting (see pp. 21, 27–29). What is indisputable is that the passing of gifts in itself creates a structure of precedence. As Isabelle Clark-Decès put it, "What is handed out [during exchange] is a position in a social order that is first and foremost hierarchical, a rank in a social sequence, so that not merely things and services but social distinctions move through the social landscape" (2018: 197; also Marriott 1959).

2. *Hierarchy is action-based and so inherently dynamic.* Insofar as status does not rest on a the transcendent value of purity, but on what people owe one another—their rights and responsibilities (*haqq*)—hierarchy is grounded in action and is therefore open to change. Unlike the abstract caste taxonomies generated by Brahmans and British colonial officials, *jajmānī* relations generated hierarchies through ongoing mutually constitutive interactions. Status was not given but earned by enacting one's social duties. The right to work was an alienable privilege, not an inalienable entitlement. Surely, the right and the attendant status were often inherited by successive generations, but this inheritance had to be constantly maintained by nominal, and what might look like practically "unnecessary," tasks like sharpening tools, again and again, and through ritual performances. Failure to do one's duty could forfeit that right. *Haqq* could be broken, by both sides. An ironsmith who failed to sharpen tools during harvest risked not only losing his job, but also being thrown out of the village. And a *jajmān* who failed to give his workers their due exposed himself to attacks and boycotts (see below). One's *haqq* could also be sold, so that workers could, and occasionally did, choose profit over respect and standing (Wiser 1936: 43). Nor was the *jajmānī* hierarchy a stable pyramid of rank, a monopoly of power with a single *jajmān* on top. Wiser described instead a system of asymmetrical reciprocity, an order of akin to the Austronesian precedence (see p. 30). While the chief landlord in the village was the head *jajmān*, all others were at once patrons and servants to one another:

> The priest, bard, accountant, goldsmith, florist, vegetable grower and so on are served by all other castes. In turn each of these castes has a form of service to perform for the others. Each in turn is master. Each in turn is servant. Each has his own clientele comprising members of different castes which is his "jajmani." (Wiser 1936: 10)

3. *Hierarchies hold power responsible,* offsetting the asymmetry of wealth and power with an asymmetry of obligations, which places the greater onus on people who are better enabled to act. While a carpenter was entitled to his share of the harvest, even if he did not happen to do any work for the patron that year, the patron was always expected to provide the customary share of the harvest and payments to servants. This duty was firm. Wiser tells a story

about how, when one year a *jajmān* decided to sell off the harvest that he owed his servants, they "unyoked the ox carts [loaded with the grain he was about to take to market], brought a scale and weighed out the grain themselves, distributing it to each of the '*kam karnewalas*' [workers] as required." The furious *jajmān* complained to the police, but the officer "sympathized with the villagers and they were sent away with a warning. If many *jajmāns* treated their '*kam karnewalas*' in this way," Wiser adds, the "Jajmani System would soon break down" (1936: 128). A hierarchy can be legitimate only when those with more care for those with less, when they enable their lives. Otherwise, such relations stop being viable and disintegrate into exploitative inequality, rebellion, and desertion.

4. *Superiors depend on their subordinates.* Whenever this ceases to be the case, hierarchy collapses into inequality. The crucial distinguishing feature of *jajmānī* relations is the patrons' dependence on their servants, ritual as much as practical. Every servant was not only an occupational specialist, but (just as Hocart wrote) also a "priest" responsible for an aspect of the ritual, whose correct performance was crucial for the maintenance of the patrons' standing. The patrons were thus at their servants' mercy, they were their ritual dependents. Servants could, and did, withdraw their services to press demands.[12] The requirement of largesse constitutive of the *jajmān's* status and role meant that no matter how much patrons tried, they could never monopolize resources. Failure to share with their servants could, and frequently did, result in strikes that left villages full of rotting carrion, which the striking Chamars (leather-smiths) refused to remove.

While anthropologists rarely write about *jajmānī* or *birat* relations today, as if these relations have vanished or are no longer relevant, their persistence has been observed across India by immersive ethnographers, and not only in the supposedly conservative Rajasthan (Gold & Gujar 2002: 27; Bharucha 2003; Snodgrass 2006), but also in Madhya Pradesh (Krishnamurthy 2018), Tamil Nadu (D. Mines 2005; Clark-Decès 2018) and West Bengal (Sen 2017). In Rajasthan, few landholders now dole out their harvest among their *kamīn* (workers), as did the Gujar *jajmāns* described three decades back by Raheja (1989). And yet some service rights are still honored today. In villages around Begun, barbers still make weekly rounds and their patrons still give them sums of cash or grain, even if no beards needed shaving that day, and even if patrons always tried to give less than the barbers demanded. Even Kanjars act as patrons to barbers who come to shave them every week. And the barbers' wives continue to work as midwives and come daily post-partum to give newborns massage in return for customary payments. Every year many genealogists still come around to record family histories. Many such relations have survived great changes, often in new, attenuated or commercialized forms.[13] Even if the production of scythes has largely been mechanized, ironsmiths find new employment as cleaners, nannies, or peons for their customary patrons. Suresh, whose grand-father played drums for the Rao's grandfather, now drives the Rao's car.

Once, when I was staying with him and Baiji, their family genealogist (Charan) came to update his register of births, marriages, deaths, and prop-erty purchases made in the previous year. At the time, Suresh was out of work, and they were struggling to make ends meet; and yet they still gave the Charan 1,000 rupees, a large sum that amounted to a quarter of their family's monthly income from the rent of the upper floor, a sum with which Suresh parted with difficulty, complaining to me that it's the kind of thing he cannot afford, but must do. We shall also see, in chapter 7, an elaborate exchange between a family of Kanjars working as bards and their Gujar *jajmāns*. At births, weddings, and funerals a family representing each of the *kamīn* castes performs customary ritual services and receives in return customary gifts. As we shall see, these are exactly the kinds of rights that many Kanjars struggle to secure from landhold-ers who employ them as watchmen (chapter 7). Some *birat* attachments have even traveled from villages to cities, where hereditary servants still often assume first dibs on a job, so jobs often go not to the most qualified, but to those with hereditary rights of service. The entourage of a Member of Legislative Assem-bly (MLA) with whom I conducted fieldwork in Jaipur (in 2013–14) is also full of his family *kamīn* from his native village. Many Rajputs who have moved to cities, but who have kept their fields and farmhouses in their villages, continue to honor their servants' *birat* rights, giving them money and "gifts" at annual festivals and life-cycle proceedings. A friend of mine, a Gujar who moved to Jaipur from a village in northern Rajasthan thirty-odd years ago, is still arrang-ing hospital beds for his family's *kamīn* from his native village and putting up their children when they come to take university entry exams.

The material details of such relations have always varied and changed over time, but the basic normative principles instantiated in *jajmānī* relations—the principle of donor-service exchange, meritorious action, mutual responsibility, interdependence, and co-constitution—have remained largely intact. They are not confined to intercaste patronage, but operate on a much broader temporal and social scale, stretching outward to electoral politics (Price 1989; Price & Ruud 2010; Piliavsky 2014) and even global migration networks (Osella 2014; Koskinami 2018), and reaching inward into relations within castes, clans, families, and households (Good 1982: 26; also Raheja 1988b). This ubiquity of *jajmānī* relations in South Asia—their presence in broader political and economic networks, within and between polities, between and within castes, in ritual and intimate settings—is precisely what many critics invoked to show that *jajmānī* relations never added up to a timeless, self-contained, village-bound "system."[14] And so they pronounced *jajmānī* studies dead (Fuller 1989).

This was a rather odd conclusion to have drawn. Surely, the ubiquity of *jajmānī* principles makes their study *more* important—not less—than even ethnographers of village relations themselves had realized. But the critics confused the normative with the descriptive, the relational *principles* that *jajmānī* exchange exemplified for a material system of transactions (Piliavsky 2014c). But if we study relational principles rather than the material content of transactions, we see nothing of a static (let alone bounded) "system" of transactions, but a normative logic of personhood, relatedness, and collectivity. This logic is not about inherent, existential rights or identities, but about socially positioned entitlements, about rights that are continually earned and sustained in relations.

Whither the *Ancien Régime?*
Begun is a palimpsest of the *ancien régime*, in which a discerning paleographer can read the history of local relations. At the foot of the citadel, beyond the empty moat where pigs and cows now graze on refuse, lies the market square of the town. This is where buses and motorbikes push their way through fruit and vegetable carts, piles of bangles, and water pots stacked precariously between shops and eateries, and where one can buy anything from hardboiled eggs and single cigarettes to tractors and knock-off antibi-

otics. At the southern end of the square stands a pink-painted shrine to the twin goddesses Lal Bai and Phul Bai. These were the co-wives of a former Rao, who attained divinity by mounting his funeral pyre in an act of *satī*. They are the patron goddesses of the town, to whom local women come asking for sons and men for better salaries. The town radiates outward from this point, with several alleyways running south and west.

Each alleyway is also a bazaar lined with shops that trade in clothes, furniture, crockery, haircuts, medicine, fertilizer, and silver and gold jewelry, among other things. The wares on offer in these bazaars give clues to the town's social topography. Each bazaar is also a residential quarter, a *mohallā*, that has traditionally been occupied by castes that traded in its specialist wares. The *mohallās* are not uniform, single-caste neighborhoods. People have always moved in and out of them, changed trades, gone to work or study abroad and in cities, sold or rented their houses. But the neighborhoods still retain their caste identities. They are still said to "belong" to one or another caste; there is a goldsmith *mohallā*, a barber *mohallā,* a Brahman *mohallā,* and others, and they are still occupied mostly by the traditional resident-castes. Each *mohallā* is also graded by status, with the historically highest ranking families living nearer the center of town, closer to the citadel.

The town as a whole has the concentric shape of a mandala, with occupational sections graded by rank running from the center to the periphery. This layout is readily visible on the streets. Walking outward from the fort to the town periphery, you will watch fine two- and three-story houses give way to single-story buildings, then to unplastered brick houses and finally to tiny, one- or two-room homes made of adobe or the brown slabs out of which poor villagers make their homes. There are a few bigger, two-story houses on the outskirts of the town, but these are concrete, new-money homes of the local businessmen or farmers active in the "land mafia" (*bhūmī dal*), and they stand in striking contrast to the old ornate houses of central Begun. These azure-painted houses, with rooftop terraces, finely wrought balconies, intricate plasterwork, and carved wooden shutters, each unlike the other, are the homes of the old town elite.

When I first visited Begun in 2005, I assumed that this must have been a high-caste neighborhood of Rajputs or Brahmans, who, I had been told, held a customary monopoly in Rajasthan over painting their houses blue. Indeed, my first hosts in Begun, the lawyers who introduced me to Kanjars and who lived in the center of town, were Brahmans, like several other lawyers I was introduced to. But once I settled into fieldwork and started making friends in Begun, I realized that people from all kinds of castes practicing all kinds of trades had hereditary, family homes in the center of town. Cloth merchants and potters, bards and makers of sweetmeats would invite me for meals in their mansions in the center of town. I had thought that this must be the new order, that families with new money, independently of traditional caste status, now owned property in the center of town. But one day, when I was having lunch on the rooftop of a cloth merchant's house, a man called out to me from the rooftop across the street, asking me to visit his house where, he said, he had many "old things" to show. This was Suresh, and so I ended up in Baiji's house. They were drummers, highly polluted in the Brahmanical purity calculus. And yet they lived in the very center of town in a grand, old house, part of which they were renting to a schoolteacher's family. Suresh explained that they were no ordinary Dholis (drummers), but royal drummers (Raj Damamis), who had served the Raos for generations. The house was gifted to Suresh's great-grandfather by the Rao's grandfather, Anop Singh, in gratitude for training his concubines to sing and dance. They were the old town elite.

The houses just outside the center were a mixed lot. Some belonged to wealthy farmers and merchants who had recently bought houses in Begun, but many were still occupied by families that had been there for a long time. These were families from the service castes who worked, not for the Rao, but for the townsfolk. There were barbers and florists and priests, just as there were in the center. But their houses were much less ornate, and often newer. They had no wooden shutters, balconies, or porticos. Though plainer, these houses were overall in a much better state of repair. Unlike royal servants, most of these families had not lost their employment and so had managed to maintain and expand their homes, educate their children, upgrade to more lucrative trades, even travel abroad. This second circle was also where the shopkeepers (Baniyas) lived. These were people with money, but no special standing. No one bowed to them as they walked through the town. Finally, on the outskirts lived the low-ranking sweepers, potters, and carpenters, but also Brahman priests employed in the town and in nearby villages.

This layout of the town gave the lie to the purity-pollution model of rank. The old town elite mixed families from supposedly pure castes (priests, bards) with the supposedly polluted (washermen, cobblers, barbers), who all occupied privileged standing not because they were ritually pure, but because they were bound to the Raos. These were all royal servants (*rāj kamīn*), the core of the servant family in Begun. The town was arranged not by degrees of ritual purity, but by degrees of proximity to the chief family. Many of the *rāj kamīn* families were by now in decline, and some were reduced to poverty. Some had sold their homes, and others, like Baiji, rented them out to make ends meet. And yet the older generation of these families still commanded visible respect in the town. Although a widow, whose late husband was a drunkard who had plunged the family into debt, Baiji was one of the royal servants. So, when she went around town wrapped in a Rajput veil, dressed in the manner of her family's patrons, people in the marketplace bowed her a quiet respect. She was the daughter of the *ancien régime* and, despite the changes that I shall soon discuss, she still held a position of honor in the town.

Royal Brigands

Farther still, on the outermost periphery of this mandala, lay the two Kanjar hamlets whose residents descend from the Kanjars who too were once in the Rao's service. This is how they arrived in Begun. In 1897, a peasant rebellion (*kisān āndolan*) broke out in the neighboring estate of Bijoliya. This was India's first large-scale peasant uprising, which spread through Mewar, reaching Begun by 1921 (G.S. Sharma 2005: 58–60). Its local hotbed was Mandawari, the home of farmers whose descendants would later stage the Kanjar pogrom. Back then, the farmers demanded the abolition of excessive taxes (*lāg, lāgat*) and unremunerated labor dues (*begār*) levied on them by the landlords (*jāgīrdārs*), and the permission to cultivate opium poppy. Fear that this would spark an all-India revolution akin to the Russian reached Delhi. Troops were dispatched by the British, two farmers killed, and the uprising quelled temporarily (Gupta & Bakshi 2008: 328–32).[15] Imperial government, however, held the Rao responsible for policing and punishing rebellious farmers, on

pain of punishment, which he was in no position to do.[16] By 1921, Rao Anop
Singh had ceded most of his judicial and fiscal rights to the British and had
little control over his domains. He managed to have several protesters ar-
rested, publicly flogged, and beaten with shoes, which only provoked further
unrest, with riots breaking out across Begun and farther across Mewar.[17] He
appealed for help to the Maharana (the king of Mewar), but the Maharana
too was out of his depth, himself looking for help with the uprising from the
British Resident (Saxena & Sharma 1972: 268).[18] And so the Rao was forced
to negotiate with the farmers and, after a year of talks, accepted their conditions. The British were furious and demanded that he reverse the settlement
and suppress the uprising (Gupta & Bakshi 2008: 328–32).

This is when the Rao appealed to the trusty old method of controlling the
peasants: he employed robber castes to harass the farmers into submission.
Taking two Kanjar families under his wing, he gave them land near Begun,
from which they could raid local farmers with impunity.[19] Hostilities between
Kanjars and Dhakar farmers (who later staged the pogrom) go back to this
time. Back then, the burglaries committed by Kanjars ranged from the theft of
a single goat (*Navin Rajasthan*, 2 April 1922) to the reported capture of twelve
cartloads of fodder together with the protesters' oxen (*Rajasthan Kesari*, 29
May 1921: 1). The peasants knew this system of strategic theft well; they knew on
whose behalf the thieves did their work, and so they appealed to the Maharana
to protect them from the attacks, which they said were sponsored by the Rao.
But the advantage of such backhanded arrangements was their deniability. In
response to inquiries into the case of the stolen fodder, the Rao replied that
"there are many lawless bands that wander in and out of my territory committing dacoities. I have no knowledge of their thereabouts and certainly no
control over their activities."[20]

This was the official record. But the story I pieced together from the accounts of local Kanjars, farmers, and Rajputs was this. In 1922, the Rao's grandfather, Anop Singh, invited the families of two Kanjar brothers, Laliya and
Bhimiya, to Begun, giving them 2 *bīghas* (half a hectare) of land a kilometer
west of Mandawari. Prior to that, the brothers were employed by one of the
Rao's clansmen on a nearby estate, where in 1920 a dispute broke out between
their familities and the Sansis, another robber caste, resulting in the death of

a Sansi man and the expulsion of Kanjars. When they arrived in Begun, Laliya and Bhimiya got into a brawl with the local Kanjars already in the Rao's employment, killing one of their men. The Rao did not throw them out (remember, he needed their help), instead adjudicating a truce between the two Kanjar groups. In Old Shambhu's words,

> *The Rao divided our land* [deś bāṇṭ kar diyo]. *He explained to us* [hamjotā karāyā]: *you will stay on this side and you will stay on the other. From that day on, we do not go there and they do not come here, we do not hunt pigeons there and we do not take their wives; we do not eat or drink with them and they do not eat or drink with us* [vāke-māke koī aṇ-paṇ nahī hai]; *and we do not give and we do not take; they do not come to our* panchāyat [*council*] *and we do not go to theirs.*

The Rao marked the boundary between their territories with a platform (*chabutarā*), which local Kanjars still honor as the dividing point between the lands of their two rival factions, or "brotherhoods" (*birādarīs*) (fig. 2.2; for more, see Piliavsky 2013a).

The platform, which Kanjars turned into a shrine of Rao Anop Singh, where he is still worshipped, memorializes the short-lived royal patronage that they had once enjoyed. The government of Mewar, both the Maharana and the British Resident, condemned the Rao's lenience toward the peasants and his "Bolshevik settlement" with them (Gupta & Bakshi 2008: 328–32). In 1930s the Rao was removed from Begun, which fell under crown rule. Anop Singh went into exile in Mount Abu, a hill station in southern Rajasthan, where he remained until his death in 1947. Once again, the Kanjars lost their patron, but the legacy of this bond lives on. Kanjars took me repeatedly to the Rao's platform to show off their pedigree. Until this day, they do not steal from the Rao's lands, and the women still veil from him, as they do from a family elder.[21]

Robbers to Criminals

The imposition of crown rule in Begun brought with it big changes for Kanjars. They were now classified as "criminal tribesmen" and placed in penal colonies set up for their "reclamation" under provisions of the Criminal Tribes Act, in force across British India since the 1870s. By the 1930s, the

FIGURE 2.2 The Kanjar cenotaph constructed by Rao Anop Singh in the 1920s. It still demarcates the boundary between the territories of the two Kanjar brotherhoods in Begun. Photo by author.

criminal tribes machinery had run amok, and all kinds of nomadic castes, such as the Banjara and Rebari cattle traders, were criminalized under the act (e.g., Radhakrishna 1989). But, as I have argued elsewhere, the original purpose of criminal tribe legislation was not the settlement of the nomads, but the demobilization of robber castes patronized by the local chiefs. Robber castes were a crucial fiscal and political force deployed by the chiefs in rebellions and negotiations, for extracting resources and policing their domains. As such, they impeded attempts to rein India's landed chiefs in. Kanjars were among the first to be criminalized—a crucial element of the *bellum* to be quelled by the Pax Britannica. The rajas were equally keen to disable robber castes, through whom rebellious under-chiefs wreaked havoc in their kingdoms, allying with the British in a systematic campaign to eradicate robber groups. The kingdoms (or "princely states," as the British called them) of Central and Western India became the sites of the earliest experiments in criminalization (Piliavsky 2013c).[22]

Like India's other newly branded criminal tribes, the Kanjars of Begun were placed in reformatory settlements.[23] By the time of India's independence, there were sixteen criminal tribe colonies in Rajasthan (then Rajputana), four of them in Mewar, whose Maharana, Bhupal Singh, was an ardent supporter of the criminal tribe "reclamation campaign."[24] In August 1930, as soon as Bhupal Singh assumed control of Begun, the two Kanjar hamlets were turned into criminal tribe colonies.[25] Their residents were not locked up (Mewar could not afford that), but their movement was severely restricted by roll call conducted three times a day—at 10 am, 5 pm, and 2 am. To absent themselves from the colony, its Kanjar inmates had to procure passes from the inspector in charge. Should they fail to turn up for roll call or be found outside the colony without a pass, they could be subjected to fines, penal labor, and incarceration.

But the system did not work in quite this way. The criminal tribe administration was, from its inception in 1871, perennially underfunded and understaffed. Reformatory colonies often scattered soon after their formation, and officers in their charge often had little real power over their inmates' movements. In the end, control of criminal tribes substantially passed into the hands of the Salvation Army, which conveniently volunteered to reform them at no cost to the British government (Booth 1916; Tolen 1991). In Begun, the record of roll call, which I found, termite-mauled, among the Rao's papers, during a clear-out of the citadel's record room, bears traces of chaos. Within six months of the settlements' founding, the initially tidy entries made three times a day by the inspector disintegrate; days and weeks of roll-call entries are missing, and, even where he does conduct a roll call, an increasing number of residents appear to be "absconding," just as in the current police records, which I shall discuss in chapter 4. By the summer of 1933, within two years of the colonies' existence, the record of roll call all but entirely petered out. The inspector's last extant note reads: "Kanjars are absconding with greater frequency."[26]

The threadbare paper record hides behind it a more complex story that was still within living memory when I conducted my research. According to three old Kanjars in Begun, who still remember the colonies, which were formally disbanded only in 1952, when the Criminal Tribes Act was repealed, seven local Kanjar households were "adopted" (*god me liye*) by the inspector (for more on police adoption, see chapter 4). He allowed their members to absent themselves for long periods and turned a blind eye to their exploits while punishing others in their stead. These Kanjars also received various "gifts" from the inspector.[27] These privileges came at a price: a share of the Kanjars' profits and other services they could provide for the inspector.[28] Within the space of a few years, the adopted families passed from the service of the Rao into that of the police. The current system of police patronage, which we shall see in the next chapter, is an heir to this. Kanjars saw this new relation with the police in much the same terms as their former ties to the Rao, and their descendants still do. They even saw this attachment to the police as leading to a higher level of patronage. One Kanjar elder, born into an "adopted" family in one of the colonies, said that their master was not really the inspector, but rather the man whose agent he was: the king of Mewar. And so instead of seeing time in the colony as incarceration, he spoke of it as a golden era, a time of patronage and protection. Rolling up his sleeve, he showed me a number tattooed on his forearm: *this is the Mewar number*, he said. I saw the mark of a concentration camp victim. But to him, it was not a mark of former privation, but an "award" (*inām*), as he called it, a gift from the king (*darbār*), a mark of royal service, a cherished sign and proof of their relation. Inspectors themselves seem to have nurtured their patronal image, styling themselves *anndātās*. Remembering the days of the colony, another old Kanjar from an adopted family reminisced:

> When Rao-ji left Begun, we became Maharana Sahib's servants. The In-charge Sahib [*the inspector*] told us—Mewar darbār is the new boss [sarkār] in Begun and he will be your new anndātā. Oh, and how he fed us! He gave us land and buffaloes and we got money to build pukka houses. He said: as long you do not steal in Begun, I will give you passes and you can go as far as you wish. So, we went and whatever we brought back, we shared with the In-charge Sahib. And in this way we lived well. No one was hungry.[29]

In time, some members of these adopted families were even appointed by the inspector as his assistants and were entrusted with, and rewarded for, keeping an eye on the colony. They became the local Kanjar elite, who boasted the patronage of the Maharana, via the inspector, whose protection gave them the wealth to support this claim. This relation was short-lived. When the colonies were disbanded, in 1952, the Kanjars were once again left without patrons.

Chapter 3

THE PEOPLE WHO WERE NOT THERE

EARLY ON IN MY FIELDWORK I was in Jaipur, Rajasthan's capital, and far from Begun, drinking midday whiskeys with some Rajputs and keeping myself abreast of current gossip. Our conversation drifted leisurely from polo-ground drama to the inauguration of a new zinc factory, upcoming weddings, and recent kills made by man-eating panthers on the border with Madhya Pradesh. I mentioned, cautiously, that I had heard that Rajput families used to patronize Kanjars and other such "criminal castes." Expecting tacit suspicion at best, I held my breath, prepared to blame the midday heat and the spirits for the implied accusation of criminal involvement. Instead of suspicion, my remark was met with enthusiasm and an outpouring of stories about the bizarre beliefs and habits of Kanjars. My Rajput friends said that Kanjars had many secret practices, about which they knew a great deal. They knew that Kanjars spoke secret tongues, traded in magic potions, could mysteriously vanish on the spot and outrun police vehicles; that they trained wall-climbing lizards for house burglary, married their own sisters, ritually defecated on the rooftops of burgled houses, and sacrificed human children to bloodthirsty deities. In fact, my Rajput friends knew so much about Kanjars that one of them even suggested that there was no need for me to rough it among the Kanjars because I could learn all I needed to know about them—their secrets—from the present company and other similarly "knowledgeable people." How my friends had got hold of the Kanjar secrets was yet another mystery. None of these city people had ever met a Kanjar. But what they told me, they said, was an open secret, a "truth" (*sachch*) known among Rajasthanis and offered to deserving guests.

The Secret Robber Caste

The idea of a secret outlaw caste has had a long career in South Asia. Ancient Indian texts, ranging from epics and folk tales to legal and liturgical treatises, are full of forest-dwelling robber castes. Like my friends in Jaipur, ancient authors had a lot to say about professional bandits' hidden lairs, thieving techniques, secret tongues, and magical potions. For them, robber castes were exotic and dangerous, magical, powerful, uncivilized, other (Piliavsky 2015a). The trope of secrecy received a new lease of life under British rule. Colonial anxieties about India's "criminal fraternities," which first focused on the murderous cult of thuggee and later on criminal tribes, ran with this old trope of secrecy. In the early nineteenth century William Sleeman, the British officer who first "discovered" and later "eradicated" thuggee, described Thugs as members of a closed society with its own secret argot, *modi operandi*, omens, and bloodthirsty rituals, which he described in voluminous catalogues (Sleeman 1836; 1839; K. Wagner 2007). This was a convenient claim, as it is through claims to "mystery unveiled and mastered that a group of officers of the Political Department had lobbied for operations against this [Thug] 'murderous fraternity'" (Singha 1993: 83). The subsequent campaign against "criminal tribes" deployed the same set of images. Turning his attention to the newly discovered "fraternities of hereditary robbers" (1849), which served as a prototype for the criminal tribes in later colonial legislation, Sleeman described their underworld (where Kanjars figured prominently) as a pan-Indian "secret criminal society" (Sleeman 1849: 1:360, 391).

The mystification of robber castes got a second wind after India's independence. Retaining their criminal identity in official practice, if no longer in statute, Kanjars and other now "denotified" castes continue to be treated as peoples external to moral society and the rule of law. In 1998 the chief minister of Madhya Pradesh lamented that the state's educational programs had little effect on "the criminal instincts" of Pardhis (a denotified tribe), which were nourished by the "hidden nature of their society, which is resilient to the ideas of modern education" (*The Telegraph* 1998).[1] A newspaper article about Kanjars accused of poaching peacocks described them as descendants of "famed highway plunderers . . . said to be habitual criminals and always carry country-made pistols and crude bombs with them." The police can never catch them because Kanjars "disappear on the spot into their secret lairs" (P. Srivastava 2005). While local monographs on denotified tribes call for their "upliftment" by way of integration into mainstream society, official accounts continue to propagate their mystification.[2]

Stories of magic and secrecy fill the records of village police stations. Wherever there are Kanjar settlements, these read not as records of all local crime, as they should do, but as records of crimes committed only by Kanjars. The Mandawari Village Crime Note Book (VCNB) opens with a characteristic account:

> This area belonged to the chief of the Begun estate. The chief used to live here. He used to collect land revenue. But after the feudal system was abolished, the revenue was collected by the tax collector. This area is 300 years old. People of the following castes reside in this area: Rajput, Brahman, Balai, Regar, Rebari, Dhakar, Sutar, Nai, and Kanjar. Kanjars live in the southern and western corners of the village. These people are involved in burglary and cattle theft. They kill and steal goats. In the village there is a primary school, the village council headquarters, an accountant office, and other government offices. Agriculture is the local people's main occupation. Kanjars are involved in crime. . . . They have their secret [*gupt*] methods [of stealing] and their own argot [*pārasī*]. It is very difficult for the police to catch them. (Mandawari VCNB 1973–present: 3)

Another document, the *Compendium Concerning Kanjar Gangs*, a kind of Kanjar ethnography compiled by the police, opens with the following:[3]

> The Kanjar caste is a criminal caste. From ancient times these people have roamed about committing group crime [including] theft, roadside burglary, looting, and dacoity [gang robbery]. They are a caste that is addicted to crime. They are very difficult to find because they can run very fast and when they commit a robbery, they disappear into the jungle or across the [state] border (CDSPO).

The *Compendium* proceeds to describe the deities worshipped, garb worn, and foods consumed by the Kanjars. It goes on to mention miraculous bone-setting practices, which involve the patient's overnight immersion in a barrel of cow dung, and a practice of rearing lizards for wall-climbing burglary. A segment entitled "customs and habits" (*riwāj aur ādat*) tells readers that Kanjar youths are considered unmarriageable until they take part in at least two burglaries.

The same terms and images—lizards, addiction to crime, magical healing techniques, secret tongues, and supernatural endowment—are as central to the official Kanjar story as they are to rumor in the bazaar, which fills official documents, where it is recast as professional expertise and consequently as official knowledge. The VCNBs kept on file in every police station are a rich repository of this official hearsay. A section of the Mandawari VCNB reads as follows:

9 August 1995
Today I came to the village of Mandawari to investigate case #264, 265/95 and I inspected the area. The village people believe that "Anand" associates himself with Kanjars and takes their stolen goods. This will be investigated. The entries are complete and correct. Signed, SHO [Station House Officer] of the "Begun" police station.

17 December 1996
The SHO checked the area during his patrolling session and blocked off all passable roads for the inspection. No Kanjars were found. The entries are complete and correct. Signed, SHO of "Begun" station.

12 September 1997
Today the Kanjar settlement was raided for the arrest of "Raj." He was not found. Most Kanjars run away upon the approach of the police. They cannot be caught. The entries are complete and correct. Signed, SHO of "Begun" station.

16 December 1998
The SHO came together with the police force in search of the criminal

"Suresh" in relation to case #273/98 with accusation under IPC [Indian Penal Code] section 379 [theft]. He raided the settlement and made the arrest. He checked for the presence of the criminal "Gopal," who was not found to be present in the village. But we heard that he visited "Begun" town. His accomplices cannot be found. The entries are complete and correct. Signed, SHO of "Begun" station.

11 May 2000
Today we made a patrolling round of the village, talked to the village people and collected information from reliable sources. The entries are complete and correct. Signed, SHO of Begun station. (Mandawari VCNB 1973–present)

The primary sources for such chronicles are the stories that villagers tell about their Kanjar neighbors. The constables "hear that so and so visited the town" or that "the village people believe that so and so associates with the Kanjars." The information is always gathered from "reliable sources" and the entries are invariably "complete and correct." This particular VCNB, which documents thirty-four years of patrolling one village, records only one actual exchange between Kanjars and the police: a particularly earnest officer described a lecture he gave to Kanjars about the evils of drinking, thieving, and eating meat (the chief vices in both Brahmanical ethics and the current discourse of uplift). Otherwise, the record is filled with reports of Kanjars' disappearances. This may raise a reader's smile, but for villagers, as well as for my well-heeled friends in Jaipur, they are matters of obvious fact. When I relayed the contents of the VCNB to local farmers, they nodded in approval: *Of course,* said one of them. *Everyone knows that Kanjars can disappear—they have magic—nobody knows how they speak and how they steal and where they go and where they come from.*

Self-Mystification
But what do Kanjars themselves make of all this? When I first arrived in Mandawari, my Kanjar hosts insisted that no one outside their community knew their language. It was not just unknown to outsiders, but unknowable. As Kanjars explained, this "insider language" (*āpas kī bolī*) did not lend itself to

learning as such, but propagated itself as instinctive, inherent knowledge, among born-and-raised Kanjars. As I slowly picked up the Kanjari dialect (which turned out to be a slightly modified form of the regional Mewari language), consternation spread: either I too had magical powers, much like the Kanjars themselves, or I had been sent in by the government (*sarkār*), itself subject to much mystification. As I picked up more words, Kanjars themselves began to insist that there was yet another level of secrecy to their language, a secret tongue (*pārasī*) beneath the level of everyday speech. This tongue turned out to be a professional argot consisting of no more than a few dozen phrases and words. As my friends in the settlement taught me more of this language, others insisted on the existence of two, four, or even a dozen other secret tongues, so that no matter how much I tried, I would never have their "total ge" (*ṭoṭal jānakārī*).

Nonetheless, the diligent Ramesh persisted in teaching me the tongues, which turned out to be a kind of "pig Latin," formed by standard substitutions of phonemes and additions of prefixes. Our lessons were highly transgressive, and this thrilled him.[4] Each time I produced a *pārasī* phrase or even a word on Ramesh's instigation, my other Kanjar neighbors were stunned. Since I could not have possibly learned this as children learn English in school, I must have absorbed them by a peculiar natural predisposition. As it became apparent that I was beginning to grasp the content of most conversations in the *pārasī*, the Kanjars of Mandawari reached a consensus: I must have been a Kanjar in a previous life.[5]

Another domain of secret knowledge is the "eighty-four wisdoms" (*chaurāsī buddhiyã*), which were known only to Kanjars, and which Ramesh promised to teach me toward the end of my stay.[6] When we finally drove my motorcycle beyond the boundary of the *bastī* and settled under a banyan tree for my long-awaited lesson, the "eighty-four wisdoms" (of which he could remember only twenty-seven) turned out to be a varied collection of thieving *modi operandi*, ancestral practices, and regulations regarding matters like bride price and incest. As many of the wisdoms replicated the speculations I so often heard in the bazaar, I had to hide my disappointment. The long-awaited revelations of ancient mores and secret practices, from the use of wall-climbing lizards to human sacrifice, reiterated what I had thought to be tall tales on the lips of others. So why hadn't I seen any wall-climbing lizards or human sacrifice in Mandawari? Well, these were very old practices, explained Ramesh, and although Kanjars no longer sacrificed humans or reared lizards, it was important for them to know their people's secret distinguishing signs (*gupt pahachān*). Their divulgence, he warned, would bring on the Kanjars' ruin. Old Shambhu once said to me: *our secrets are our watering well*—a source of livelihood.

The Landlord and the Watchman

The Kanjar secret hides behind it an entire terrain of offstage relations, in which Kanjars play a pivotal role. When I first moved to Mandawari, with a head full of Kanjar magic and mystery, I was surprised to find that in the evenings, when I returned from my trips to the town, there was often a farmer or two lounging on rope beds and chatting with Kanjars. Some were the very men who told me about the Kanjar mysteries. Some came for a drink, but most were there on business. It turned out that most Kanjar men in the area are employed as watchmen (*chaukīdārs*) by farmers, whose fields, orchards, houses, and villages they guard. Watchmanship is a racketeering business: protection from the threat that the watchmen themselves pose. They try to make sure that no one from their village steals in the village under their watch. If something goes missing, the watchman's job is to trace the culprits and retrieve stolen goods.

Apart from policing, the Kanjars' other responsibility is to negotiate conflicts that arise in their patrons' families. But why do respectable families need Kanjars to resolve their quarrels? Why would they let them into their families' innermost lives? All relations in Indian families are hierarchical, as we learned from Baiji in chapter 2. Relations between husbands and wives, parents and children, older and younger siblings, sisters' husbands and brother's wives, relations between various kinds of uncles and others, are not equal. Even twins are unequal, because one will have emerged first from the womb. This hierarchy is attended by a whole host of asymmetrical communicative conventions (Piliavsky 2011). Rules of communicative precedence—about who can say what to whom, how and when—frame the way that family members interact with each other. The right to command or demand, to insist or even to initiate conversation is the prerogative of superiors. A woman or a younger person may supplicate or plead (often effectively), but they cannot legitimately insist. In ordinary circumstances, this endows communication among familiars with a striking elegance of economy, unencumbered by the courtesies of "pleases" and "thank yous;" most messages are conveyed through a single glance or a semi-gesture, to which people are meticulously attuned. Everyone knows where each person stands and what is conveyed. When conflicts arise, however, things get difficult. Communicative transgressions, which threaten superiors' honor and standing, are highly provocative and can quickly escalate into violence (Piliavsky & Sbriccoli 2016). A wiser youth avoids crossing her elders. But how can a young person address a complaint they may have against a superior without sparking a family feud and causing the family's loss of face? Or how can a big man approach another as a supplicant?

This is when they need outsiders, people with no rank at all, to negotiate. Life in North Indian villages, as elsewhere in India, teems with various go-betweens, people who bridge the gaps in ranked communicative conventions, people who save people's and families' honor, and who prevent feuds. (See Chris Bayly's [1996] account of this communicative backstage cast of spies, runners, gossips, and informers who gathered intelligence, conveyed messages, negotiated deals, provoked or intimidated opponents, and mediated disputes—the kinds of characters who populate Kipling's *Kim*.)[7] While playing a crucial role in upholding the polite veneer of local society, such agents are themselves normally outsiders to it.[8] Spies, messengers, and negotiators have long been drawn from the ranks of peripheral persons and communities: forest tribes, nomads, beggars, ascetics, street performers, or itinerant bards. Kanjars are the ultimate go-betweens—mystified and excluded from respectable life, they end up in its innermost crevices.

They are remarkably good at bringing about reconciliation. In the months I spent in Ramesh's house, he must have defused two dozen potential feuds. Some negotiations can be long and laborious, requiring from the watchman a great deal of patience, delicacy, and diplomatic skill. In the summer of 2008 Ramesh got involved in a case of theft that took place in one of the Gujar families who employ him. His job was not to investigate the matter (the perpetrator was already known), but to ensure the amicable restoration of stolen goods.

The wife of the youngest of three brothers in this family stole five goats from the household of the eldest and sold them in a village some 20 kilometers away. The victim could not confront her, because men cannot speak to the wives of their younger brothers, a separation maintained by keeping physical distance and by veiling.[9] Any attempt at a dialogue with her would violate her, his, and the family's honor.[10] Besides, as Ramesh explained, it was shameful for the elder brother to "beg" (*māṅganā*) for the return of the goats. The family needed an "outside man" (*bahār kā ādmī*) to instruct or counsel (*samajhānā*) the woman.[11] *I,* Ramesh added, *am just such a man!* As an outsider, Ramesh could speak and be spoken to by both sides of the conflict, and in the course of the following months, he made several visits to both parties, delivering their concerns—and finally threats—to each other. He ultimately managed to convince the woman that resolution was the right and proper thing to do. She paid the price of the goats, of which Ramesh got one-fifth as commission.

When diplomacy fails, Kanjars resort to more aggressive techniques: the nocturnal raid (*gaimi* in Kanjari), at which Kanjars are experts and which has long been central to South Asian politics, at all levels. A nocturnal raid is a standard method of intimidation. Successful raiding contests end with a resolution, the restoration of stolen goods, and the reinstatement of rapport between the parties in conflict. Or they can provoke protracted feuds.

Plunder has long been integral to statecraft on the subcontinent (Gordon 1969; Vidal 1997; Kasturi 2002: chaps. 5 and 6). Recommended in the third century BCE in Kautilya's treatise on statecraft, it is still in wide use today.[12] Indian rulers of various ranks—from heads of states to landed gentry, village heads, and individual landholders—have long employed the services of professional raiders for tax collection, intimidation, and intelligence (Gordon 1969; Kolff 1990; S. Guha 1999; Skaria 1999; Mayaram 2003; K. Wagner 2007). Most of these were hillsmen and itinerant groups, some of whom eventually attained Rajput status. This has long been a common practice. As early as 1774, Warren Hastings, the first Governor General of India, referred to the landholders of Bengal as the "nursing mothers" of criminal groups (O'Malley 1925: 305–6). And in 1809, Thomas Broughton, a British envoy to the Maratha court, wrote that the youngest son of the Raja of Jaipur employed Meenas to raid his father's lands to get him to grant him an estate (1892: 85, 105). Later Sleeman observed, "A

Rajput chief, next to leading a gang of his own on great enterprise, delights in nothing so much as having a gang or two, under his patronage, for little ones. There is hardly a single chief, of the Hindoo military class, in the Bundelcund, or Gwalior territories, who does not keep a gang of robbers of some kind or other, and consider it as a very valuable and legitimate source of revenue" (1844: 1:188). This raiding politics was alive and well in nineteenth-century and early twentieth-century Rajasthan (Vidal 1997; see also Tod 1920 [1829–32]: 2:493).

In early July, when all were having tea while I nursed pneumonia on a *charpoy*, an elderly Gujar herdsman, whom I recognized as one of Ramesh's employers, appeared on the doorstep. Producing a bottle of moonshine, he lowered himself purposefully onto the *charpoy* next to Ramesh.[13] He explained that his elder brother, with whom he shares a field, had decided to appropriate a quarter of his land. Two days ago our guest woke up to find that the low stone wall separating his fields from his brother's had moved a meter into his land. A younger brother, he was in no position to demand the restoration of the boundary. He said that he had tried to "beg for an answer" (*jawāb māṅganā*), but his brother ignored his approaches. The dispute needed to be resolved quietly, without the police or courts.

Ramesh used to work for the elder brother (the one who had moved the wall) until he stopped paying him. This was an opportunity to redress an old grievance, to show just how indispensable his services were, and hopefully to regain his employment. Five bottles and three hours later, during which it conveniently turned out that both had suffered a great many injustices at the encroacher's hands, they decided that Ramesh would burgle the offender so as "to seat" (*baiṭhānā*) or "press him down" (*dabānā*), to lower or diminish him by "showing their weakness" (*kamajorī dekhānā*). Commissioned theft can achieve this effect in two ways. First, by making their homesteads vulnerable to penetration, it shows them up as incapable of self-defense. A man of good standing, idealized in the figure of a sword-bearing raja, has to be able to protect, an ability that burglary assaults. This is why penetration in its own right, even without burglary, is often sufficient. Second, by forcing victims to "beg" (*māṅgnā*) for the return of their possessions, burglary places its victims in the supplicant's inferior role. Such inversion of the relative standing of the parties in conflict places the sponsor of the raid in a superior position, from which they can make demands. One farmer who likes to hire Kanjars to "seat" his cousins and neighbors explained that after he had Kanjars "collect the harvest" (*ugāī uṭhānā*) from his cousin's home, the cousin was forced to ask him to give back what they took from him. He said:

> *He came begging like a dog to return his wife's gold. So, I told him—now you too will have to give me an answer, where is that money I lent you last year? So, he returned the money, which [until then] he refused so much as to talk about. And he got his gold, but not without interest* (baṛhī).

Commissioned theft does not simply compel compliance by blackmail, it makes otherwise prohibited negotiations possible by a momentary inversion of rank.[14] The younger Gujar brother wished to accomplish just this: to "lower" his elder brother and so put him in a position to heed his demands. As he himself put it, he wished "to press [his brother] to answer [*jawāb denā*]." A few minutes past midnight on the following moonless night of *amāwas* (the best time for nocturnal raids) Ramesh dispatched two of his younger brothers to extract the 2 kilos of silver that the Gujar said were hidden in his brother's bedroom. By four in the morning, the party was back and whispering excitedly. The silver was exactly where it was said to be. Since it was the hot season, the family were sleeping out of doors, so the Kanjars had no trouble doing their business.

Within a fortnight of the burglary, at five o'clock in the evening, the drinking hour, a Gujar man bearing a bottle of hooch appeared at the gate of Ramesh's house. This was the victim of the recent excursion, who in the course of the following months proceeded to make regular visits through which he negotiated the return of his silver for a payment of 300 rupees, and the reinstatement of my host's position as his watchman. The relationship between the two brothers did not mend instantly, but the boundary between their fields was restored to its prior position. Not all raiding contests end in amicable resolutions. Instead of "begging" for the restoration of goods, victims may set their own thieves onto the assailant, and the thieving contests can turn into months or sometimes years of escalating, reciprocal assaults that can end up in bankruptcy, murder, and irreparable rifts. The countryside is full of cautionary tales about relentlessly proud Rajputs who ruin themselves by refusing to compromise in thieving contests, which often turn into something akin to negative potlatches, sorcery matches, or lawsuits. Not everyone plays such raiding games fairly, and some may use gangs of thieves to extract debts and interest or to avenge, or "ruin" (*barbād karnā*), a rival. In such cases theft becomes an attack on the relationship instead of a communication aimed at its restoration.[15]

When negotiations disintegrate, it is Kanjars, who usually come under attack.[16] Whereas open family brawls threaten communities' honor and integrity, violence against Kanjars is unproblematic. Remember: they are socially external and so morally dispensable. The same is true in reverse. And Kanjars have few qualms in meting violence against outsiders (*kādzās,* hereafter Kadzas) to their caste. Disagreements between Kanjar watchmen and their employers can quickly escalate into violent clashes. And it is not always clear who has the upper hand in them. Ramesh was once beaten by one of his Gujar patrons, who suspected him of burgling his house on behalf of one of his neighbors. Ramesh was deeply offended, not just by the blows of the staff, but much more so by the implied accusation of infidelity. He flew into a rage and threatened his abusive employer not only with withdrawing his own protection, but with burgling the man's family "to the last skirt" (*yek ghāgharā na chhoṛke*). Within days he substantiated his threat by setting the Gujar's motorcycle on fire, a move I thought would certainly land him in jail. *Even if I go to jail,* Ramesh said, *I will come out in two months and then you will see—I will not leave a single peanut in his stores, and he knows that! He has seen what I can do, so he knows that it is better to avoid meddling with the police.* Ramesh was right, and the case did not end up with the police. Instead, the Gujar's family members, fearing further violence from Ramesh, negotiated a truce. The offense on both sides was grave, and reconciliation took more than four months of frequent exchange. Eventually, peace was restored when the Gujar was convinced to sell a horse to Ramesh for half its value. Ramesh bought the horse, which he now rents out for weddings.

Raids have long been a way to claim Rajput patronage in South Asia, and today it is a way to claim the patronage of the police. One day a Rajput friend of mine from a village near Begun woke up to find the entire contents of his living room—a coffee table, chairs, stationery, and even curtains—neatly arranged in his front yard. The burglars took nothing, but they left a clear message. The terms of sharing a field, on which he had been unable to agree with his cousin for months, were soon negotiated and courteous rapport between them restored.[17] This was striking. A year earlier, when I was reading about "criminal tribes" in the West Bengal state archives, I came across an identical story, reported in 1923 from Calcutta. A British police sub-inspector, just posted to the area, was approached by the local Kanjars who offered him their services. They explained that, being new to the area, he would have trouble policing it without their help, and that they were happy to work for modest compensation. The officer sent them away, refusing their services. The following week, however, he found the contents of his office laid out on his lawn. Nothing was missing, but Kanjars soon found employment as police informers (Pinhey 1925).

Patron-Policeman

The Begun police can do no better today without Kanjars. Even while filling notebooks with stories of Kanjars' vanishing acts, officers cultivate close ties with the most important Kanjar thieves and gang leaders in their jurisdiction. In fact, one can usually find a constable in civilian clothes loitering in Kanjars' settlements or chatting with Kanjars in the Begun bazaar. Some are looking for information on recent thefts, others for a cut of their profits, and others yet are vying for weekly protection fees (*hāfatā*). Thus, the protection racket works in both directions. *There was a time*, says Old Shambhu,

> *when the police were the Kanjars' biggest enemy. No Kanjar would ever give the police any information. Not on pain of death. But now the Kanjars have grown weak. They like their meat and their bread hot every evening. They don't like to sleep in the jungle. I slept in the jungle most of my life. So they tell on their brothers and keep their easy life. But what is this life that they live? What kind of life can an informer* [mukhabar, in Kanjari] *have?*

Muttering some curses under his breath, he looked past me, spat, and walked away.

Old Shambhu grew up in an era of enmity with the police, an era that ended in 1991, when, following the pogrom, the police "adopted" the Mandawari Kanjars and began collaborating with gang leaders (a practice established in the 1930s, as we saw in the previous chapter). In return for information and a share of the Kanjars' loot, the police now keep informers and their associates out of jail. Local farmers take a dim view of this police collusion with Kanjars, and with good reason. If the old order of watchmanship (*chaukīdārī*) presupposed that the watchman-thief would thieve *outside* his patron's domains, under the new order of police adoption Kanjars can thieve with impunity only *inside* their police jurisdictions. This means that their raids are tightly focused on the neighboring villages, from which they often steal several times a week.

This arrangement suits many Kanjars since in exchange for information and a share of spoils, policemen turn a blind eye to their exploits, write off arrest warrants, and make court cases redeemable for moderate fees. Whereas thieves without patrons in the police may get their charges dropped for 100–200 percent of the value of property they have been accused of stealing (this is usually grossly inflated), adopted thieves normally pay only 25–50 percent. Besides, as Old Shambhu said, once perennially on the run, adopted Kanjars now sleep soundly at home after their raids.[18]

Not every Kanjar enjoys police protection, and those who do not end up in jail, again and again, for burglaries perpetrated by their protected neighbors. This splits the community. *The young boys are idiots*, says Old Shambhu:

> *they think the police are their parents* [mā-ī-bāp]. *They even dress like the fucking cops. They think the head of the station loves them. They think he is the new* jajmān. *All they are doing is bringing ruin to their community. They are spoiling relations. Look—all the brothers in Mandawari are fighting. Why do you think? You will see—soon there will be another attack on the village. The farmers won't put up with this for very long. These kids have forgotten what the police did to us. When the farmers start shooting, they will see what this mother-and-father is like. They'll sell them like dogs. Do they care whether we are alive or dead?*

The young boys are not as plainly happy with police patronage as Shambhu implies. For many collaboration with the police is a shameful, if necessary, part of life, not something they like to discuss openly. By day, Ramesh makes deals with police constables, and by night he curses them to the sky. He needs their protection. He is adding a second story to his house. He has planted an orchard. He has bought a horse from his Gujar *jajmān* as part of their reconciliation.

His daughter-in-law is now pregnant with her first child. He can't afford to be in and out of jail, like before.

One drunken evening, when Ramesh was feeling especially sentimental, he recalled a story his mother told him before she died in the pogrom. Her father was a very fine hunter. One day one raja and his people were in hot pursuit of a mad elephant that had killed some people in a nearby village. Deep in the jungle, the raja's party stumbled across some tents pitched there by the Kanjars. Terrified of the noise made by the hunting party, the Kanjars hid inside, and only her father stepped out to greet the raja. The raja said to him that they had lost the elephant's trail, and her father offered to help. He knew all the signs in the forest, and so he took them down the elephant's path. As they reached a clearing in the forest, they saw an elephant charging straight at them and bellowing like a train. The men started running, and the raja was left all alone. This is when her father took his bow and arrow, and shot the elephant straight through the mouth. The raja took Ramesh's grandfather into his entourage and settled his family in Dewas, a fief north of Begun. *Back then*, said Ramesh,

a jajmān *really took care of his people. Whatever problem they had, if someone was ill or needed money for a wedding, the raja would provide. When they had disputes, he would help them solve those too. Look at our Kanjars now: their brawls go on and on and on. There is no one who can end them. No one big. No one above them. Good patronage ties do this, too—they bring peace and justice to communities. Or so people say.*

Don't the police protect you? I asked.

The police? asked Ramesh, as if he did not hear me properly.

Those bastards [saleh] *just come and eat our money. Inspector Sahib tells us that he will protect us, like he is some big man and a* jajmān, *and then his sidekicks* [chamachās, *referring to constables*] *come and eat up our money. You see them here begging* [māṅg khāte] *every day from house to house: "give me 50 Rupees, 20 Rupees, give me a bottle of* madh." [He mockingly mimicked a high-pitched, tearful voice.] *They'll take anything.*

And what of the Gujars who hire you as watchmen? I asked.

We used to have good relations, but you see—everyone now just wants money. You saw what that Gujar did to his own brother? You saw what he did to me? What kind of jajmān *is that? He is a very—veeerrry—small man,* he drawled comically.

This is patronage gone topsy-turvy. The care and generosity with which the patrons of bygone days (purportedly) treated their clients have given way to crass greed. Instead of "feeding," the patrons now "eat." Instead of providing, they profit; instead of caring they consume. Even more shamefully, the constables "eat" indiscriminately "from everyone's hands." The virtuous past, a fanciful golden age when patrons were generous, women were loving, and men were brave, is a staple of South Asian folk historiography, a story of perpetual degeneration. And it is a leitmotif in Kanjars' oral histories, too. What their stories convey is that their relations with patrons, whether farmers or the police, are venal and treacherous, and (as we shall see in the next chapter) have long been so. Such patrons cannot be relied on, practically as much as existentially. They will not protect you when you need their protection, they offer no support and no concerned care. These relations do not offer belonging or social substance. Whereas Kanjars speak a great deal about former Rajput and Gujar patrons, patrons who "kept" them in the time of the kings, and about their patron deities (whom we shall meet in chapter 5), Kanjars' current patrons afford them little respect. Often, they only bring trouble.

Proper patronage ties—ties that command respect, entail social belonging and generate social substance—must be acknowledged publicly. Local castes, clans, and families with good standing all have proof of patronal belonging. As we have seen in the previous chapter, they have lands and houses that have been granted to them. Some have copper certificates (see chapter 6). They wear clothes (in the style of their patrons) that display service ties. Kanjars have almost none of this (but see chapter 4 for their attempts to demonstrate patronal bonds). They may well work for farmers and the police, but these dealings are generally—and in their essence—screened from view. The secret sphere in which they operate is no doubt their "watering well," as Old Shambhu said, a source of profit, but this very secrecy also makes it a domain of vulnerability. For the many Kanjars who have no patrons among the police, this carries tangible consequences. They are subjected to persistent predation, "erroneous" convictions, and prolonged spells in jail without trial or evidence.

Even for well-established informers, police patronage can be fickle, and they often find themselves as vulnerable as their unprotected caste mates.

Right after I left Begun, Ramesh was put in prison for some months by a new and hostile head of police station. When Kanjars disappear into jails for months at a time or are murdered by upper-caste neighbors, nobody is surprised: they are, after all, master illusionists, ever vanishing into the jungle.[19] This is how one jailer explained to me the absence of seven Kanjar inmates from his records: *Nobody ever knows where Kanjars are—they are always coming and going* [āte-jāte rahate]; *sometimes they are here and other times they are not. How can I keep track of them?* The sphere of secrecy is a space of vulnerability, violence, and abuse. Those who populate it do not exist for the order of respectable life, being expelled from it by the discourse of mystification as well as all the genuine secrecy that dealings with them require. The outsider is necessary but also expendable, someone who can be gotten rid of with no harm done. *What matter is it to anyone whether the Kanjars are there or not?* one farmer said. They were not really there in the first place.

Chapter 4

THE PERILS OF MASTERLESS PEOPLE

THE KANJARS' TROUBLES BEGAN at least five hundred years back, but probably long before that. In 1590 Abu'l Fazl, the Mughal emperor Akbar's court historian, wrote that there were Kanjars in the imperial court. "Men of this class," he remarked, "play the p*akhāwaj* [drum], the *rabāb* [lute], and the *tāla* [cymbals], while the women sing and dance" (Abu'l Fazl 1873–94 [c. 1590]: 3:257). And in 1727 Jean de Thévenot, a French visitor to the court of Shah Jahan noted that, "the women and girls of this caste . . . have no other occupation but dance" (de Thévenot 1727 [c. 1661]: 5:151, my translation). These Kanjars were traveling entertainers of the kind one still sees occasionally singing, drumming, and ropewalking on the Indian streets, but they had the fortune of gaining the favor of India's grandest patrons, its emperors.[1] Akbar loved his Kanjars, and especially their women, whom he dubbed "Kanchanis," meaning the "blossoming, gilded, or golden ones" (Abu'l Fazl 1873–94 [c. 1590]: 3:257; Bernier 1891: 273).[2] "Handsome and well dressed," wrote Aurangzeb's French physician François Bernier, the Kanchanis "sing to perfection; and their limbs being extremely supple, they dance with wonderful agility, and are always correct in regard to time" (Bernier 1891 [c. 1660]: 274). The Kanjars who frequented the imperial court were no waifs and strays. As Shah Jahan's Venetian doctor Niccolao Manucci remarked, they were "more esteemed than other [dancing girls]. . . . When they go to court, to the number of more than five hundred, they all ride in highly embellished vehicles, and are clothed in rich raiment. All of them appear and dance in the royal presence" (Manucci 1907 [1708]: 1:196).

The Kanjars not only sang and danced, but also traded in a wider variety of pleasures. An Anglican chaplain who traveled to Western India in the late seventeenth century was rather taken by their charms:

> Dancing Wenches, or Quenchenies [who] entertain you, if you please, with their sprightly Motions, and soft charming Aspects, with such amorous Glances, and so taking and irresistible a Mien, that as they cannot but gain an Admiration from all, so they frequently Captivate a zealous Rich Spectator, and make their Fortunes and Booty of the Inchanted Admirer. (Ovington 1928 [1689]: 257)

By the early nineteenth century, Kanjars were so well known as courtesans that the Englishmen who set out to work for the East India Company read in the *East India Vade-Mecum* that the "kunchenee ... dance and sing for the amusement of the male sex, and in every respect are at their command" (Williamson 1810: 1:386). Some Kanjar families across Northern India and Pakistan are still in the sex trade, which they practice in Rajasthan's roadside hamlets as much as in dance bars in Lahore and Bombay (see Saeed 2001; Agrawal 2004; Brown 2006; later in this chapter).[3]

In the early days of the Mughals, Kanjars were free-range entertainers who moved between palace and city, performing both in the royal court and the bazaars.[4] Although they were frequent visitors to the imperial court, they had not yet become court artists.[5] And so the Kanchans described by Abu'l Fazl and those eyed by Manucci in the bazaar may well have been very the same people, known back then as either "Kanjars" or "Kanchans" (Akbar's pet name for them). By the eighteenth century, however, things had changed. What was once a single community of traveling performers had now split into two. The lowly marketplace entertainers, who came to be known as "Kanjars," a word that acquired negative undertones, and the courtly elite known as "Kanchans," which became an honorific.[6] The split in status mirrored the split in patronal arrangements. Some of the dancers managed to secure formal service rights at the Mughal court, while others eked out a living in the bazaars. By the early eighteenth century, under Shah Jahan, the relation of Kanchans to emperors was already highly formalized: they were expected "to attend twice a week at court, for which they received pay, and to perform at a special place which the king had assigned for them" (Manucci 1907 [1708]: 1:196). "When they came to [the court] on the Wednesdays to pay their reverence at the *Am-Kas* [inner reception hall], according to an ancient custom, [Shah Jahan] often detained them the whole night, and amused himself with their antics and follies" (Bernier 1891 [c. 1660]: 273–74). Shah Jahan's puritanical son Aurangzeb disapproved of his father's indulgences and prohibited Kanchanis from entering the royal quarters. And yet their service ties were already so well fixed that, "complying with long established usage, [he did] not object to their coming every Wednesday to the *Am-Kas*, where they ma[d]e the *salam*" (Manucci 1907 [1708]: 1:274).

The difference between Kanchans and Kanjars was not only one of income. Kanjars who failed to fix ties with royal patrons and so were left to dance in the marketplace acquired the status of beggars—a masterless, stray folk. While those who danced for a single grand patron became the darlings of high society, concubines and even rivals of queens, those who danced for anyone who was willing to pay became not only socially marginal and morally suspect, but also axiomatically "loose."[7] By the late nineteenth century, the word "Kanjar" was already "so proverbial that it [was] a common thing amongst natives to term a quarrelsome foul-mouthed woman a 'Kunjurnee'" (Gunthorpe 1882: 80). And by the early twentieth century, "Kanjar" was simply "the ordinary word for pimp or prostitute" in the Punjab (Rose et al. 1911: 3:474, also 454–55; Ibbetson 1916 [1883]: 288–90). A current online dictionary of British South Asian slang tells us that "Kanjar" is "a pimp" or "a person who don't care even if they are banging their own sis," or simply "one who has earned the anger of a fellow Pakistani neighbor" (www. urbandictionary. com). More generally, the word refers to all kinds of socially stray and morally loose people: tramps, prostitutes, beggars, vagrants, thieves, bastards, or pimps. Today parents may say to their ill-behaved children: *Kanjarõ kī taraf mat karo!* (Don't act like a Kanjar, don't be a bastard!).

Kanjars tell their own story of their downfall. There once lived a remarkable woman called Bajori Kanjari. She was a dancer, a ropewalker, a magician, and a living goddess (*śakti*), the daughter of goddess Sakti and god Dev Narayan, the patron god of the Gujars, the great North Indian herding caste. Renowned for her beauty, Bajori Kanjari performed tantalizing dances and ropewalk-ing tricks for her patron, the king. She was the Kanjars' ancestress, and her story goes like this. One day the raja was merry with drink, and he decided to throw a big party. To entertain his guests, he stretched a rope between two mountain peaks and challenged Bajori, his favorite *danse*, to walk from one to the other end. If she managed to walk the length of the rope, he promised that he would grant her half of his kingdom. As the guests gathered round to watch, Bajori took up her balancing rod and set out on her long walk. She went farther and farther until she was so far away that they could barely see her in the distance. At this point, the queen, who was standing by quietly, realized that, should Bajori succeed, the king's drunken jest would cost him (and the queen's son) half the kingdom. So the queen took out a sword and sliced the rope in half. This is when, to everybody's amazement, instead of plummeting into the lake below, Bajori rose to the sky. She was, after all, a goddess. As she made her ascent, she put a terrible curse on the king, the worst kind of curse that can befall a king. He was to have no more progeny, and Mewar was to have no more royal heirs.[8]

The curse came true. The king in question, Maharana of Mewar Jawan Singh (r. 1828–38), died without issue, and the next seven kings, right up to the current one, had to be adopted. This is not just the Kanjars' story. The kings tell it, too. They call it "the tale of the dancer's curse." In fact, they marked the event with a cenotaph, known as "the dancer's platform" (*naṭnī kā chabutarā*), which now stands in the middle of Lake Pichola, right in front of the royal palace, in the very place where Bajori made her ascent. Meant to propitiate the divine dancer, the cenotaph stands as a stern warning to patrons who may fail in their dues (Masters 1990: 81–82). Bajori not only cursed the kings, but also decreed that no Kanjar should ever serve a Rajput again, for trust between Kanjars and Rajputs was forever lost. Kanjars also say that they once served Maharana Pratap, Rajasthan's greatest hero king who defied Akbar, winning against him a Pyrrhic victory in the Battle of Haldighati in 1576. The Maharana's fort in Chittor (then the capital of Mewar) fell to Akbar, the Rajput army dispersed, and the many peoples who fought alongside the Maharana, including Kanjars, acquired the dubious freedom to roam, as the old folk say, "in the jungle," hunting and thieving and plundering the highways.

India's Vagrants

These stories are charter myths that offer an etiology for the Kanjars' current predicament. They are part of a large genre of narratives on the subcontinent built around the trope of lost or severed patronage bonds as the cause of social misfortune. All kinds of low castes tell such stories, but they are especially common among the lowest of the low—among India's "vagrants" (e.g., D. Mines 2014). Outsiders refer to them by many different names, but the vagrants themselves share a remarkable sense of unity, recognizing one another as members of a single society (*samāj*). I say "remarkable" because this society includes people who speak dozens of different languages, ply all kinds of trades, and are scattered right across South Asia—from Sri Lanka and Tamil Nadu to Pakistan and Bengal. What unites them is not only the outsiders' negative solidarity, but also the substantive bonds of a shared language, patron deities, commensal relations, origin myths, and indeed often traceable ties of kin. In different places they are known by different names, but they call themselves Bhantus (m. *bhāṇṭu*, f. *bhaṭāṇī*), using a pan-Indian endonym akin to the European "Rom." The gentiles are known as Kadzas/Kadzis (m. *kādzā/kājjā*, f. *kādzī /kājjī*), again like "Gadjo" in Roma.[9]

The Bhantus' exonyms, or the caste names by which others call them, give a sense of the jagged history of their movements from place to place, from trade to trade, and from one master to another. Nat, Dom, Sansi, Bagri, Beriya, Hurukiya, Dhadi, Kucchbandhi, Moghia, Pardhi, Badhik, and Kanjar are only some of the many names that Bhantus go by in Northern India. Some of these names refer to the trades they were known for, others to the names of erstwhile patrons, and others still to the names of places where they once lived.[10] In common parlance, however, and unlike other caste names, they bear no association with a particular trade, person, or place. These names reflect the social indeterminacy of such groups, and refer always to social (and moral) outsiders, to "vagrants." Although most Bhantus have now settled and adopted the exonyms as their caste names, until recently they were known by different names in different places, their caste identity shifting rapidly with their movements. So, the 1881 Census Report recorded more than 100,000 "Kanjars" as living in the North-Western provinces (Plowden 1883: 1:18, 302), ten years later, there appeared to be only 29,186 "Kanjars" in all of Hindustan (Baines 1893: 206). One colonial officer gave a good account of how such changes happened:

[The Bhantus] are known by a multitude of names, and the names vary every hundred or so miles of space. This is what happens:—Say Massānia's . . . camp is in Oudh. People will say, "Here are the Berihas." Massānia treks to Aligaṛh; the public in Aligaṛh will exclaim, "Here come the Habūras." In Delhi and Karnāl, no one will have any doubt that Massānia's people are Kanjars. In Ferozepur, they become Kīkan; in Multan, Gedari; and in Sindh, Gīdiya. (Williams 1889: 38)

This caused substantial confusion among colonial officials and ethnographers who struggled to come up with a precise description of the "Kanjar caste." While Kanjars in one place claimed to be Sansis, Sansis in another said they were Kanjars; Kucchbandhis insisted that they were Beriyas, and Kanjars and Haburas each claimed that the other was a subset of their caste; others yet reported that Kanjars were a segment of the Jat, Habura, or Banjara castes; and some Kanjars said that Sansis and Beriyas were both Kanjar clans. Sansis, in their turn, insisted that Bagris, Badhiks, Gidiyas, Haburiyas, Kichaks, Kanjars, and Moghiyas were all Sansi clans.[11] Just as the Bhantu castes were impossible to name, they were even more difficult to pin down to an occupation, the chief marker of caste. Those known as Kanjars alone have plied a huge variety of trades, ranging from rope-, mat-, and toy-making to prostitution, snake charming, trapping, dancing, and theft.[12] Despairing of finding the true Kanjar caste, British officials concluded that the name is "used in a very loose manner" to describe a "much subdivided" body of "loosely allied communities" or "an aggregate of vagrant tribes of a gypsy character."[13] Modern ethnographers have been no more precise, describing "the Kanjar caste," as a collection of "various small nomadic communities" or "a large amorphous set of communities" (Singh 2004: 5:1539; Agrawal 2004: 225n).

So, why such confusion? Some of it has been driven by force of circumstance and some by the Bhantus' own strategic adoption or abandonment of their names. Because historically the Bhantus have been on the move and because they have often had only tenuous links to settled society, whatever name was already locally associated with vagrants would stick to all new arrivals. At the start of my research, people who were described to me as Kanjars or Sansis by my middle-class friends actually called themselves Banjaras, Kalbeliyas, or Kuchchbandhis. Some have successfully shed the labels of disrepute. So, a

"Nat" family I met in Northern Rajasthan turned out to be close relatives of my "Kanjar" hosts. Before India's Independence the family lived in Mewar, where they were given land by a local raja. But then life got tough: in the 1930s they were put into a penal colony along with other "criminal tribes," and following Independence, once the colony was disbanded, they were persecuted by the police. So, in the late 1950s they upped and moved to the north of the state in an attempt, as one elder put it, to *divorce the native country and the name Kanjar.* They adopted the new, "clean" title of Nat, meaning "dancer" (from *nāchanā,* "to dance") and started ropewalking and dancing for village audiences. Much better, he explained, to have a name that refers to a proper occupation than to have one that refers to none. What he meant by a "proper occupation" was something particular that could be offered in service to others:

> *You see, dancers dance for their masters. Even if they travel a hundred thousand miles, they have masters* [jajmāns] *of their own. But who is the prostitute's master? Every man. And who is the thief's master* [mālik]*? You know—thieves, like your Kanjars, have masters, but who* [which master] *will admit to that? It takes a king to say to the public: I feed the Kanjars. And where are such kings nowadays?*

That has been the strategy for many Bhantu communities, who have tried to drop the vagrant names in favor of more respectable occupational titles like brush maker (Rachbandh), snake charmer (Sapera), stonecutter (Sankat, Patharkat), or woodman (Lakrhār) (Nesfield 1883; Crooke 1896a: 3:137–38). As Rose noted in his *Tribes and Castes of the Punjab,* "Sansis in Hindustan and the Districts of the Punjab east of the Ghaggar river are known as Kanjars," and "wandering Sansis style themselves Kanjars only in the Delhi territory and parts of the east, dropping the name when they approach the Sutlej" (Rose et al. 1911: 3:474–75). As another colonial police officer noted, "Very little really is known about the Kanjars [because] they generally hide their identity [and] seldom admit they are Kanjars" (Gayer 1909: 55). And little wonder. Here again is Williams on Massania's troubles:

> If Massānia is hard pressed, and the Kājas [Kadzas, gentiles] gather to-gether with bludgeons and sharp-edged instruments to attack and drive him away, he will protest that he and all his people are Cangaṛ (the name

by which the basket-makers go), and the Kājas may, or may not, be appeased. (Williams 1889: 38)

Often, the Kadzas are not appeased. A people I met in Bhopal, who I was told were Kanjars, told me that they were not Kanjars at all, but Kuchbandhis (brush makers, it being better to make brushes than to "beg"). But they were branded as Kanjars in the 1930s during the creation of a criminal tribe colony in Bhopal. They have been unable to shed this "stamp" (*chămp*), as one of their women told me, ever since.

The Bhantu vagrants are not to be confused with India's nomadic communities. In India, all kinds of castes practice itinerant trades, but many of them are not outcasts, like the Bhantus, but on the contrary command respect. Banjaras, for instance, who trade in cattle and salt, Gadoliya Lohars (nomadic ironsmiths), Bhopa singers of epics, or the transhumant Rebaris who trade in camels and sheep enjoy great respect in settled society. Recall Rao Hari Singh's admiring comments on the Gadoliya Lohars (chapter 2). The problem for Bhantus lies not in mobility as such, nor in their landlessness, but in the lack of social attachments.[14] Banjaras and Rebaris may move a great deal, but they have a steady circle of patrons, whom they visit on their annual rounds. They may be spatially mobile, but socially they are firmly fixed. The Bhantus conversely have had no social anchors. Moving from Lahore to Kolkata to Bombay, they would put on ropewalking and snake-charming shows; make toys, ropes, and baskets; or practice thieving and prostitution, offering their services to anyone who was willing to pay (Waterfield 1875: 28; Wise 1883: 86). While Banjaras, Rebaris, and Bhopas were associated with specific trades, which assumed tightly specified service attachments to particular patrons, names like Kanjar, Sansi, or Kuchbandhi (which refer to no particular trade) have become entrenched as titles for socially unsettled, indeterminate vagrants—both fascinating and dangerous, but certainly external to mainstream, respectable life.

Bards

Bhantus themselves tell their own story of longstanding patronal attachments by virtue of being hereditary bards. They say that the very word "Bhantu" comes from the word *bhat*, or "bard." Bards who write family genealogies and sing their praise have long been much sought after on the subcontinent. From the early medieval period, and increasingly with the elaboration of the Rajput "great tradition" from the sixteenth century onward, genealogy emerged as the cornerstone of good social standing and political legitimacy in Western and Central India (Kolff 1990: 72, 110).[15] To be a Rajput, the status to which many groups across Central and Western India have aspired, it was not enough to own land and have the protection of an overlord, one also needed a pedigree, complete with sacred (*purāṇic,* or "epic") lineage, divine origins, and a patron deity (*kul devatā* or *kul devī*) of one's own. From the sixteenthth century onward, "every royal clan depended on a line of bards for its recognition" (Tambs-Lyche 1997: 61),[16] and by the mid-seventeenth, when the Rajput model became entrenched as the benchmark of social status and political legitimacy, "genealogical orthodoxy" was firmly established as an essential aspect of respectable standing (Kolff 1990: 73). In 1891 the British Census commissioner lamented that "the affairs of State are falling into the hands of [non-Rajput] castes," all of which claim Rajput status. "The beggar's book [genealogist's register] outworths the noble's blood" (Baines 1893: 204, quoting Shakespeare, *Henry VIII,* act 1, scene 1, lines 184–85). All upwardly mobile aspirants to Rajput status, from major landholders to hillsmen and leathersmiths, relied on the production and maintenance of pedigrees. And so bards were in high demand among communities of all standings.[17]

Originally, most bards came from the ranks of the vagrants. In fact, the name *Charan,* or "genealogist," derives from the Sanskrit word *chāra,* meaning "motion" or "wandering about" (Monier-Williams 1876: 321).[18] As communities of patrons secured royal or aristocratic standing, their bards, too, rose in status. In Western India the history of Rajputization, or the emergence of a Rajput elite (see p. 35), resulted in the rise of two classes of bards: the elite bards (Charan eulogists and Bhat genealogists) who served Rajputs and other dominant communities,[19] and the lowly Bhats (genealogists) and Nats (dancers and ropewalkers) who served various low-status castes (Russell 1916: 339; Snodgrass 2004: 275–80).[20] From the thirteenth century, while royal Charans and Bhats occupied some of the highest social positions, just below their royal patrons, the bards of low ranking communities have remained on the periphery of social life. Many of those who would take up the bard's trade came from communities of wandering entertainers: snake charmers (Jogis, Kalbeliyas), musicians (like Dhadhis, Langas, Manganiyars), dancers, ropewalkers, and acrobats (Nats). Kanjars have figured prominently among them.[21]

Prior to their dislocation from positions of authority in the colonial period, royal bards were equal, or even superior, in status to royal Brahmans (Tessitori 1917; Vidal 1997: 92). Like royal Brahmans, they held a place of honor in the court and received permanent tax-free land grants (*muāfis* or *śāśans*) (Waghorne 1985: 11; *Imperial Gazetteer of India* 1908: 24:100).[22] In Rajput kingdoms, royal bards had the standing of landed nobility and were listed in British accounts among the "leading men of the [Rajput] State," alongside Rajput nobles, state officials, and royal priests (Bayley 1916 [1894]: 46, 11, 25).[23] Indeed, royal Charans and Bhats were so revered that they were treated as sacrosanct and inviolable: the sacred brothers or sons of their patrons' clan goddesses (*kul devīs*), referred to as the Deviputra (Sons of the Goddess) (Shah & Shroff 1958: 249). As such, they were legally "classed together with 'the cow and the Brahman' whose slaughter was forbidden" (Qanungo 1960: 40).[24]

Bards of low-caste communities, however, ended up at the opposite end of the rank scale, not only because they had lowly masters, but because their service ties remained indeterminate, inchoate. Although engagement in a respectable bardic profession improved these vagrants' lot, they retained the reputation of socially loose vagabonds who "come and go" (*āte-jāte*) and "eat from everyone" (*sabhī kā khāte*). Within the broader bardic community, they bear the pejorative accolade of "begging bards" (*Brid-dhārī* or *Bradesarī Bhāṭs*) (Russell 1916: 2:338), and in colonial caste catalogues they were placed at the bottom of the rank scale alongside camel men, barbers, mendicants, laborers, and other "persons of disreputable occupations" (e.g., *Census of India, Ajmer-Merwara* 1901: 2:pt. 1:120).

What is important to understand is that bardic work in itself was not in disrepute; royal and low-caste bards did identical work: they wrote, performed, and recorded panegyrics and genealogies (*bansāvalīs* and *piḍāvalīs*). Differences in their status did not depend on the prestige or ritual purity of their occupation, but on the status of their *jajmāns*. Bards who served Rajputs were the elite, while the bards of Gujars or Bhils were the riffraff. Their standing was not only a matter of who their patrons were, but also, crucially, of the quality of their service attachments: the more exclusive and durable were the bards' bonds to their *jajmāns*, the higher was their standing. Patrons' claims to antique pedigrees and their bards' claims to antique service attachments mutually reinforced. The genealogies were both proof of the *jajmān's* pedigree and proof of his bard's service, which was as old as the pedigree that he had recorded. Patron and bard, each afforded the other a claim to a clear "origin"—one genealogical, the other patronage-based, but both existentially crucial. Visible signs of patronal bonds (titles, property, land grants received from *jajmāns*) further anchored the bards' claim.[25] Although today many bonds between bards and Rajput *jajmāns* have dissolved (as genealogy has lost its former appeal) and many bards have taken up new professions, they still like to show off the gifts, honors, and land that their forefathers had received from *jajmāns*, and to display genealogical registers as markers of their service attachments. The royal bard of Begun explained (fig. 4.1):

> *You can see how far Raoji's genealogy* [piḍāvalī] *goes and that is how long my forefathers were tied to his family. You see, this land and this house here were given to my grandfather by our Rao Sahab's grandfather. Everyone in Begun knows that. And everyone respects us because they know that we have been with Raoji's family from the very origins of their clan.*

Itinerant, low-caste bards could make no such claims. However long-lasting their ties to *jajmāns* may actually have been, they accumulated little proof of their attachments. Receiving no formal titles or land from their patrons (most of whom had no land to give), they remained "beggars" in respectable people's eyes. Although, as I shall discuss in chapter 6, mobile bards have done their best to flaunt their attachments through flamboyant performances, their apparently erratic movements make them appear as socially stray, morally wayward, untrustworthy, and threatening. In conversation with a farmer in Begun, I once observed that the itinerant bards do the same work as the royal Charans and Bhats, and that they should, therefore, be treated as members of the same *jātī*. This is what he said:

> *We do not see it this way. You see, we know that the royal bard* [rāj kavī] *has been singing for Rāo Sahābjī for a very long time. He has land and a house. We know the hand from which his family has always taken bread. But with these roaming bards—who knows where they have come from and where they*

will go? How do we know how many hands feed them? They come and go. We see them as beggars and vagabonds.

The perceived uncertainty of the mobile bards' attachments to patrons—accusations of indiscriminate "eating"—aligns them with other vagrants. The *jajmāns* themselves also often distrust their bards, whom they suspect of dancing and singing en route for anyone who might be willing to pay. Their suspicions are not entirely unfounded. I first encountered a group of Kanjar Bhats when Ramesh, my Kanjar host, spotted a cluster of their tents just outside a tribal Bhil village. Parking his motorcycle quietly in the shadow of a big mahua tree, we stopped to chat with them. At the sight of an approaching motorcycle, the Kanjars grew wary, becoming particularly nervous when they learned that my Kanjar companion was from Begun, where their Gujar *jajmāns* reside. One of them drew Ramesh aside for a brief chat. When we left, Ramesh said:

FIGURE 4.1 Bhanwar Singh Rav, royal bard (*rāj kavī*) of Begun, reading out his couplets (*dohās*). Poetry is no longer in demand, and his son (left) does not compose couplets. Photo by author.

Bastards [sālahs]*, here they are dancing for Bhils and somewhere else they will be dancing for drummers and washermen; and he asks me not to tell his* jajmān. *What do I care for telling? Sooner or later he will lose his* jajmān's *trust and that will be the end of his business. Everyone knows that they beg from everyone. Kanjars they are, but small Kanjars. They disgrace our caste. This is why we don't give our daughters to these beggars.*

Spies

As we have seen in the previous chapter, the Bhantus' secretive, elusive position has its advantages, making them perfect agents of surveillance, intelligence, and backstage negotiations, who, as I remarked already, have long been essential to South Asia's statecraft. So much so that in the seventh century the author of a Sanskrit epic, *Śiśupālavadha,* wrote that "statecraft without espionage seems to us like the science of grammar without the Paspasha [the introduction to Patanjali's great commentary on Panini's Grammar]" (Durgaprasada & Sivadatta 1914: 2, 112). Authors of ancient statecraft treatises have always advised kings to employ various spies to inform them on the proceedings in their own and neighboring kingdoms.[26] From antiquity, the ability to know, and to rule knowingly, while maintaining the face of politeness in relations with one's neighbors and subjects, relied on the maintenance of a secret intelligence force. The best people for this purpose were always various itinerant folks. In fact, the Sanskrit word *chāra* means not only "to wander" but also "to spy" (Monier-Williams 1876: 321). In his *Arthaśāstra,* Kautilya tells the king that to keep an eye on his servants, he should assemble a cohort of "wandering spies" (*sanchāra*) from among actors, dancers, singers, musicians, jugglers, prostitutes, buffoons, wandering heralds, and bards (Kautilya 1967 [c. fourth century BCE]: 1.11–12, 2.27). And he recommends royal spies who do not actually come from wandering communities to dress up as itinerant actors, picture reciters, dancers, puppeteers, and the like (1.12). Kamandaki, the author of another well-known statecraft treatise, *The Elements of Polity* (*Nītisāra* c. 400–600 CE), also writes that intelligence agents should be either *jāṅgalī* (uncouth, savage) folk or should disguise themselves as mendicants, traveling merchants, ascetics, forest dwellers, and mercenaries (Kamandaki 1896 [c. 400–600 CE]: 190).

While we know that the once-itinerant royal bards have been employed as messengers, negotiators, and secret intelligence agents (Vidal 1997), the employment of lower-caste itinerant bards for similar purposes has not been well documented.[27] A handful of sources, however, suggest that low-caste itinerants, and among them most often itinerant bards, were often so employed. Abu'l-Fazl tells us that the migratory Meos of Mewat worked as runners and spies for Akbar (1873–94 [c. 1590]: 1:252).[28] Bhil and Sahariya tribes, as well as Banjara and Rajka cattle traders also gathered information and carried messages within and between Rajput states.[29] Indeed, in Central India Sahariyas are still known as Rāwats, from the Sanskrit term *rājā-dūta*, meaning "king's messenger" (Mandal 1998: 192). This practice has persisted well into twentieth-century polity. In Mewar in the 1920s and 1930s, Maharana Bhopal Singh employed two illiterate beggars, who gave him detailed reports on the goings-on in his kingdom.[30]

Secret intelligence agents were not only employed by royals. Landholders of all stripes used itinerant peoples to spy on rivals and negotiate conflicts with them (Servan-Schreiber 2003: 279), and in Mughal India "merchants and rival nobles employed wandering spies and agents to obtain reliable information from the entourages of the great [noble] men" (Richards 1995: 61). As we have seen in the previous chapter, sensitive matters, such as thefts, elopements, or land disputes, called for hidden negotiation means: in princely and market-place politics, each man needed a backstage *dalāl* (go-between). As C. "Bayly observes, in the 1860s,

> rather than informing the police, . . . a man who suspected someone of cattle theft would have the animals traced by his private agents and would then hire a professional go-between (*dalāl*) to confront the suspected criminals. A large portion of the value of the animals would be recovered, but absolutely nothing would have come to the notice of any official agency. (Bayly 1996: 334)

Much like the royal bards, the low-ranking Bhats gathered information, and helped to resolve disputes and to negotiate deals. According to one Kanjar I met, whose family are still employed as bards by the Rajputized Koli hillsmen,

> *Our ancestors worked in the business of espionage* [jāsūsī kā kām karte the].
> *If there was a need for warring with another raja, how would [a raja] learn*

about his enemy's state of affairs? As Nat-Bhats, we put on performances [tamāśās], *we danced and sang and then we found out that this raja gave such a gift to another raja and then we advised [our* jajmān *raja] that he should give the same [to keep his honor]. And we brought news about the other raja: how much money he has in his coffers, how many men, how big an army, how many field guns. In this way we gathered all the information [jānkāṛī] and would tell our raja that [his enemy] has five hundred field guns and ten thousand soldiers, so [we would tell him], go there with twenty thousand soldiers. For this service we received gifts [dānpurn] and a contribution [chandā] from the harvest [collected by each] household. The rajas gave us whatever we asked for: guns and swords, cloth, pots and pans, and liquor [śarāb].*

As we have already seen, this system lives on and Kanjars still work as backstage agents of enforcement, intelligence, and negotiation for Rajputs, farmers, village communities, and the police.

Thievery as a Vocation

In keeping with the local dictum that "it takes a thief to catch a thief,"[31] most watchmen were themselves members of thieving groups, themselves the threat from which they protected others.[32] But hiring thieves as watchmen was never a stable solution. Here is one account by a colonial officer, who employed itinerant Moghias to police Meena highway robbers.

The excesses of the Meenas were thus put down, but it soon appeared that the country had only been freed from one evil to fall into a greater, and that the Moghias were professional robbers and dacoits of no mean order . . . , they became so formidable, that the very authorities who had introduced them had, as a measure of self-defense, [had] to treat with them. [As] they were expelled, their wealth immediately purchased them shelter and protection elsewhere, and from their new residence they revenged themselves on the territory they had been driven from, either by robbing its people or bringing it into trouble by committing outrages in it. The authorities as their only resources had then to entertain fresh Moghias as watchmen. This secured the protection of their own territory, but sooner or later brought them into difficulties with others, the Moghias whenever opportunity offered robbing or committing excesses elsewhere. The history of the past is said to have been a succession of expulsions and fresh entertainments.[33]

Village communities, landholders, and kings had long employed professional thieves as watchmen, escorts, mediators, and spies.[34] Although some thieving groups managed to secure lasting patronage ties, and some even acquired land grants and hereditary rights of office, for most, patronage remained a highly uncertain arrangement.[35] Unlike drummers, barbers, or priests, who enjoy publicly recognized service rights, thieves worked in the murky sphere of hidden negotiations that lack the security and recognition of public trades. Employed for protection, resource extraction, rebellion, conquest, protection, and dispute resolution, thieves were often used furtively and temporarily; failure to perform their duties, accusations of infidelity, or conflicts inside thieving communities themselves easily sent such groups and their fragments adrift.[36]

When contention defied dialogue and words failed, negotiations called for more potent communicative means. So, *dalāls* often served not merely as messengers or information brokers (C. Bayly 1996), but also as raiders. Traveling ascetics often doubled up as messengers, spies, and gun-bearing toughs, and Bhil chieftains asserted their protection rights by raiding villages and caravans (Kolff 1971; S. Guha 1999; Skaria 1999). Mughal rulers conducted their combat through robber bands, Marathas established dominion by methodical plunder, and Rajputs founded kingdoms, rebelled, and feuded by rustling cattle and marauding the countryside.[37] Apart from being an important, and sometimes the sole, method of procuring resources, robbery was also integral to diplomacy, used to subjugate and sway rivals by penetrating their domains. In fact, robbery was so central to South Asian politics, wrote Shulman, that "cattle-raiding was considered a standard feature of the relations between neighboring 'kingdoms'" (Shulman 1980: 289).[38] Or, as Skaria observed, "The very act of leading raids was crucial to imagining a raja, his bravery and his daring. To rule, in other words, was to raid" (1999: 145).

The turbulent, ever shifting and fragmenting political structure of South Asian polities demanded a great deal of muscle. On every political level—from Mughal emperors to Maratha leaders, Rajput kings, small landholders, and Bhil chiefs—eclectic cohorts of robbers were mobilized to help extract resources, conquer, and govern; bands of marauders ranged from the ten-thousand-horse professional armies to a motley handful of thieves (Gordon 1969: 427–29).[39] While some of these troops were professional mercenaries, like the Pindaris in Western India, most were made up of all kinds of landless, uprooted men in search of patrons, prestige, and land: immigrants from Central Asia, displaced chiefs, migrant workers, peasants driven off their lands by wars or droughts, peripatetic traders, mendicants, pastoralists, hillsmen, and vagrants.[40] For different kinds of marauders, plunder had different meanings. While for settled communities (Rajputs, farmers) and professional nomads (herdsmen, itinerant traders) thieving may have been a source of income, it was not a source of identity. For many tribal and vagrant communities, however, theft became the anchor of social selves. Engagement in thievery, long recognized as a legitimate (if not a wholly respectable) vocation on the subcontinent, held out the promise of patronal ties and, through them, to a respected standing (see Piliavsky 2015a).

Historically, in Western India (as elsewhere on the subcontinent) the robber reputation has been nurtured by tribal communities. Koli and Bhil hillsmen famously cultivated the reputation and ethos of professional thieves in order to maintain their rights to levy dues and claim the patronage of Rajput chiefs, who employed them as raiders, go-betweens, escorts, and watchmen (A. Forbes 1856: 1:104; S. Guha 1999: 52; Skaria 1999). Bhils in the Gujarati highlands still boast of their thieving prowess and of being "Mahādev's thieves" (Skaria 1999: v), and in rural Mewar Gujar herders pride themselves on being the boldest rustlers of buffalo herds, insisting that once upon a time they "went along with the Kanjars," and were so like them, that they considered them younger brothers. Of course, they say all of this in private, after a drink. Publicly, they are just as averse to Kanjars, whom they, nonetheless, employ in secret. The reputation of professional thieves gives special moral license to burgle. In North India tribal communities, long after their settlement and the development of primary identities as farmers and herdsmen, have continued to take advantage of the robbers' repute. In the tumultuous days of the 1857 rebellion the roads to Delhi swarmed with Gujar bands (Dalrymple 2007: 185, 145n).[41] By now, most Minas and Gujars have established themselves as respectable communities in Rajasthan: many are employed in government service, and some wield considerable political power. Their renown as bandits, nonetheless, lives on in people's narratives and in their own tall tales of past thieving feats.[42]

Over the course of the nineteenth century, hill tribes like Minas and Bhils, which had long dominated the robber trade, gradually left this career as they found steady employment (as watchmen, escorts, and guards hired by heads of states, gentry, and village communities) (Broughton 1892 [1809]: 85–86, 105, 233). Some of them settled, some even receiving permanent land grants, and took up farming.[43] As Gordon observes, "after 1815, the British were occupied with establishing regular relations with various levels of the prevailing power structure [in Central and Western India] and with destroying the large-scale marauders ('Pindaris' and tribal groups)," with the result that "smaller-scale groups (such as 'dacoits' and 'Thugs') flourished" (1969: 429). If in the early decades of the nineteenth century John Malcolm, a Scottish freebooter, remarked that in Central India Bhils "have not yet abandoned their habits, but their robberies are upon a very limited scale to what they were a few years ago" (1832: 1:525),[44] by mid-century, further gentrification and colonial "pacification" of hill tribes in Western India had seen their gradual settlement and incorporation into Rajput polities and later the British state.[45]

As the hill tribes left the robber's path, the vagrants took their place on it.[46] By the 1830s, Bhantus were already acquiring the repute of hereditary robbers, quite independently of their Gujar or Mina patrons; many were working as watchmen.[47] Colonial accounts of this new class of robbers suggest that most of them were indeed Bhantus rather than nomadic or tribal groups. The most thorough, but by no means the only one, of these accounts are "thuggee" Sleeman's reports, where he repeatedly wrote that his dacoit informers called themselves "Bhantu" (1849). The list of "dacoit tribes" he compiled in the 1830s included Sansis, Beriyas, Bagris/Baoris, Badhiks, Haburas, Kalbeloyas, Moghias, Pardhis, Kanjars, and Nats—all of which, as I discussed earlier, are names that Bhantus go by.[48] Sleeman also noted that the dacoit tribes had not always practiced banditry, but had historically been engaged in various itinerant trades, like genealogy or entertainment. He wrote that Kanjars, who figure prominently in his catalogues of Thugs and dacoit tribes, "were itinerant tradesmen, wandering with their herds and families about the country . . . [or] vagrant Musulmans, who followed armies and lived in the suburbs of cities, and in the wild wastes" (Sleeman 1836: 162, 144).[49]

Just as earlier Rajputs and British officers employed Minas and Bhils for intelligence, military, and policing tasks, the newly gentrified Minas and Bhils started employing Bhantus as their *dalāls,* not only as bards.[50] In 1809, Broughton observed that the landholding Minas who were employed by Marathas "assured [him] that they could, upon any pressing occasion, assemble a body of twenty thousand men." Of these, they claimed, "nearly a third were sprung from one family, the founders of their tribe; the rest are aliens, who have been incorporated at different times into the community" (1892 [1809]: 105). Although Broughton gives no details about who made up this Mina auxiliary force, we know that in 1824 the Koli hillsmen of northern Maharashtra gathered their intelligence and supplies of food through the itinerant servants of local landholders (S. Guha 1999: 53). In all likelihood, the Minas' troops described by Broughton were also substantially Bhantus.

Bhantus often joined their patrons' gangs, so that a number of their gangs described by Sleeman had Sansi, Moghia, or Kanjar members, but were led by their Bhil, Mina, Rajput, or Jat *jajmāns* (Sleeman 1849: 406; 1836). Indeed, Kanjars still pride themselves on having once raided the countryside together with their Gujar, Bhil, Mina, Koli, and Jat *patrons*—the "true castes of thieves" (*sachche corõ ke jāt*), as they say—who taught them, as Ramesh insists, the art of thieving. This is how Old Shambhu described the Bhantus' arrival in the plunderers' trade:

> *Kanjars here in Mewar were employed mostly by Gujars, Malis [gardeners], Minas, and Bhils. Our brotherhood [birādarī] ate [khāte the] from the Gujars. We kept their genealogy [bansāvalī] and songs of praise [piḍāvalī]. Wherever there were Gujars—in Tonk and Devgarh, on the Manasa and Khari Rivers, in Kota and Mewar, everywhere in Rajasthan—we had our jajmāns. Around here, you know, Gujars were the biggest gangsters [ḍākūs]. They robbed on the roads and rustled cows and buffaloes [pāḍās]. They were our jajmāns and we went with them whenever they looted. Sometimes they sent us to loot for them and sometimes we went together with their parties. And so, gradually everyone in Rajasthan came to know us too as the toughest bandits, just like the Gujars.*
>
> *Then, Gujars slowly took to work in the fields. Their herds grew and they moved less. [Many of them] received land from the Rajputs and they stopped stealing so much. Bhils and Minas—who were once also great gangsters—also*

slowly settled. Since the old days, Minas were great friends [of the kings] and you know that here in Mewar Bhils have always been the king's oldest companions [sāthīs]. You see how many villages they have got around here? They all received land from the king. Here near Begun many Gujars, Minas, and Bhils were settled when the Marathas left, after the reign of Rana Bhim Singh ji [r. 1778– 1828]. By that time, some Kanjars still ate their jajmāns' protection, but many were already in the "business of theft" [chorī kā dhandhā]. They were looting all around Rajasthan and in Indore and Ahmedabad and even in Lahore.

My grandfather did some bards' work for Minas, but that was a new business for him because our people have been thieves "from the time of kings" [rājā-mahārājā kā jamānā] and thieving is our old work. . . . It is the same with Sansis and Moghias, who are also "old-time thieves" [purāne jamāne ke chor]. Even today, there are still some Gujar, Mina, and even Bhil gangsters [ḍākūs], but these days Kanjars are the greatest thieves [sab se baṛe chor].

While most Bhantus known as "Kanjars" have sought to shed the label and the stigma that attached itself to the name, some claimed the epithet as their caste name and with it the license to engage in underhanded, illicit, or illegal trades like prostitution or theft. They turned the pejorative into a prerogative of their own. In the words of a young and resourceful Kanjar, "a *badnām* [bad name, disrepute] is an idiot's ruin and a clever man's watering well."[51] Professional identity, however morally dubious, meant not only that those who called themselves "Kanjars" could seek employment as raiders, watchmen, spies. It also held out the promise of entry into polite society, if only through the back door. As thieves, or prostitutes, Kanjars did find employers, but proper patronage was much harder to come by. It is not enough to have employment. Bonds must be based on a promise of perpetual care and need to be publicly recognized.[52] The secretive nature of most Kanjar trades has meant that relations between them and their patrons remained invisible to, and not legitimized by, public opinion, leaving Kanjars unrecognized as a people with proper social attachments and keeping them excluded from respectable life.

Chapter 5

HOW TO MAKE AND EAT A
GODDESS IN NINE DAYS

DEVI LAL IS THE OLDEST Kanjar in Rajasthan. He says that he may be a hundred, perhaps a hundred and ten years old. When he was young, Devi Lal was a very dangerous thief. He used to steal camels in the Thar Desert, drive them for hundreds of miles south, and sell them all the way down in Kutch. Back then, he had more gold than he knew what to do with; he had two wives, a horse, and a dozen sons, all but one of whom have died by now. Devi Lal has done time in several kingly jails, and in the 1930s he lived in a criminal tribe colony. This is where he got his tattoo—the blurred line of digits 8-2-5-6-7— that decorates his wrist, and which he showed me with pride. Today Devi Lal lives with his youngest surviving wife in a tent made of blankets and scraps of plastic stretched over some bent sticks. No road leads to Devi Lal's house, and my motorcycle tires were punctured every time I came to visit. Devi Lal spends his life on a charpoy smoking beedis, drinking tea, and telling stories to anyone who comes to listen. Not many do, and he was thrilled to tell me about his life. The first story he told me was about the Kanjars' most important local patron and about his father, Myalia, a formidable thief.

Myalia Kanjar was a great thief. He was famous in all of Mewar. He had this special bond with the goddess Joganiya. She gave him great strength, and the police could never lay their hands on him. How many goats and buffaloes did he kill for Mother Joganiya?! But one day the king of Mewar threw him in jail at the old fort in Mandalgarh. You have seen the walls of that fort! Nobody has ever managed to run from it. But Myalia asked the goddess to grant him release. Day and night he pleaded with her, and finally the Mother granted his wish: he ran from the prison by night and nobody saw him go. He climbed the wall and jumped right down. You have seen that wall. No man could have survived the jump, but Myalia fell into the tree branches and was saved. Now, with the shackles and chains binding his hands and feet he couldn't go far. But at that time a herdsman from a Gujar caste was cycling past. Myalia told the Gujar to take him to the temple of Joganiya. Seeing the shackles on Mya-lia's feet, the Gujar grew frightened. But what could he do? Everyone knew Myalia, and the Gujar knew that Myalia would kill him if he did not take him along. So, he put Myalia on his bicycle and brought him to Joganiya's temple. There with his own eyes he saw how Myalia's shackles automatically fell off and Myalia was left standing free. You can still see those shackles and chains at the shrine of the goddess.

By common account, Kanjars are a "heroic stock" (*bahādur kom*) distinguished by their strength, pluck, and cunning, the dispositions necessary for thieving, a "heroic business" (*bahādurõ kā dhandā*) akin to hunting or war.[1] People say that these virtues bespeak the Kanjars' "special relation" (*khās sambandh*) to the goddess (*devī*), who personifies the force (*śakti*) that animates the Hindu cosmos. The goddess has myriad forms, including the classic goddesses of Sanskrit mythology and her innumerable local avatars. The chief goddess in southeastern Rajasthan is Joganiya Mata (yogi mother), also known as the "goddess of thieves" (*chorõ kī devī*). Joganiya is know to favor the Kanjars: she blesses their thieving raids, ensures rich spoils, and shields them from the police. Proof of this patronage is in her hilltop temple, which has a display of shackles and chains deposited by escaped jailbirds over the years as signs of gratitude for her help (fig. 5.1). For Kanjars, Joganiya's tutelage is not only useful; it is an existential boon. A priest at the Joganiya temple explained:

When the Mother grants a boon [bar-dān] to petitioners [māṅgne-wāle], she gives them her power. Then their work gets done. Because they have the Mother's power, they can do things they could not do before. The Mother grants

FIGURE 5.1 The irons of escaped jailbirds at the temple of Joganiya Mata. Photo by author.

Kanjars many boons. Kanjars always get her blessings [pātī] *first. This is why they are such formidable* [zabardast] *thieves.*

The Shape of the Community

The goddess's boons and blessings are gifts of the kind anthropologists have written much about, gifts that confer something of their donors on their recipients (e.g., Marriott & Inden 1977; Mauss 2002 [1925]; Parry 1986; 1994; Raheja 1989). As the temple priest explained, the gifts transmit to the Kanjars the goddess's particular distinguishing trait, her *śakti* (potency), imbuing them with the courage (*himmat*) and strength (*bal, ṭakaṭ*) they are famed for. The goddess is the source of the caste's distinctive nature: the ascribed mental, moral, and physical traits referred to collectively as its *khāndān*, or "collective substance," which I discuss briefly in chapter 1.

Remember that Kanjars draw a sharp line between their own *Bhantus*, and the Kadza gentiles outside. The Kanjar caste, and other castes in the Bhantu fraternity, is a classic segmentary system of the kind described by anthropologists of Africa and the Middle East (e.g., Evans-Pritchard 1940; Dresch 1989) as a set of relations organized through a structure of nested oppositions: two exogamous moieties, inside them patriclans (*got* or *gotra*), and inside these, village segments, families, and households.[2] Historically, the ranks of the *Bhantu* fraternity have swollen and shrunk, as its members moved from one to another of its constitutive castes, members of other castes joined the Kanjar clans, and Kanjar families split off or migrated to and from new clans. This mobility, nonetheless, operates within—and is made possible by—a rigid structure of complementary opposition, which organizes the most significant exchanges and relations among Kanjars. Women and bride price (through isogamous, cross-cousin marriage), resources, business contacts, and information all flow most readily between the two moieties. Most gangs are also cross-moiety alliances, and training in the thieving trade relies on trans-moietal exchange.[3] It is customary for young boys to run away from home and live for several months and sometimes even years in their father's sisters' or mother's brothers' villages. These villages become their "second homes" (*dūsarā ghar*) for life: the place where they learn the tricks of the trade, make lifelong friendships, join a gang, and find future wives. For most boys, this second home remains the chief source of funds, intelligence, bail sureties, and contacts with landholders, informers (who point out property to steal), and the police, all of which are essential to the thief's business (Piliavsky 2013a; and chapter 3 above). This sense of complementary interdependence is explicit among Kanjars. As Old Shambhu reflected one evening over a drink: *What are we* [*men of our moiety*] *without the others* [*men of the other moiety*]*? Whom would we marry? There would be nobody to give to and take from* [len-den koi na hogā]. *Who would we be? What would our Kanjar society be?*

Unlike in African and Middle Eastern segmentary systems, where people value the closest and smallest segments (clans and families are most important there), most Kanjars value the biggest, most encompassing segments most. One may think of this order as a structure of hierarchical encompassment in which households are encompassed by families encompassed by clans encompassed by moieties. As we shall see, each segment has its own patron goddess—or rather a different form of the same goddess, who, like the caste itself, is segmented and ranked, correspondingly. Each family, clan, and moiety has its own form of the goddess (see figure 5.2). When Kanjars explain why they value the more encompassing segments more, they say that they have greater *śakti* and unity (*yektā* in Kanjari). As the level of encompassment drops from caste to moiety, clan, family, and household, the segment weakens and disintegrates into a fractious mess. Kanjars insist that because moieties are strong and cohesive, they bring good fortune, integrity, and strength to their members. Families and households, on the contrary, are weak (*kamjor*) and so mired in squabbles. This is why, they say, boys always abscond from homes, abandon their fathers' gangs, and betray their brothers. And this is why husbands and wives always fight.

The pantheon of the Kanjar goddesses, in which each form of the goddess embodies one or another caste segment, mirrors the structure of the Kanjar caste. Just as every Kanjar belongs to one of the two moieties, each claims the aegis of one of two moiety goddesses: either Almodi or Ashapal. When Kanjars first meet, they may not have heard of each other's clan, as these differ from place to place, but they can instantly establish the other's moiety by asking: "which Mother do you belong to?" and indeed this is often the first question they ask. This clarifies whether the other is their "sister" or "brother" from the same moiety, or "wife's sister" or "wife's brother" from the opposed moiety, and thus how they ought to relate. Like the moieties themselves, the goddesses Almodi and Ashapal are segmented into a number of ranked forms—the "great," the "small," and the "nascent"—associated, respectively, with the level of a clan, a family, or a household (fig. 5.2).

Attachment to a moiety goddess does not only locate Kanjars within their caste, it is also a measure of their good standing, a sign of being a "proper" (*khāndānī*) Kanjar. If a clan or a family or a person is in disgrace for some reason, Kanjars say that their ties to the Mother (goddess) must have been severed (*ṭuṭījā*), or that the Mother has abandoned them (*chalījī* or *choṛ dīī*).[4] If patronage by the regional goddess anchors Kanjars in broader society, bonds with caste goddesses locate them within the caste and are greatly valued by Kanjars, who spend much of their time nurturing these ties. Service offerings to the caste goddesses are part of daily alimentary practices, especially the drinking of liquor and the butchery, preparation, and consumption of meat. Every bottle of *madh* that Kanjars brew and drink is offered first to the goddess by spilling a little onto the ground while invoking her name. Every goat and sheep they steal, slaughter, and eat is sacrificed to the goddess in an act of service that cements their relation to her. *Proper,* khāndānī *Kanjars always*

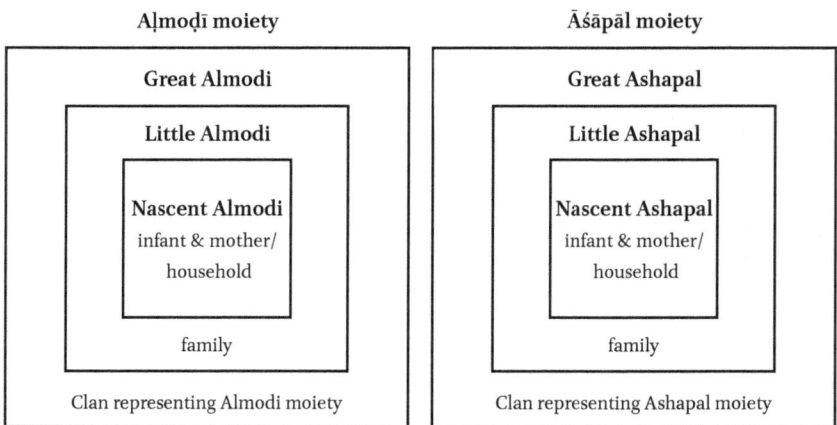

Aḷmoḍī moiety	Āśāpāl moiety
Great Almodi	**Great Ashapal**
Little Almodi	**Little Ashapal**
Nascent Almodi infant & mother/ household	**Nascent Ashapal** infant & mother/ household
family	family
Clan representing Almodi moiety	Clan representing Ashapal moiety

FIGURE 5.2 The major divisions of the Kanjar caste. Diagram by author.

serve their Mother, says Kalla. *When we sacrifice meat to her, this is how we serve her* [unnochī sevā karte hai]. *This is how we get our* khāndān. In return for offerings of meat and alcohol to the goddess, Kanjars receive from her the gifts of strength, boldness, and humoral heat (*garmī*) that make them who they are. This is why the goddesses are known literally as "givers" (*deyārīs*). As Old Shambhu put it, a properly sacrificed animal quite literally *makes the Bhantu* [*bhāṅtu banātā*]. How exactly, we shall see just below.

Kanjars' neighbors accuse them of being "addicted" to meat and alcohol, something that NGOs for "Kanjar upliftment" preach against. But for Kanjars themselves, the consumption of meat and alcohol is an existentially vital process through which they maintain their communal substance—a substance that must be earned diligently by serving the goddess every time they eat and drink. During the eighteen months that I spent in Ramesh's house, hardly a day passed without a well-lubricated, meaty feast. These were not just drunken parties, although we did get drunk (a real challenge for a "participant-observer"), but shows of being a proper Kanjar, one in constant communion with the goddess. Not every Kanjar can afford daily meat and drink, but those who do—mostly successful thieves—enjoy the esteem of proper, *khāndānī* Kanjars with strength and courage enough for success in their caste trade.

This consubstantive process does not run in one direction. Inasmuch as the goddess's gifts create her devotees, their services also create the goddess in a process that Kanjars straightforwardly call "making the Mother." The most important annual offering of service to the goddess takes place during the autumnal festival of Bari Navaratri, literally "nine great nights."[5] This festival is so central to the Kanjar sense of collective existence (and collective pride) that my Kanjar friends often insisted that this was what I must write my book about. As Ramesh explained, during the festival Kanjars *create a map of the Kanjar society* [kanjar samājõ kā nakśā banāwe]. *You can see our caste as it really is!*[6] Navaratri involves two main rituals: offerings to the goddess, and the initiation of children. Both revolve around animal sacrifice. Over the course of the festival, as Kanjars sacrifice animals and initiate infants, the celebrations move from a quiet, domestic affair to a raucous, public festival. The goddess appears in a succession of avatars (*rūps*), each of which receives its own appropriate offerings from its own segment of the caste.

Navaratri is also when every Kanjar is born. Babies are of course born throughout the year, but they only become Kanjars at initiation during Navaratri. The celebrations culminate in the haircutting rites (*laṭī caṛhānā*), which are the Kanjars' first communion, in which the babies receive from the goddess their *khāndān,* and their name. Prior to initiation, infants remain nameless, they do not wear proper clothing, eat with others, or receive proper burial and mourning rites if they die. They are babies, but not yet Kanjars, which is to say not people yet. For the mothers, this is also a time of post-partum isolation, a vulnerable, transitional time. Mothers and babies have their own goddesses, known as the Birth Mothers (*bey mātās*), to whom new mothers make offerings during Navaratri. On the first day of the festival, the new mothers make egg-shaped icons of their nascent goddesses out of ghee, water, and cow dung (fig. 5.3). Over the following seven or eight days, they make offerings of milk and boiled rice to the goddess, which they also give to their infants. One young mother, Indra, explained: *the Birth Mother is like a child—very innocent, vulnerable. She is so small, so weak [kamjor]. We take good care of her and she eats milk and rice.*[7] Kanjars say that it is because their goddesses are so weak that newborns and their mothers are highly susceptible to illness and death.[8]

On each night of the festival, the senior households of every family light oil lamps and offer ghee, incense, cow dung, and coconuts to their family goddess. This form of the goddess is known as the Little Mother (*nannī mātā*), an avatar that ranks above the Nascent Mother, but below the great moiety goddess we shall encounter shortly.[9] Little Mothers are more potent than Nascent Mothers, but weaker than the Great Goddesses of Kanjar moieties and clans. As protectors of households, Little Mothers are meant to keep their residents from quarrels, illnesses, poverty, and the police—a task at which the goddesses often fail. Kanjars say that it is because Little Mothers are weak that relations in Kanjar families and households, between parents and children, and between siblings, are volatile. Brothers often do not speak to each other, sometimes for years on end. And even when they are on speaking terms, they usually avoid visiting one another or sharing meals.

Kanjars blame this fractiousness, this disunity (*yektā koī*) on the frailty of the Little Mothers, and on the fact that entire families hardly ever offer her services, except during Navaratri. Services offered to Little Mothers are more

FIGURE 5.3 The nascent goddess in her egg-shaped form with a few grains of rice stuck to her. Photo by author.

extensive than those offered to Birth Mother, but they are still rather modest affairs. As Ramesh explained:

> *If Little Mothers had more strength, our villages and families and brothers would stick together. But how can they [the goddesses] have strength, if we do not give it to them? There is no unity in our families. There is no family in this village where brothers light a camphor lamp to their goddess together.*

Or, in the words of his brother Hari Ram: *how can the Family Mother be strong if we do not serve her? It is the caste that makes its mother.* If the offer of services to the goddess would improve their lot, why don't Kanjars put greater effort into serving her collectively? *They did,* said Old Shambhu, *but those were the old days.* They always are. What is true is that often Kanjars simply cannot get together to offer her services because they are so frequently not on speaking terms. It is a vicious cycle, with family discord being both cause and effect of the Little Mothers' impotence.

On the final days of Navaratri, the villagers carry the *mūra*t (icons) of their family goddesses to the open shrines where they transform their Little Mothers into one of the two great moiety goddesses.[10] On the eve of the installation, Kanjars hold the all-night vigil (*rāti jugā*) to rouse (*jugānā*) the deities with bright lights and raucous devotional songs (*thālī*). They emphasize that the vigil does not only make the goddess "accessible, approachable, and active," as some scholars of popular Hinduism have suggested (e.g., Erndl 1993: 102), the vigil actually *creates* the Great Goddess (fig. 5.4). Encouraging me to join in the singing, Ramesh enthused:

> *The more of us get together and the louder we sing, the more things we offer,* *the more ghee we burn, the greater our Mother becomes. Why do you think* *our Mother has so much strength* [ṭakaṭ]*? Because we celebrate* [manāte] *Navaratri with the most bustle and pomp* [dhum-dham se]*, more than any* *other caste.*

FIGURE 5.4 Great Ashapal adorned with a shawl, rupee notes, and flower garlands. Photo by author.

The morning after the vigil, Kanjars construct makeshift altars on which they will later perform final rites of sacrifice. But these altars are not just places of sacrifice; they are themselves forms of the goddess. Kanjars say that the making of altars is itself a *pūjā*, a service central to the act of "creating the Mother." Kalla explained: *When we make the Mother's altar, we pay homage* [pūjte] *to her. We make our Mothers. We give them form* [rūp] *and then we offer them services* [sevā karte]. Clans of each moiety construct an altar in a shape particular to their moiety goddess: the Ashapal clans make something they call a *chauk* (a patch of ground outlined with cow dung), and the Almodi clans erect a superstructure called the *teyda* (fig. 5.5). The altars are later decorated with flags, flowers, and various offerings, among which Kanjars set up the goddesses' images, adorning them with shawls and garlands of flowers or rupee notes.[11] Since each altar is itself a form of the goddess, the fact that one should be vertical and another horizontal is an essential expression of the opposition between Almodi and Ashapal. One has to oppose the other in form as well as in substance, and Kanjars (they struck me, time and again, as born structuralists) explained this explicitly to me.

Within each moiety, each clan further decorates its goddess's altar to match its own distinctive features. The Chatrawat clan of the Almodi moiety construct a second story, called the *upparmāḷī* (or *dāgḷī*), on their vertical *teydā* altar, while the Karmawat clan of the Ashapal moiety shape their horizontal *chauk* into a triangle. The altar structure and the arrangement of offerings can be further elaborated with details particular to a given village segment of a clan. Kanjars who wish to distinguish their segment can also add special features to their service. So, while the purpose and overall sequence of the ritual remain stable, there is a lot of room for improvisation, for pursuing the ritual's ethnogenic purpose in new, creative ways. As the services are constitutive of the goddess, doing so also reinforces the segmentation of the goddess into the variety of her clan- and village-specific forms. Chatrawats in one village make the offerings of rams' ears, and Karmawats in another village veil their goddess during sacrifice. Old men from the clan that makes offerings of rams' ears explained that they started doing this about two decades ago to distinguish themselves from another, less respectable Chatrawat family that moved to a nearby village. The goddesses—who are at once possessive and segmented—who embody

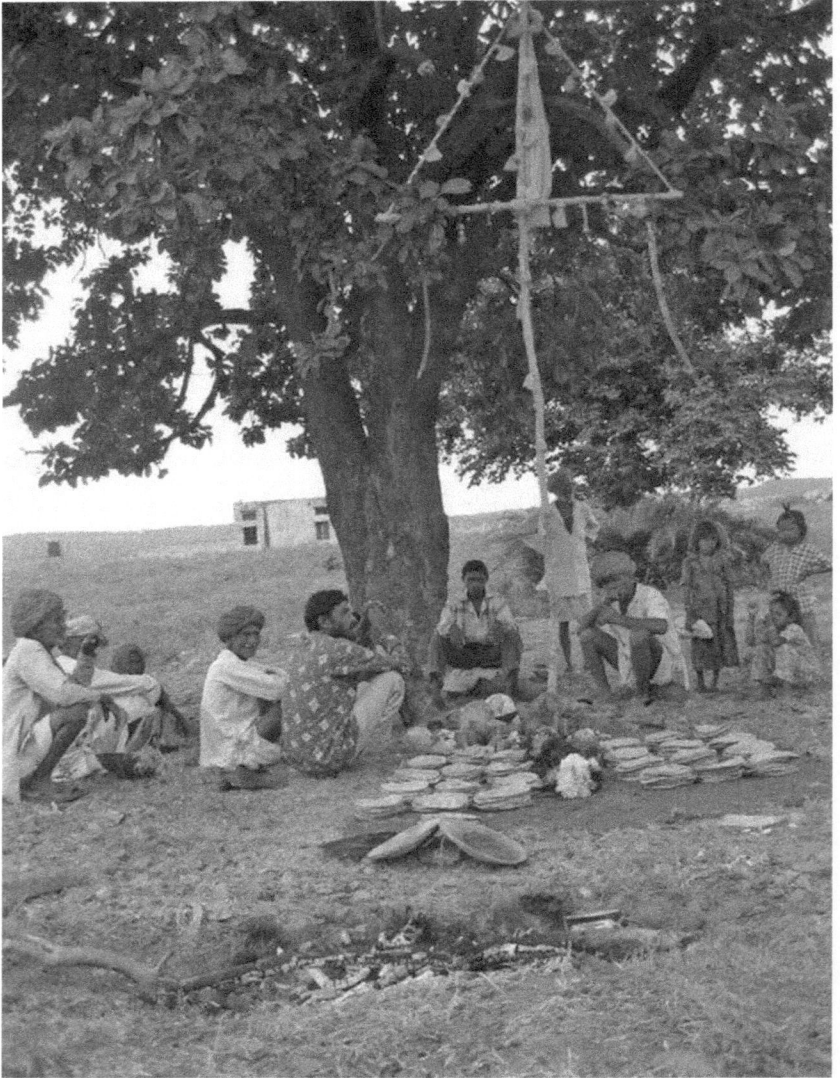

FIGURE 5.5 A *teydā* altar erected by the Bamanawat clan of the Almodi moiety. Photo by author.

the tension between unity and distinctiveness, values that run in conflictual ways through Kanjars' social lives and find expression in their fractiousness and simultaneous insistence on uniqueness and unity. The conjunction of unity and difference runs in greater or lesser measure through much of what South Asianist anthropologists have long thought of as "caste": an order of unity and differentiation, connectedness and specificity. The order of segmented patron gods, from Kanjar goddesses to the different avatars of Lord Vishwakarma worshipped by engineers, reflects this order.[12] The Kanjar Navaratri, however, reveals this principle with a particular clarity and intensity.

Feeding the Goddess

The goddess's chief avatar, which makes an appearance at the end of the festival, is the sacrificial animal itself, which is known as the goddess's form (*rūp*), image (*mūrat*), and nature (*prakṛti*). Each goddess receives one of two sacrificial animals: rams (*miṇḍās*) from the Almodi moiety, or he-goats (*tsāḷi s*) from the Ashapal. The animals are further differentiated by the color of their clan. The Karmawat clan sacrifice only black goats, the Chatrawat only white rams, the Chandawat only silver or mottled rams, and the Singhawat, red. As embodiments of the goddess, the sacrificial animal receives offerings before sacrifice: rice pudding (*khīr*) and *madh*, which the Kanjars sprinkle over them. In the moments immediately before their slaughter, the animals are offered another service of sprinkled water and alcohol, ghee, cow dung, and some sacrificial *kuśā* grass, which Kanjars tie across their mouths (fig. 5.6).[13] Contrary to the Brahmanical logic of sacrifice, Kanjars see this preslaughter service not as a rite of purification,[14] but as an offering of service made to the goddess in her animal form. The animals are thus both victims and recipients of sacrifice: *When we make burnt offerings* [dhūp lagāte] *to these goats*, said Kalla, *we serve our Mother. The Mother goes inside* [ghus jāti] *the goats.*[15]

Eating the Goddess

To pay proper service to their goddess, Kanjars must slaughter her, not in an act of deicide, but in one of transfiguration which transforms the goddess into her final avatar: into meat consumed by her devotees, who thus turn into a community (*samāj*). Kanjars pour the blood that gushes

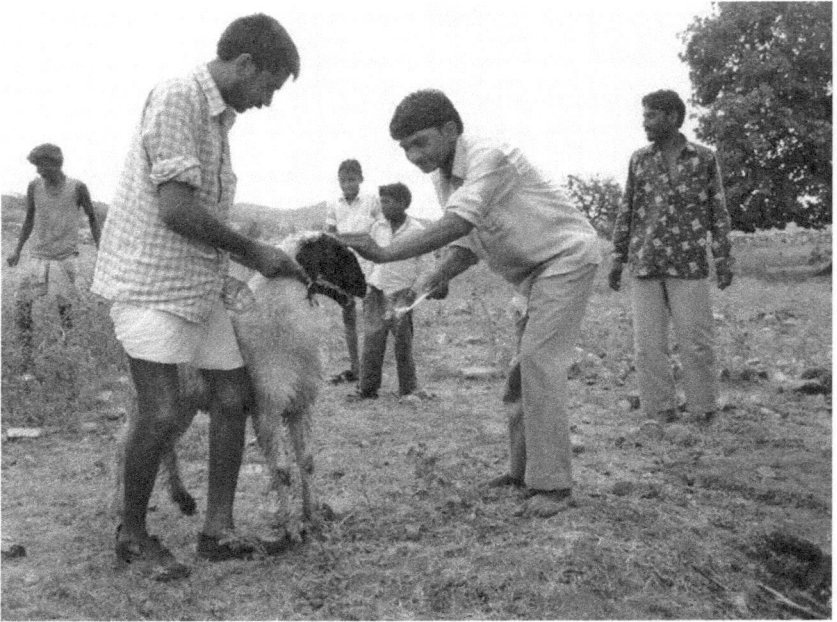

FIGURE 5.6 Bamanawat men making offerings to the Great Almodi they are about to eat. Photo by author.

from the neck of the sacrificed animals over the goddess's image, an offering called the "blood service" (khūṇ sevā). Without the blood service, they say, the animal's life will have been "spoiled" (bigaṛā huyā) or simply "wasted" (ujāṛā); its flesh (gulli) will not turn into meat (boṭṭi) that can be eaten in the final act of communion with the goddess. Kanjars call this sacrificial meat as the "gift of meat" (boṭṭiyāchin dān) from the goddess, or simply the "mother's meat" (mātā-jī ke boṭṭiyā̃). Exasperated by my relentless questions, Old Shambhu explained: Where is our Mother? When we eat sacrificial meat, she goes inside us [ghūs jāwe]. She lives in every piece of meat that we eat. When we sacrifice goats, when we eat their meat, she goes inside us. Simple enough. As an act of eating the deities, Kanjar sacrifice is closer to Catholic communion than Brahmanical rites, where devotees consume the deity's sacred leftovers (prasād), but which do not result in their transfiguration.[16]

The consumption of rams and goats puts flesh onto the moiety opposition. When each goddess appears and is eaten in this way, members of each moiety take on the distinct material properties of each kind of meat. As Kanjars say, "one becomes the goat one eats" (*jo tsāḷi ko khāwe, vo tsāḷi ho jāwe*). Whereas the sinewy meat of goats, humorally hot (*garam*) and potent (*tej*) in texture and flavor, gives special strength (*ṭakaṭ*) to the Ashapal clans, the soft, fatty mutton of rams makes the Almodi clans more gentle (*mulāyam*) and generous (*udār*). As one old woman explained, this distinction makes the Ashapal Kanjars better thieves, but makes the Almodi Kanjars softer and more peaceable. The opposition of moieties is further demarcated by each moiety's totemic consumption, or conversely avoidance, of the gallbladder (*aḷmoḍā*), from which the name "Almodi" derives. The organ contains the essence of the Almodi Mother, and at initiation infants born into the moiety receive a taste of raw sheep's gallbladder, which elders swipe across their lips along with a sip of *madh* (fig. 5.7).[17] Few babies enjoy the process, and their initiations are always filled with much wailing and hilarity among the adults. But the mirth of the moment belies its seriousness, for this is when children first eat the goddess, receive their *khāndān,* and join the caste.

Even though food and drink are central to Navaratri, the festival involves no communal feasts. Instead, meat and bread (the latter prepared by the initiates' parents on special hearths), are half-cooked (*maḍḍā*).[18] At the end of the sacrifice, each family carries away its own share of meat and bread, which they later cook to completion and eat in the isolation of their homes. This final preparation and consumption of food is the goddess's final service.[19] The absence of communal feasts may suggest that communal solidarity is not what the rites are for. But Kanjars insist that this is the very aim of the festival. One young woman explained: *when we eat the Mother's meat and roti, our society comes together. Just then Kanjars forget their squabbling. The clans and villages become one.* Kanjars do not, however, achieve communion by reciprocal exchange or sharing of food; they commune instead by eating their goddesses, each household separately. The goddess's body, quite literally incorporated by each Kanjar, becomes the Kanjar "community," and the two become one. As Ramesh put it, *because the Mother is inside us, you can understand our society as her form or you can say our society is the Mother's body.* Or, as one woman said, *the Kanjar caste* is *the goddess's body, isn't it?*

FIGURE 5.7 The haircutting rite (Bamanawat clan of the Almodi moiety). An elder snips locks from the child's and mother's heads, and administers liquor and gall-bladder to both. Photo by author.

Khāndān

To an outsider, the Kanjars' dealings with their goddesses may appear as peculiar as the Kanjars themselves. Yet in all their eccentricity, Kanjars enact a widespread relational formula that I laid out earlier. The shorthand I used in the prologue for this relation was "patronage," and in chapter 1 I suggested that the hierarchical bond between "donors" and "servants" amounts to mutually constitutive co-creation. Through the Kanjar goddess ritual, we can now see how this actually works, close-up. The donor-servant relation is not just a set of transactions through which persons and communities *interact*, but a process from which they genuinely emerge.

Anthropologists like Raheja, Marriott, and Inden demonstrated that life in rural North India revolved around the continual distribution of consubstantive gifts by dominant families to their servant clienteles, arguing that transactions like feeding, marriage, and sexual intercourse involved the circulation of persons' "bio-moral particles," some more and others less pure. Yet in arguing that upper castes insisted on a rigid exchange protocol for fear of receiving substances from below, they did not explain why the low castes should continue to engage in transactions that appeared to reinforce their humiliation. Nor did they show how exactly Indian persons and communities emerged out of transactions, only how they were maintained and re-created in them. Although people exchanged substances, they only perpetuated preexisting arrangements: the rigid hierarchies that gifts were said to maintain. However, a more careful reading of the historical and ethnographic archive, and my own ethnography, shows that patronal relations, as observed and as described by people involved in them, actively and continuously constitute persons and communities, and so contain the possibility of change.

As I have already shown in previous chapters (and as we shall see in the next), for Kanjars human patronage has never been a stable arrangement. Without a master, thieves are mere pickpockets (*jeb-kaṭ*), beggars (*māṅgne-wāle*), or vagabonds (*ghūmne-wāle*). As promiscuous receivers of gifts and their *khāndān* from a hodgepodge array of donors, people without fixed patronage bonds are jumbled, lacking in integrity, or any kind of definite and so respectable self. Thieves who do have patrons, however despised their work may be, have a place in the world; and in this jumble of uncertain patronage ties, the goddess offer a special, and existentially crucial, anchor. Here again is Old Shambhu:

Our caste has always roamed in the jungle. From olden days, we have been coming and going. No patron has ever kept us for long. Sometimes we served Rajputs, sometimes Gujars, Bhils, Minas, and now the Kanjars serve the police. But we have always been Joganiya Mother's servants; she protects us and gives us our bread.

During Navaratri both the Kanjar caste is produced, segment by segment, and the goddesses also emerge, segment by segment. As such, as Old Shambhu already said, the goddesses become maps of the Kanjar society. In his classic study of the Tamil god Aiyanar (1959 [1953]), Dumont argued that the organization of relations among Hindu gods mirrors the caste system and its relations. Human and divine societies are thus tied by an analogy and a common organizing principle. For Dumont, this principle was the structural opposition of purity and pollution. But, as we have already seen, Kanjar goddesses are maps of a different sort. They link gods to humans not by analogy, but by direct bonds of service and gift (see also Haekel 1963: 197). In rural Rajasthan divine and human societies are not tied into, appraised, or ranked through a single overarching substantive value (whether purity, honor, kingly valor, or auspiciousness). Instead, they derive their substance and social worth from a shared set of relational values. It is not persons, but relations which are ordered and appraised. The ranking of persons and communities derives from judgments about whom they relate to, what these relations are like, and how well they do in these relations—how closely they match one or another relational ideal.

Patronage is not only a central structural mechanism in the formation of persons and communities across the region, but also a normative conception. This is clearly audible in the Kanjars' insistence on just how good and worthy the rites of Navaratri are. Whereas in the rest of their lives Kanjars may be nobody's people—masterless people held in contempt by the social mainstream—the festival is their chance to put on a show of life as they would have it. When they described to me with great relish every nuance of the give-and-serve process, of how they create the goddess and how they "eat" her, they were not only imparting the correct ritual form, but telling me how very important everything that Navaratri puts on display really is.

Chapter 6

WHO AND WHOSE

WHILE RELATIONS WITH PATRON GODDESSES are stable arrangements, easy to maintain in the ideal ritual form, ties to human patrons are fickle, always pregnant with the threat of betrayal. In this chapter we shall see how changes in relations with human patrons fragment the Kanjar society, splitting it into different ranks and ultimately even different *jātīs* that no longer eat together or intermarry. Just as differences between patron goddesses organize the divisions and relations between the society's structural elements (clans, moieties), differences in relations with human patrons generate internal differences of worth. This contentious process of differentiation will show just how important belonging is to being. That to be really is to belong.

Remembered connections to human patrons are central to the identity of each Kanjar clan, which Kanjars define through links to a patron caste, whether remembered or (very occasionally) still extant. The status of patrons affects the clan's rank, placing the servants of Rajputs above servants of Minas and Bhils. It is not only the status of patrons, but also the quality of relations with them that really shapes Kanjars' judgments of one another, and their intra-societal rank. It shapes whether they think they would allow their children to marry one another or whether they would sit down together for a cup of tea, whether they judge one another admirable, tolerable, or beneath contempt. The more a relationship approximates the ideal donor-servant bond—the more fixed and durable it is—the greater is its value and the higher is its parties' esteem. Kanjars who have managed to convince others that they have the most durable ties with particular patrons have the greatest respect within their caste. *And*, as Ramesh once said, *everyone wants to marry their daughters into their families*. Those who have, conversely, failed to secure, or lost, such bonds are the riffraff among Kanjars.

Remembered connections to human patrons, or *jajmāns*, is what constitutes a clan: a Kanjar clan is a group of people with a shared memory of a patron caste. The status of (mythical) patrons bears on the intra-caste status of the clan. A clan thought to have once served the Rajputs would stand above a Gujar-serving clan. Even more important to the reckoning of relative worth is not just the status of the jajmān, but the *quality* of the relationship to him: its fixity, tightness, longevity. Kanjars who have managed to establish the most durable ties with specific patrons enjoy the highest esteem in the community, and those who have failed to secure, or have lost, such connections are the lowest. As I note in chapter 1, the same principle applies to the evaluation and ranking of persons and groups in Rajasthani society more generally. But the Kanjar case offers a particularly revealing example.

In Rajasthan Kanjars are broadly divided into three occupational segments—the bards known as the Kanjar Bhats, the prostitutes known as Banchras or Nat Kanjars, and the thieves known simply as Kanjars. Each segment has its own relative standing within the broader Kanjar society. In simple outline, Kanjar thieves, who have generally managed to secure the most durable ties with important patrons (Rajputs, Gujars, policemen), enjoy the highest standing, and the prostitutes, who are engaged in the most haphazard array of relations with a great number of varied patrons, have the lowest. Bards are in the middle. Today the three segments form largely discrete spheres of exchange and alliance, whose members do not collaborate professionally, eat together, or intermarry.[1] Each is further subdivided into subsegments, each of which is further ranked. While this taxonomy is generally agreed by all Kanjars, an agreement reflected clearly in their marriage practices (on which more shortly), it is an order in flux, and rank is always subject to negotiation. Because the presence, character, and forms of relations with patrons are continually shifting, with some groups losing patronage ties and others forging new ones, the whole of the Kanjar society is subject to ongoing fragmentary motion, through which segments of the community form distinct status groups, split away, move outward, and ultimately form separate communities, which acquire different names, such as Bhat, Banchra, or Nat, and which eventually form discrete castes.

The Rules of *Birat*

Bonds between patrons and servants are locally thought of as constituting an ongoing transfer from *jajmāns* to their subordinates of something known as *birat* (also pronounced *barat, bart, birt, brat, vrat,* and *brit*), a concept usually referred to as *"jajmānī" (a word less frequently used in Rajasthan) in ethnographic literature* (as discussed in chapters 1 and 2). Locally, the concept of *birat/jajmānī* is understood in the following way. Every person has to perform certain tasks to maintain their physical and ritual being, and doing those tasks gives them a place in the social world and so makes them a person. Each one of these tasks, from keeping one's home clean to eating and getting married, has an appropriate form that constitutes a ritual, whether life-cycle or quotidian. Each ritual in turn reaffirms one's social existence. These tasks are distributed within one's family and broader local caste group, so that this kind of ritually constituted self is necessarily collective.[2]

Means permitting tasks can be delegated to specialists outside of one's own caste. As more and more tasks are delegated to others, the person becomes bigger and bigger and, as such, expands and rises in society. In the words of one high-ranking Rajput,

> *A man is as great as the society* [samāj] *that he can support. We know that a man is great if five different Gujar clans alone bring milk for his children. Look at the rulers of Mewar: they had a servant for each and every task—one man made their bed, one man tied their turban, and two noblemen guarded their bedroom. They had servants to do each tiny thing for them. Each man in Mewar was his servant, so we say that the Mewar* darbār [*ruler*] *is as great as Mewar.*

The more servants are incorporated into the *jajmān's* sphere, the greater he is. Or, in the words of a local adage, "a man is as big as his circle of relations" (*jitnā baṛā ristā, itnā baṛā ādmī*). Just as the greatness and potency of the Kanjar patron goddesses are relative to the size and fortitude of their community of devotees (see chapter 5), the status of *jajmāns* is contingent on the size of their service communities.

The delegation of labor is conceptualized as the transfer of *birat*, which, although commonly glossed as "patronage," means more precisely a "right to service." Even if a community has been in a patron's service for many generations, the right of *birat* is not something they *have*, something that belongs inalienably to a caste, but something that they must *receive* continually from their *jajmān*. Like khāndān that is transferred continually by goddesses to their Kanjar devotees, *birat* is something that belongs to human patrons and must also be transferred continuously, as a sort of running loan, to their servants. The language of *birat* reflects this logic: the *jajmān* "gives *birat*" (*birat detā*); the servants "take *birat* into their keeping" (*birat rākh rākhte*) or "fetch their *birat*" (*birat māṅgte*) when they serve their patrons; and they are thus referred to as "askers" (*māṅgne-wālās*) or "*birat* doers" (*biratkārīs*). *Birat* refers to both the right of service and the right to the payment received in return; as such, it designates the gift-service *relationship* rather than either the gift or the service itself.

Two hours' drive south of Chittorgarh city there is a large Kanjar village of almost two hundred homes. This village, called Gopalpura, houses one of the few remaining Kanjar bard families in Rajasthan. Every year, its residents travel from July to May, leaving Gopalpura vacant for most of the year. In July, at the end of the hot season, every household in the village sets out on a "begging tour" (*māṅgatā*), during which each will traverse up to two thousand kilometers (by foot, bus, donkey, and horse cart); each will go as far as Bombay, Pune, or Delhi, and visit up to three hundred villages, hamlets, and suburbs on their way (see map 6.1). To cover such distances, the bards keep a very tight schedule, traveling almost every day and putting on performances (*khel*) for their *jajmāns* on most evenings.

The annual *khel* performance is the central moment of the affirmation of bonds between the bards and their *jajmāns*, and the main occasion for exchange between them.[3] Much like the festival of Navaratri described in the previous chapter, the *khel* is a ritual capsule of the donor-servant relationship that concentrates its basic principles in time and space. Like the rites of Navaratri, *khel* is a mutually constitutive act. As the *jajmāns* offer gifts and

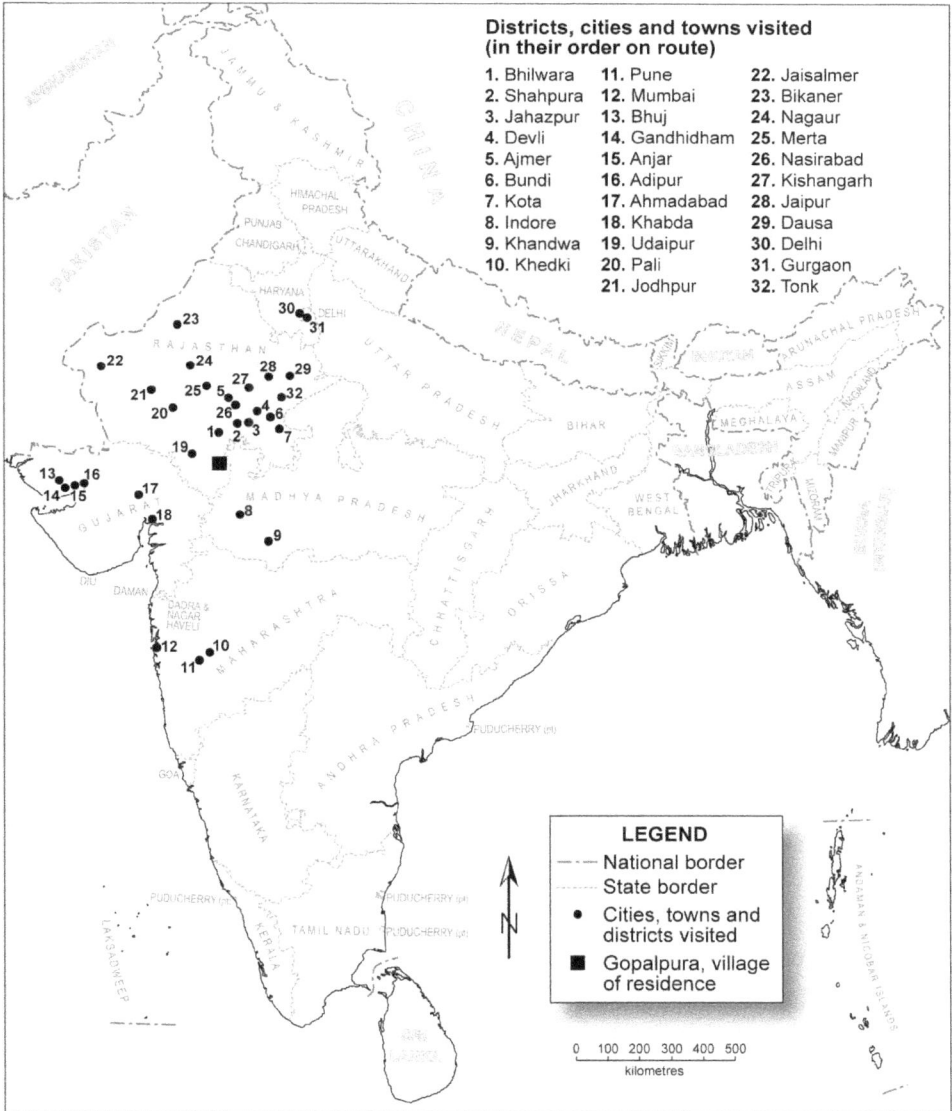

Districts, cities and towns visited (in their order on route)

1. Bhilwara	11. Pune	22. Jaisalmer
2. Shahpura	12. Mumbai	23. Bikaner
3. Jahazpur	13. Bhuj	24. Nagaur
4. Devli	14. Gandhidham	25. Merta
5. Ajmer	15. Anjar	26. Nasirabad
6. Bundi	16. Adipur	27. Kishangarh
7. Kota	17. Ahmadabad	28. Jaipur
8. Indore	18. Khabda	29. Dausa
9. Khandwa	19. Udaipur	30. Delhi
10. Khedki	20. Pali	31. Gurgaon
	21. Jodhpur	32. Tonk

LEGEND

–·– National border
······· State border
● Cities, towns and districts visited
■ Gopalpura, village of residence

0 100 200 300 400 500
kilometres

MAP 6.1 Places visited annually by one Kanjar Bhat household from Gopalpura. Based on maps drawn by David Watson of the Department of Geography's Cartographic Unit, University of Cambridge.

FIGURE 6.1 An elderly Kanjar Bhat (seated behind) looks on as his wife, eldest son, daughter-in-law, and oldest grandson perform *khel-tamāśā* for their Gujar *jajmāns* (Dhul Khera village just outside of Begun, 5 February 2008). Note the ropewalking setup in the background. Photo by author.

bards their performances, each party reaffirms its role in the relationship and its standing with respect to the other. The event, which is usually staged in the center of the village, is a very public occasion. And, as such, it allows patrons to show off their generosity and servants to display their fidelity, the qualities fundamental to the respectable standing of each.

The *khel* is divided into four parts (usually performed in this order): the genealogical recitation (*bardhānā*), the performance of panegyric verses (*śubhrāj*), a ropewalking routine, and the entry into the bards' ledger (*pothī*) of the births, deaths, marriages, and transfers of assets that took place in the previous year (fig. 6.1). In return for their services, the bards receive a variety of payments and gifts.

For *jajmāns*, the significance of *khel* goes beyond the upkeep of pedigree. It shows them as people with a divine and glorious, well-documented source of collective self—which, as we have already seen, is crucial to good social standing—and provides them with a special opportunity to display their largesse.[4] Public display, which (as I shall discuss in more detail in the following chapter) is central to the establishment of personal honor and integrity, is a crucial aspect of such performances. As a Gujar *jajmān* of one Kanjar bard household explained, *a* jajmān *is as big as the turban he gives to his servants* [kamīns]. *When we give gifts* [ināms] *to our Bhats, the village people see that we, Bor Gujars, are a great caste. It is important that the village people see how much we give to our servants* (fig. 6.2).[5] Unlike inconspicuous, routine services of sweepers or washermen, the bard's *khel* provides an occasion for a spectacular display of *jajmānī* largesse. The consciously conspicuous performance, with its raucous drumming and singing, and the massive ropewalking contraption that Kanjars always mount in the center of the village, leaves no villager unaware of it, drawing a lot of attention to the grandeur and generosity of patrons, to their role as the "givers of bread" (*anndātās*).[6] For weeks before the bards' visit, the Gujars reminded me incessantly that I must not miss the show.

FIGURE 6.2 Left to right: A Kanjar Bhat from Gopalpura, his grandson, son, and Gujar *jajmān*. Photo by author.

Gifts presented to bards on such occasions are highly varied, but always include fixed sums of cash (*inām*) turbans (*pagh*), and usually also dress, cloth, food, smoke, drink, and sometimes even cattle. While the patrons are quick to dole out chai, large turbans, and brightly colored shawls to their clients, their feet often go cold when it comes to parting with cash, the transfer of which, although heavy on the *jajmāns'* pockets, is not nearly as useful a display as the tying of turbans. It is bad value, when it comes to adding to the *jajmāns'* reputation. The bards, nevertheless, drive a hard bargain here, refusing to inscribe in their ledgers the genealogical detail of households that have not paid. At the performances I attended, to cajole their *jajmāns* into paying up, the bards placed a list of patron households on display and loudly called out payments as they were being made. They then wedged the notes visibly into their ledger, which they wielded before the villagers, my camera, and the approving *jajmāns*. Within an hour, the bards succeeded in coaxing payments out of all fifteen Gujar households in the village, walking away with an impressive total of 1,500 rupees. In 2008, when I recorded the occasion, each patron household was formally expected to part with 100 rupees (a sum equivalent to a day's wages for manual labor on government-funded construction sites). Thus, in one evening, the bards collected fifteen times a manual laborer's daily wages and half of a police constable's monthly salary, which at the time amounted to 3,005 rupees. Such plentiful collections are not common, and Kanjar Bhats often struggle to receive any cash or even gifts in kind.

While the cash sustains the bards' business in practical terms, it is the use of clothes that most prominently displays their ties to patrons. Clothes akin to those of the patrons is one of the most important markers of their attachment to *jajmāns* and inheritance of their *khāndān*. Clothing received by servants—shawls, turbans, cloth, bodices, skirts—is identical in its pattern to that worn by the *jajmāns,* and indeed in many cases was once worn by the patrons. The manner in which these are worn (skirt length, the way in which the turban is tied), however, must differ (and the patrons insist on this), lest asymmetry of status between them should be obscured. Thus, clad in the garb of their *jajmāns*, service communities (and this does not apply only to Kanjars or wandering bards) are readily identifiable as servants of particular castes.[7] As the brightest marker of communal selves,[8] clothing, including the all-important turban (*pagh*),[9] is the most visible badge of belonging to one *khāndān*. It gives servants their social substance. It is their anchor. As Brahmini, a Kanjar Bhat woman, plainly put it, *when we put on the* jajmāns' *shawls, skirts, and turbans, we wear their khāndān, and everybody knows that way that we are the Gujars' bards.*[10] Pointing to her husband, dressed almost indistinguishably from his Gujar *jajmān* (fig. 6.3), she laughed: *look, there is but a syllable's difference between Gujars and Kanjars!* [Gujar aur Kanjarŏ mẽ ek akśar kā farq hai].[11]

The transfer of *birat* engages servants in the fulfillment of their *jajmāns' dharm*, or "existential duty." With distinctive *dharm* and its fulfillment lying at the heart of local selves, *birat* thus passes a central aspect of patrons' selves to their service communities, which are incorporated, much as ancient Roman families were incorporated into the person of the *pater familias* (compare Saller 1984), into their *jajmāns' khāndān*. So, Gujars and

FIGURE 6.3   A Kanjar Bhat (left) from Gopalpura with two of his Gujar *jajmāns*. Those who did not personally know these men could not tell which is which from their clothing. Photo by author.

potters often claim that they belong to a Rajput or a Brahman *khāndān*, and Kanjar Bhats claim belonging in a Gujar or a Mina *khāndān*. As one elderly Brahman explained, *when we take* birat *into our keeping, it is our responsibility* [jimmedārī] *to keep our* jajmān's dharm. *As the keepers of his* dharm, *we become part of his* khāndān, *and he must take care of us as if we were his children.*

The standing, indeed the very social existence, of both parties depends on the continued performance of their respective duties: on the patron giving, and the servants performing the work expected of them. Patrons who renege on their duties have always risked public disgrace at the hands of their bards, who, if slighted, could publicize the tightfistedness of their patrons, either by threatening self-hurt, to exhibit the suffering caused by neglect (see chapter 4), or, more commonly, through ceremonial accusations of miserliness.[12] Kamlesh, an old Gujar, told me that when he was a child his family feared the bards' ridicule songs. *It was a matter of honor* [ijjat kī bāt], said another elderly Gujar, *that we were not thought of as misers* [kanjūs], *so we always gave our bards their* birat. Even if such tactics were not always effective, and are increasingly less so these days, references to penny-pinching in insult poetry derive their abusive power from the fact that generosity, the benchmark of superior standing, was always easy to question and undermine (compare Harlan 1992: 122; Snodgrass 2006).[13]

In exchange for their patrons' generosity, the servants owe not only work, reverence, and obedience, but, most importantly, loyalty to their *jajmāns*. The servants' disloyalty is seen as a sign of the patron's inability or unwillingness to satisfy or control his subordinates. So, the fidelity of the servants is a matter of great significance for *jajmāns*. As Ram Singh, the *ṭhākur* of a nearby village, who maintains a sizeable servant entourage, explained,

> *If people see my workers* [kām karne wāle] *begging from somebody else, they will think: he is poor, stingy, or weak; he has no control over his own servants. If my servants beg from somebody else, it is as if my wife and children are eating another man's food. The people who will see this will say that this man does not keep his* dharm, *that he does not keep his family well and that his household and his life had gone astray* [ghūm gaye]. *It is just like that with our servants. As long as we keep them, they must be true to us and take from no one else. This is our duty* [dharm] *and honor* [ijjat].

Because servants are incorporated into, and are thus constitutive of, the patron's service family—and indeed of his person—the substantive integrity of the *jajmāns'* communities and individual selves relies on the faithfulness of their servants. The *biratkarīs* (servants, people with a right to service) may lose much of their skill, remain idle for years, or altogether abandon their hereditary occupation,[14] and yet retain their *birat* and its contingent entitlements.[15] Sometimes, they collect annual payments without doing any work. Promiscuity on the part of the servants can put the relationship in jeopardy, and accusations of unfaithfulness can be used by *jajmāns* to retract their service rights.[16]

The fracturing of patronal ties amounts to a loss of integrity and proper standing, in broader society as much as among their caste mates. This can be catastrophic for service communities, resulting in the loss not only of their livelihoods, but also of the source of social standing, and even of their position within their caste. As we saw in chapter 4, low-caste bards who lose their patrons acquire the repute of vagrants, whom no other Kanjar will marry (even if outsiders see all Kanjars as vagrants). Reflecting on the current erosion of their *jajmānī* ties, Bima, a young Kanjar Bhat, remarked: *these days we are not only losing our daily bread, we are losing our honor* [ijjat] *and our khāndān.* For mobile communities like the Kanjar Bhats, who "roam about" for most of the year and are thus suspected of promiscuous "begging," assertions of loyalty—relational fixity—are all-important. Thus, the *khel* is mostly a pledge of allegiance. Each family of practicing Kanjar Bhats owns a much cherished "copper letter" (*tāmbā pattar*), which functions as a kind of work certificate and is presented to patrons at every *khel* as evidence of the bards' service rights (fig. 6.4 and, for a recently manufactured *tāmbā pattar*, fig. 6.5). Although such certificates are meant to be summaries of patrons' family histories, their text is typically more a proof of the document's authenticity. The short, 364-word text of one such letter contains eight assertions of the certificate's authenticity and fourteen oaths.[17] The patrons' genealogy (*bansāvalī*) recited during the *khel* is also punctuated with oaths of loyalty to the patrons as refrains. But patrons never fully trust their wandering bards, whose fidelity is ever threatened by the temptation of profit that can be made on the side (see also chapter 4).[18] And so the Gujars suspected their Kanjar bards of infidelity:

> *The bards come and go and we never know whether they dance for others or remain true to us. People say that they see them dancing and singing for*

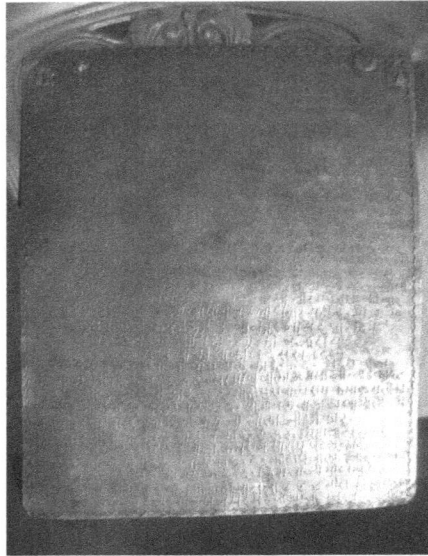

FIGURE 6.4 A copper plate (*tāmbā pattar*) for a Bor Gujar clan kept by a Kanjar Bhat family in Gopalpura. The plate records the patron family's descent from divine and human ancestors. Photo by author.

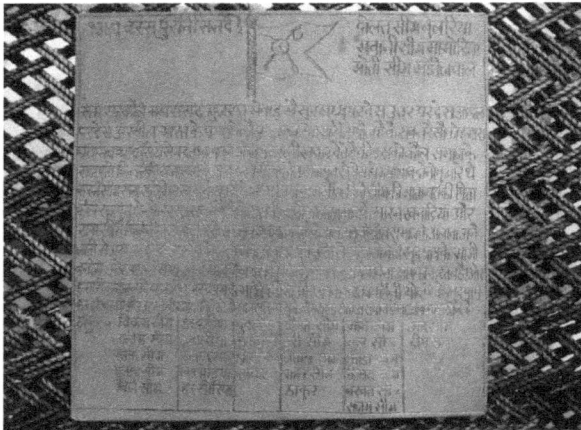

FIGURE 6.5 The *tāmbā pattar* (copper certificate) of a Koli clan kept by a Nat Kanjar family in northern Rajasthan. The certificate provides a synopsis of the *jajmāns'* genealogy, insistence on the relationship between mythical ancestors of Kolis and Kanjars, and a list of senior clansmen from the patron community. It is dated, improbably, 1351 *Vikram Saṁvat*, or 1294 CE. Compare this to another such certificate used by the bards in Gopalpura and thought to be authentic (see figure 6.4). Photo by author.

Bhils. Who knows—maybe they are even dancing for sweepers [Bhangis]? Why should we feed them if they go around selling our birat? *If we give them money, it is like feeding an unfaithful wife.*

Ties Undone

Many *jajmāns* no longer patronize bards. Pedigree has lost much of its former currency for socially aspiring communities, many of which now look to political or bureaucratic connections, as well as education, as sources of prestige. Hereditary ties between many bards and their patrons have thus been substantially undone (Snodgrass 2006; but see my notes on their persistence in chapter 2). Whereas fifty years ago a Kanjar Bhat caravan was a common sight on the Rajasthani byways, today the Gopalpura Kanjars are the last Kanjar bards left in all of Mewar. According to the elders of Gopalpura, about half of the *jajmāns* they entertained twenty years ago no longer employ them, and those who still do give much less: cash needs to be prized out of their pockets and gifts of cattle are virtually nonexistent. The generosity I witnessed is largely a shadow of bygone days.[19]

Many bards have, nonetheless, found new ways to make a living and occasionally even to prosper. Over the past few decades the Kanjar Bhats have increasingly supplemented, or altogether replaced, their dwindling *birat* incomes with cash made by entertaining other villagers on their way.[20] Kallu, an old woman from Gopalpura, related how her family started "selling *birat*," when she was a child:

> *One year when there was a drought we came to serve our* jajmāns *and they sent us away. They said—go, we have no money and no food to give you, go! Still we did our work. We set up the rope and I danced for them, but they did not come out to see and nobody gave us even a cup of tea. The same happened in the next village and in another one. Then we had no grain with which to make bread. So, we went and sang some songs in a Bhil encampment nearby.[21] And many Bhils came and they liked our work, so they gave us some vegetables and some wheat. And so our stomachs were filled.*

Such work can be lucrative. Villagers are often happy to share a basketful of grain and a few rupees for an evening of entertainment, and a night's performance in a small village can bring in few kilos of wheat and a few hundred rupees. With the audience expanded in each location from a handful of patron households to the entire village, daily collections can amount to 100–300 rupees. So, at the end of their 2007–8 tour, one Gopalpura family brought home 20,000 rupees, a large sum by rural standards.[22] And so a number of Kanjar Bhat families in Gopalpura were able to build pukka concrete and brick houses, and some even managed to buy small plots of land, which they have little time to cultivate in their busy travelling schedule (see fig. 6.6).

Such income, however, comes at a social cost, earning the Bhats the disrepute of beggars, both inside and outside their caste. Other Kanjars say that, having forfeited their *birat* "to fill their stomachs" with anyone's, even the sweepers', bread, Kanjar Bhats have become "half-castes" (*ādhī-jāts*).[23] Having betrayed their *jajmāns*, they lost their *khāndān*. Kalla explained:

> *They take everyone's gifts and they eat everyone's khāndān. So, what is their khāndān? What is their caste? They have no caste, and we no longer see them as Kanjars. Only drunkards and no one else in our brotherhood sells* [bechtā] *their daughters to them.*

Even though the Gopalpura Kanjar Bhats can be quite well off, respectable Kanjar thieves altogether avoid contact with them. Only the poorest and most degraded of them will give their daughters in marriage to Bhats, usually for an exorbitant bride price.

The collapse of the bards' standing in the Kanjar society has led to a dramatic shrinking of intra-caste exchange and alliance relations. The community previously maintained relations—gave and took women in marriage, lent to and borrowed money from, visited, and exchanged information and contacts—with a wide community of Kanjars, going as far afield as Agra, Indore, and Pune. But today, because most Kanjars are in the thieving trade and consider themselves above the degraded bards, the extent of the bards' marrital and professional bonds has shrunk dramatically: over the past two generations, nearly 90 percent of marriages in Gopalpura have taken place with two neighboring Kanjar Bhat communities, and most of these (60.6 percent) are confined to their own village.[24]

Although the residents of Gopalpura accept their inferior standing, they are loath to admit to working for anyone but their patrons.[25] It was only after several

FIGURE 6.6 A Kanjar Bhat in front of his house in Gopalpura. The ground floor
was built in the late 1950s, and the upper story was added in 1998. The owner, here
posing with his donkey, recently bought 3 *bīghās* of land, where he now grows
peanuts. Photo by author.

bottles of *madh* on one long evening that we had a more candid discussion of
the transition to the new, more commoditized form of their trade. Even then, it
was important for them to prove that they still had the right of *birat*. Kalpesh,
a young Kanjar Bhat, tried to explain that the sale of their performances was
a variant of *birat* relations, called *āyat*. *Āyāt*, he said, was like *birat*, with the
exception that servants could receive gifts from a wide range of *jajmāns*. But as
he persisted in his explanation, an awkward silence fell over our drinking circle.
Ramesh later explained that they grew ashamed. I was a guest, and I had paid
for the drink that evening, and it was no good to lie to me like that.

   Āyāt refers to short-lived, contractual exchange of services, a sale that does
not bind parties into a proper, lasting patronal relation (Kothari 1994: 206). As
such, *āyat* is morally opposed to *birat*. If the durable and orderly *birat* relations
are the bedrock of loyalty, trust, and good social standing, *āyat* relationships
are a corrupting force, which leads to equally unhinged and jumbled personhood and immorality. Rajasthanis thus cite the *āyat*-like nature of merchants'
(Baniyas') transactions as a source of their moral decrepitude: *it is because, as
we say, they take from all and give to all* [sabhī kā lete, sabhī ko dete] *that we
do not trust the merchants.*

   The patrons' gifts of food, clothing, and cash have social worth for recipients as containers of *khāndān* and vessels of their incorporation into the patron's community only insofar as they are made in the context of an exclusive
and long-lasting relationship, a relation based on a promise of *care*, not just
payment for services. With gifts carrying people's nature, the regulation of their
transfer is central to articulations of status. The integrity of persons and communities relies on their receipt of substance from a known and restricted circle
of patrons, ideally a single one, with whom one would maintain an exclusive,
long-term relation. Beggars and vagabonds, who receive gifts from a motley
assortment of sources, are thus composed of a motley array of substances and
lack bio-moral integrity and social worth. As one Rajput explained:

> When a person eats from one jajmān, we know what kind of person they are
> and we give them respect. But when people start to take from everyone, there
> is confusion [gaṛbaṛ] and we no longer know what they are like or what they
> may do. This is why it is important for workers to serve and eat only from
> [their own] jajmān.

While gifts from strangers are a threat to one's status, and are accepted with much apprehension,[26] donations from regular patrons are sought after as sources of social attachment and worth.

Thieves and Prostitutes

Kanjars involved in prostitution, who entertain a hodgepodge array of patrons, rank lowest among the Kanjars. Historically, many Kanjar groups across Northern India and Pakistan have been, and continue to be, involved in prostitution (see chapter 4).[27] In Rajasthan, they are commonly known as Banchris, Nat Kanjars, or Nats (fig. 6.7).[28] While some sell sex for a few dozen rupees on byways, other such groups (mainly in central and northern Rajasthan) have attracted wealthier clients and are now financially much better off than either the thieves or the bards. The thieves, however, see them as a "fallen" (*gire hue*) lot and have cut off all commensal and marital ties

FIGURE 6.7 Anthropologist with a Kanjar Nat girl in northern Rajasthan. Photo by anonymous interlocutor.

with them (at least openly).[29] Interestingly, it is not sexual promiscuity that Kanjars cite as their "fall."[30] Rather, it is their engagement in relations with a random assortment of patrons. As one Kanjar Bhat put it,

> We see it this way: because Nat Kanjars have started selling their daughters to anyone who comes to them—Bhils, leather workers [Balais], drummers [Dholis], sweepers [Bhangis]—they have forsaken their khāndān and we no longer accept them as our relatives [ristedār].

Unlike Kanjar Bhats, who have retained (in however attenuated a form) ties with *jajmāns* and continue to claim a degree of respect within the broader Kanjar community, the Nat Kanjars can claim no particular or durable ties of patronage at all. In a desperate bid to prove themselves worthy to higher standing Kanjars, whose daughters they continue to attempt to marry (but whom even a very high bride price often fails to secure), some Nat have fabricated copper letters (*tāmbā pattars*) as evidence of their bonds with hereditary *jajmāns* (see figure 6.5). But such "evidence" fools few. Old Shambhu was approached by a Nat family with a marriage proposal. They showed him one such certificate, which, he said, *was a fake* [naqlī]*, its copper too shiny and the engraving too sharp.* He added: *My son could read it. What kind of a secret bardic language is that? We know their work. They can show us thousands of copper letters and we will still not give our daughters to them.*

The thieves constitute a status elite, if not an economic elite, among Rajasthani Kanjars. While Brahmans and merchants may treat Kanjar thieves as depraved vagrants, their own caste mates respect them as men with proper and durable bonds with respectable patrons, to say nothing of pride in their burgling skills. As I have already noted in chapter 4, the sustained success of the Kanjars' thieving business had relied historically on protection by local authorities, village communities, landholding families, and Rajput chiefs. It still does today. Belonging is not only a matter of existential significance; it has obvious practical benefits, too. Although in practice allegiances between thieves and their masters have often been highly unstable, Kanjars conceive of thieving as work that necessarily requires the protection of patrons and entails *birat* rights. The thieves known to enjoy *birat* have a privileged standing. As Ramesh explained:

Without a jajmān, *a thief* [chor] *is not a true* [pakkā] *thief. He is a thief for a day* [yek roj kā chor]—*a new player* [neyā khelāṛī]. *If you have no* jajmān, *you will be caught in a minute and—furrr—you go to prison! Or another man will kill you and nobody will say a word . . . But if a man is a thief and his grandfather and great-grandfather were thieves, we know that he has a master* [mālik] *and he has got* birat, *so we give him respect. Everyone in our caste knows that our forefathers* [bujrak] *were thieves since the days of Rām. And that is how everyone knows that we are true and original* [khandāṇī] *Kanjars and men of honor* [ijjat-wāle].

Historically, unlike bards who had been patronized by the lowly Bhils, Gujars, Minas, or Malis, many Kanjar thieves had enjoyed, and still enjoy, the privileged protection of local political elites—Rajput chiefs, other landowning families— connections with whom continue to form the bedrock of the thief Kanjars' superior standing inside their caste. Shifts in such bonds are the anchor of Kanjars' movements, up and down in rank, within their community.

The New Kanjar Elite

The legacy of such alliances remains a matter of privilege among Kanjars in Rajasthan: the Mandawari Kanjars are known as the Rao's servants (*Rāo Sahāb-jī ke kamīn*), an accolade that marks their preeminence over other Kanjar thieves who were once patronized by lesser Rajputs or by lower castes. Their superior standing shows up most clearly in the disparity of bride price given in marriages.[31] As I noted in chapter 5, Kanjars practice bilateral cross-cousin marriage, ideally "swap marriage" (*adle-badle kī śādī*), in which households exchange brides of the same generation (a sister and a brother from one would marry a brother and a sister from another). The egalitarian ethic within the community demands that the value given and received by each party in this exchange should be equal so as to maintain the families' rank parity. Remember what I wrote in chapter 1 (also see the following chapter)? Where there is egalitarianism, there is commensuration. Equality demands calculated comparison: the measurement of who has what, and of how this compares to what others have. Kanjar marriages encapsulate this principle. Value transferred in marriage has two key variables: honor (*ijjat*) and bride price (*tsāri*), whose balance is carefully calculated. When families exchanging brides are status equals, bride price payments are also equal and so they cancel each other out. This is the morally ideal, "uncalculated" kind of marriage, where no money passes hands. Any differences in honor, however, must be compensated for with bride price payments: the greater the difference between families, the more the lower standing one will have to pay. As Hari Ram explained, *if you have* ijjat, *then you will receive a high bride price and you will give little, but if your family has little* ijjat, *it is the opposite: you give a lot and receive little.* In short, honor is inversely proportional to bride price, and this differential is carefully calculated in marriage arrangements (table 6.1). The range of bride price shown in the table reflects status differences between wife givers and wife receivers. The highest bride price (150,000– 250,000 rupees) was given by the lowest-ranked Kanjar prostitutes to the highest ranked Kanjar thieves, who once served high-ranking Rajputs.[32] In marriages between status approximates (few can actually agree that they are equal), bride price remains modest (9,500–11,000 rupees).

What I have described in this chapter so far are the principles of *birat* relations, the rules of the game rather than its historical process, which has always been subject to a great deal of change. In the old system, Rajputs employed entire Kanjar families or sets of families, who enjoyed communal *birat* rights, under which all of their members were entitled to the *jajmān's* protection and support; those who were too young, too old, or otherwise incapable of thieving profitably were still in the keeping of their patron (Bharucha 2003: 222). It was only if the entire community failed in its duties that the *jajmān* could seek to break the relationship. These rules changed with the arrival of the new order of patronage by the police, which was born in Begun in the 1930s, in the criminal tribe colonies (chapter 2). Their supervisor was, on the one hand, responsible for control over inmates (which he had to demonstrate to his superiors). On the other, he was interested in securing the labor and loyalties of the inmates. The inspector struck a balance by patronizing the inmates selectively, adopting only the best thieves, while using others to fulfill his arrest quotas.

Adopted families enjoyed leniency and received land, livestock, and cash provided by the state for the development of the colonies. Others were promptly penalized for short absences and incarcerated for burglaries committed by their adopted neighbors. While adopted thieves erected two-story

TABLE 6.1 Bride wealth transferred in Kanjar marriages between 2006 and 2008 in Chittorgarh district, based on information about 42 marriages in 18 villages.

Bride Receivers (bride wealth givers)	Bride Givers (bride wealth receivers)	Bride Price (in rupees)
Former servants of high-ranking Rajputs	Former servants of high-ranking Rajputs	9,500–11,000
Former servants of high-ranking Rajputs	Former servants of low-ranking Rajputs or other low castes	3,500–7,000
Former servants of high-ranking Rajputs	Kanjar bards	(no marriage alliances forged)
Former servants of high-ranking Rajputs	Kanjar prostitutes	0
Former servants of low-ranking Rajputs or other low castes	Former servants of high-ranking Rajputs	17,500–18,000
Former servants of low-ranking Rajputs or other low castes	Kanjar bards	2,500–3,000
Former servants of low-ranking Rajputs or village communities	Kanjar prostitutes	0
Kanjar bards	Former servants of high-ranking Rajputs	0
Kanjar bards	Former servants of low-ranking Rajputs or other low castes	23,500–25,000
Kanjar bards	Kanjar prostitutes	0
Kanjar prostitutes	Former servants of high-ranking Rajputs	150,000–250,000
Kanjar prostitutes	Former servants of low-ranking Rajputs or other low castes	85,000–100,000
Kanjar prostitutes	Kanjar bards	75,000
Kanjar prostitutes	Kanjar prostitutes	0

Table compiled by author.

houses and bought more land, others became increasingly impoverished, in-
debted, and humiliated, finding themselves regularly chained to the walls of
police outposts, a spectacle still vividly remembered by the oldest of Kanjars.
When Rao Sahib was our anndātā, *nobody had much, but everyone had enough,*
remembers Shanta, one old woman, *but during crown rule some filled their
bellies while others starved to death.*

Once again, the old normative principles that framed became a vehicle of
major changes in the community, while themselves remaining steadfast. Kanjars who were previously in the Rao's service acquired new forms of employment and protection, which created new gradations of rank and a new Kanjar
elite. The nature of this elite changed as well. Not only did it shrink to about
one-tenth of what it was under the Rao (who was responsible for every Kanjar
he settled on his lands), but the terms of belonging to this elite also changed.
The new system encouraged the most skilled thieves, whose promotion relied
on their caste mates' systematic impoverishment and humiliation. With the
adopted Kanjars directly or incidentally involved in the denigration of their
caste mates, rank differences within the society (which, as we have seen, prizes
equality among families and clans) have sharpened and turned hostile, marked
by increasing hate, jealousy, and fear. As I noted in the prologue, today this
divide is readily visible in the Kanjar villages, where pukka two-story houses
of adopted families tower over the ramshackle stone homes of the others, who
now work for miserly wages on the fields of the Kanjar elite.[33]

As Kanjars from families that were adopted in colonies under crown rule
say, the replacement of patronage by the Rao of Begun by patronage by to
the colony inspector did not degrade their *birat* and honor. On the contrary,
they describe it as a *promotion* from patronage by the Rao to patronage by
the Mewar Maharana. They explain the privileges and material benefits that
their forefathers received back then as "awards" (*ināms*) from the Maharana,
who established the settlement when Begun came under crown rule (chapter
2). Those few who still remember the days of the colony describe houses that
were built by adopted families as "royal homes" (*darbārī ghar*), meaning gifts
from the Maharana, received through the inspector, but not from him. Other
Kanjars see things differently. They say that adopted thieves sold themselves
to the police (recall discussions in the prologue and chapter 3).

Whatever the views, following Independence, as Rajputs lost their economic and political standing, the police emerged as the Kanjars' chief patrons and relations with them became a crucial source of intra-caste rank. After 1952, when the Criminal Tribes Act was repealed and the colonies were disbanded, these relations were reshuffled again. The inspector was replaced with a newly appointed station house officer (SHO), for whom the Kanjars were not a priority. His range of duties was much wider than the inspector's, and was subject to more stringent supervision from above, and he was not personally acquainted with the Kanjars, who ended up, once again, on the loose. All local Kanjars, the previously adopted and others, were now subject to special policing measures, as "criminal tribesmen" until 1952, and later as "habitual offenders" under provisions of the new Habitual Offenders Act, which in 1956 replaced Criminal Tribe legislation, while virtually reproducing its provisions. Like most other "denotified" peoples, inmates of the disbanded colonies were listed as habitual offenders and subjected to the already familiar special policing measures: impromptu raids, roll call, and "preventive" incarceration (see note 1 in chapter 3).

Regular surveillance and the punishment of absences by imprisonment restricted the radius of Kanjar mobility to a distance that could be traveled within a night. The resulting upsurge of burglaries committed by local Kanjars in the Begun *tahasīl* (administrative block) soon attracted attention of the district authorities, who pressed the local police to deal with the problem. Local officers first resorted to "soft measures," as one retired officer, who was posted in Begun in the 1950s and 1960s, put it:

> *We could not control Kanjars then. We raided and we took roll call, but how could we catch them? Every time we came, they ran away into the jungle. We were in much trouble with our superiors, who were cutting our pay because Begun was rife with robberies and the culprits were free. In 1954 or '55 we finally caught one big thief from Mandawari, whom we enrolled as an informer* [mukhbīr]. *Within five years or so, five more Kanjars from different settlements in Begun came to us of their own accord and became men of the police* [pulis ke ādmī]. . . . *They were all intelligent men who understood the benefits of working for the police. This way we gained some control over their activities.*

All Kanjars thus reconscripted by the police were men formerly employed by the inspector, who had more trust in and experience of work with the police than others. They were also the most established, accomplished, and active thieves. As informers (*mukhbīrs* or *mukhbars* in Kanjari), their job was to inform on, aid in the pursuit of, and facilitate negotiations with other Kanjars. In return, they were given free rein to thieve in Begun. Like the old system of patronage, the new arrangement was also termed "adoption," and has by now been standardized to the point of bureucratization. It is expected, for instance, that SHOs should inherit informers from their predecessors, who record the details of the relationship (lists of reliable and unreliable informers, descriptions of their parties and thieving beats, and other minutiae) in a file they leave behind. By established convention, newly arrived SHOs are expected to pay a personal visit (within a fortnight of being posted) to each adopted family, to each newly inherited informer, to reconfirm the relation. In 2008, out of the eighteen Kanjar villages in the Begun *tahasīl*, twelve were adopted. The remaining six were subject to systematic harassment, which officers charging them with all local offenses, so that their residents either hid in the nearby jungle or languished in lockups with no trial or even a warrant for arrest. To secure their bail, their families had to burgle more and more, thus amassing longer and longer criminal records. This system is alive and well today.

Coppers' Robbers

The new police arrangement, which encourages Kanjars to thieve inside their jurisdictions (as opposed to outside, as before), made the thieving terrain coterminous with police jurisdictions.[34] This did not only intensify violence between Kanjars and their neighbors—which culminated in the Mandawari pogrom (see prologue and chapter 3)—but also changed relations inside the local Kanjar society. Today, the parameters of police jurisdictions are reproduced within the structure of the Kanjar community, in its thieving beats and marriage arrangements. And the territorial and hierarchical markers of police organization now largely dictate the limits of exchange, marriage alliances, gradations of status, and the structure of authority within the community. Under the old system, Kanjars traversed great distances on their burgling excursions, forming professional and nuptial bonds with other

Bhantus along the way (see Piliavsky 2013a; map 6.2). Under the new police system, such ties dramatically shrunk to the territories under a few neighboring police stations, a change that has had serious social repercussions for the Kanjar community. If four generations back Mandawari exchanged four women in marriage with the villages in Bhilwara, a different district, and as many marriages were formed three generations ago (this time in a more populous village), one marriage alliance was forged two generations ago, and none at all was secured during the most recent nuptial round. Thus, in the span of four generations alliances with villages outside of the local police

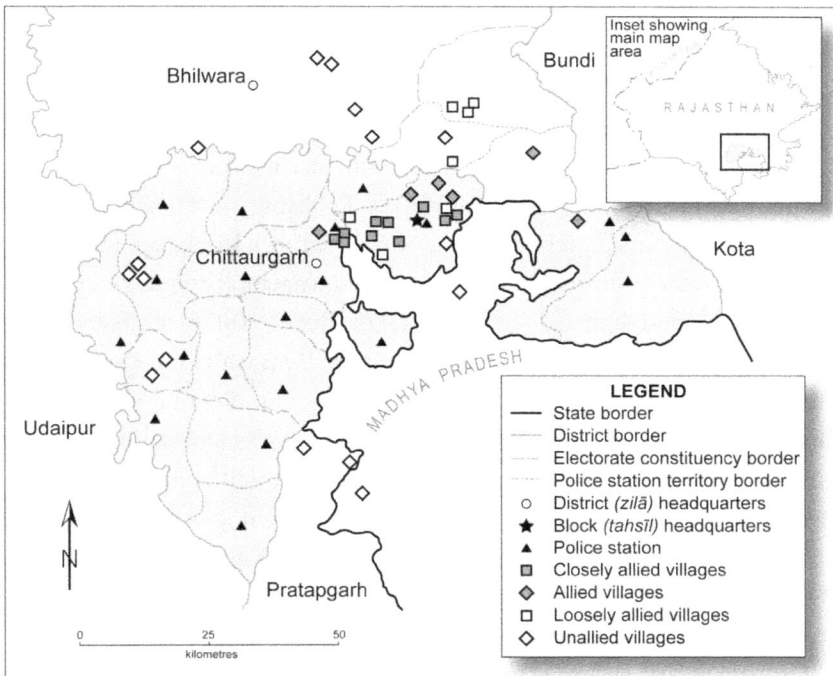

MAP 6.2 The relational reach of the Mandawari brotherhood. "Closely allied" villages are connected by more than 10 marriages (traceable over 4 generations) and are marked by frequent contact and professional collaboration. "Allied" villages are connected by 5–10 marriages and regular contact, and "loosely allied" villages are connected by fewer than 5 marriages and occasional visits. "Unallied" villages maintain no regular contacts. Based on maps drawn by David Watson of the Department of Geography's Cartographic Unit, University of Cambridge.

jurisdiction have dwindled from twenty-four (17 percent of total marriage exchanges) to four (1 percent) today. Now, more than half of the villages within the Mandawari brotherhood (recall chapter 2 on what constitutes this)—the community of professional and marriage alliances—are confined to two neighboring police jurisdictions.

The structure of rank among local Kanjar thieves has, moreover, come to mirror the structure of police rank. While the police usually adopt entire Kanjar villages, their patronage is not even. Gang bosses form relations with particular officers, whose ranking is reflected in the ranking of Kanjar gang bosses. Much as the rank of drummers and bards reflects the status of their traditional *jajmāns*, so the rank of Kanjar gangs reflects the status of their patrons in the police. Most Kanjars with patrons in the police form relations with officers in the lowest, field-working ranks (known collectively among Kanjars as *sipāhīs*): constables, head constables, and assistant subinspectors. The territory of each station's jurisdiction is divided among such officers, who are entrusted with the everyday field duties of policing these beats (see Jauregui 2016 for a detailed account of this rank structure). Unlike the frequently transferred senior officers (inspectors and subinspectors), the *sipāhīs* usually remain in one post for many years, often for the duration of their careers, when they have the chance to develop long-lasting relations with local Kanjars.[35] As employment is often inherited (multiple generations of men from the same family are often employed in the same or similar post),[36] such relationships can outlast several generations, acquiring the gravity of "traditional" (*pāramparik*) ties.[37] These are the officers one may find on most evenings in Kanjar *bastīs* in civilian dress. Local villagers say that to the *sipāhīs*, Kanjar patronage offers three things: *paise, dāṛū aur ijjat* ("money, liquor, and respect"). The officers themselves like to boast of their knowledge of Kanjar language, "customs and habits" (*rivāj aur ādat*), and connections with and influence over their Kanjar "workers" (*karamchārīs*), whom they treat as their personal clients. The *sipāhīs*, however, exercise only limited sway over Kanjar by offering or retracting small bureaucratic favors (such as writing off arrest warrants). Such favors are easily purchased with nominal payments of 50 rupees or a bottle of madh, which the *sipāhīs*, who have virtually no career advancement prospects and whose postings may have cost as much as 100,000 rupees,[38] usually accept.[39]

For SHOs, on the contrary, Kanjars are most useful as a source of intelligence that boosts their "statistics," which in turn boosts their career progress. Such officers select their informers carefully, recruiting only the most intelligent and resourceful thieves. Kanjars who acquire protection from senior officers acquire special status among their own. SHOs are rarely posted in one place for long, so relations with them are often less durable than those with the *sipāhīs*, but they entail more substantial privileges. Kanjars patronized by SHOs enjoy virtual impunity inside their home jurisdictions, are more effective at having arrest warrants dismissed, settle better deals whenever the need to pay off the police arises, and arrange much cheaper and speedier releases from jail on bail. Patronage by SHOs also allows them both to protect and harass their caste mates as complaints they file against other Kanjars will be taken seriously.[40] And so Kanjar gangs and police stations are identical in structure, indeed structurally they form a single society of their own.

The old system of headmen (*paṭel*s), or elders representing a family and acting as arbiters in disputes, is now paralleled among Kanjars, and in many villages replaced, by "bosses" or "gang leaders" (*sardārs*) who work for the police. The growing significance of *sardārs* as agents of justice means that matters for the Kanjar caste council (*jātī panchāyat*) are increasingly referred to and mediated by police and court authorities, where *sardārs* have more sway than traditional headmen. This is not only a shift of authority from hereditary headmen to gang bosses, but a more fundamental transfer of the community's legal apparatus to the sphere of state courts. Contrary to James Scott's argument for a top-down imposition of state structure onto local social life (1998; 2009), the state has rather neatly and tightly woven itself into Kanjar society, where it plays a vital role—practically, juridically, structurally—and where its forms are now reproduced in local relations (see Li [2005] and Scheele [2007] for similar criticisms of Scott).

Sardārs wield authority not only because they have better access to state resources. They are also held in high regard among Kanjars, even those who fall victim to the police because of them. Kanjar gang bosses describe work that they do for the SHOs (mostly intelligence and thieving work rather than bribery) as "service" (*sevā*) or "work for someone" (*kammā* in Kanjari), and the favors they receive in return as "gifts" (*dān*) from patrons proper, a role that officers step into gladly, doing things that are normally expected from traditional jajmāns: passing their old clothes on to their Kanjar clients and offering them food when they visit the police station. SHO patrons can be coercive, in which case both Kanjars and *sipāhīs* complain of mistreatment. But if they fulfill expectations of protection and care, their Kanjar clients call them "fathers" (*bāps*), "parents" (*mā-ī-bāp*), and "bread givers" (*anndātās*)—using the honorifics, which, as we have seen, are otherwise used for divine and human *jajmāns*.[41] However secretive and precarious, these relations confer honor on the Kanjar clients. They offer belonging, and with it offer *khandān*.

The spatial limits of the Mandawari brotherhood are now defined by the territorial configurations of the local police jurisdiction, the social organization of the local Kanjar community thus reproducing the structure of the local police.[42] As Ramesh remarked, *We are like the police: they have their land and we have ours, they guard their borders and so do we, they have their bosses and so do our villages. Each brotherhood is like a police station, except that we, Kanjars, have got no SP [Superintendent of Police, an overall head].* While the territorial demarcation is reproduced often unwittingly, Kanjars quite consciously adopt other markers of being part of the police *khanadān.* Since Independence, an increasing number of children have been given names like Sarkariya or Diptiya (from *sarkār* for "state" and "[police] deputy," respectively), and a trip to the bazaar (where I offered to buy some clothes for Ramesh's younger son, Lakshman) ended up with us buying a child-sized police uniform. That had more than a touch of irony. Although in Mandawari Kanjars do not wear police uniforms, as do some Kanjars in other settlements, they invariably have their shirts made in the print worn by the local constables when off duty. Belonging and its display, however morally ambivalent it may be, is crucial, intrinsic to being in a world where to be someone one needs to be someone's.

Chapter 7

THE NEW LORDS OF BEGUN

IN NOVEMBER 2008, toward the end of my fieldwork, I was back in the Rao's citadel for an afternoon tea. Almost a year had passed since our first meeting, when he first told me about his family and the town. Once again we sat in the mirror-work sitting room lit up by the light falling through colored glass. This time, it was not the Rao himself who met me at the door. An elderly peon in a pseudo-uniform greeted me briskly, showed me into the room, put a glass of water before me, and vanished. As I sat there waiting for the Rao, I marveled at the silence in the room. My ears were still clanging with the noise of the marketplace, but all I could hear now were the cries of the peacocks. After some time, as I adjusted to the silence, I could make out the town below, but only as a distant whisper, a murmur as if from another world. And then the door creaked and in came Ajay, the Rao's youngest son, who was now living with him. *Namaste, namaste-ji! Long time no see, nah? You have been keeping busy? How fare our Kanjars? Good, good. Papa-ji sends his apologies. He will join us shortly, but he is very preoccupied these days with the elections and all.*

These were indeed busy days for the Rao, who had decided to compete in the State Assembly elections. *Was this the Rao's debut in politics?* I asked. *Oh no*, said Ajay, *Papa-ji is an old hand in politics!* In 1967, the Rao won a seat in the Rajasthan State Assembly, where he represented Begun for the next decade. Although he ran as an independent, he joined the Congress Party and

was made minister of agriculture, becoming at age twenty-eight the youngest minister in the India. In 1977 he retired from politics and settled in Delhi.
But now that he had returned to Begun, *it was only natural*, said Ajay, *for him
to run for the Assembly.* He was, after all, the chief of Begun, to whom people
looked with love and admiration. *He was their natural choice.* But the people's
love was not enough. He also needed the support of a party. Forty years back,
the Rao won twice by a landslide. *But today the voters are greedy*, said Ajay:

> *You know how it is, they just want money. You need to buy food and alcohol for
> the campaign. And many of them now expect cash. So we need party funding.
> Maybe the Maharana of Mewar could run as an independent. He has seven-star
> hotels, so he can easily fund a campaign, if he wanted to run for Parliament. But
> most people, even Papa-ji, need help with campaign funding. Otherwise, Papa-ji
> would have no need of a party ticket. He is assured of victory because he has his
> people's trust. The people will vote for him, not for the Congress.*

He was going to say more, but the door opened and the Rao entered the room.
We stood up abruptly, bowed our greetings, and the Rao told the peon to bring
us tea, black with lemon. He was bubbling with excitement. The party candidates were about to be announced, and he could not wait to campaign. He
had just had a call from the police circle inspector (the local chief of police),
who warned him that the Congress was considering another candidate. But
the Rao laughed this off. He said that before elections policemen try to court
favor with candidates.

> *They make these calls. They offer what they call "intelligence," what they claim is
> information from the party headquarters, to make sure that when the candidate
> wins they will be on his side. They want to make sure that the new MLA does
> not put them on ice. Do you know what this means—ice posting* [baraf]*?—He
> laughed.—You know, once I become MLA, I can get him transferred to a post in
> the desert, where he'll sit for ten years. What will he do? So, they are all making
> these bogus calls. We've had calls from every head of police station.*

Such calls did not shake the Rao's confidence. He dismissed them as "silliness"
and asked if I'd like some sherbet. Why did he join politics in his youth? Was
it his dream? No, he demurred: *I was not at all into politics, I was young and I*

never joined a political party. But then the people shouted "Jay ho! Jay ho!" [Victory! Victory!]*, so I stood for elections as an independent and won.*

Feast in the Time of Elections

Meanwhile, Begun was consumed by a pre-electoral frenzy. Storefronts and temple walls, billboards and boulders on roadsides were plastered with the insignia of the Congress and the Bharatiya Janata Party (BJP), India's two national parties, which dominated the local political landscape. All day long loudspeakers in the bazaar blared out echoing loops of party slogans, clashing with mottos spewed out of megaphones by jeepfuls of young men that raced up and down the narrow streets of the town. Excitement reached fever pitch when a helicopter decanted a retired Bollywood star onto the cricket field in the center of town. Children, high on sweets distributed by the candidates, covered the rooftops of nearby buildings and hung off the branches of nearby trees. *The last time something this big happened,* joked the circle inspector, *was when the famous historian James Tod* (see chapter 2) *came to town.*

At the center of the festivities was something that the people called "feeding" (*khilānā*), something that they expected from candidates. This took a variety of forms: public feasts at which food, alcohol, and blankets are distributed; private parties thrown for persons of wealth and influence; or gifts of a sari, a plastic pouch of liquor, a blanket, a frying pan, or cash made to families or individual voters. "Feeding" is the centerpiece of election-time discussion and an important measure of assessment of candidates' worth. As such, it reveals a great deal about local conceptions of the role of the politicians, their relationship to the voters, and the popular idiom of relatedness between the government and "the people" at large. People expect to be "fed" by candidates during elections, and feasts are the subject of much lively discussion in villages and the bazaar. What sort of a meal was it? Was there enough for everyone? Were there sweets? Were they cheap sweetmeats or rich, milky *laḍḍūs*? Was there alcohol?

Known as *bhaṇḍāras* or *savāmaṇīs*, but also often simply as "feeding-watering" (*khilānā-pilānā*), feasts were everywhere: in villages, town squares, and middle-class farmhouses. They could be simple meals for a dozen or vast banquets for thousands.[1] In Begun and the surrounding villages candidates hosted smallish feasts in each neighborhood and every village.[2] The ultimate election-time feast took place on the eve of elections, during the all-night electoral vigil known as the "night of the long knives" (*qatal kī rāt*), an electoral tradition that dates back at least to the early 1950s (Adrian Mayer personal communication; Piliavsky & Sbriccoli 2016: 378).[3] During the night, or more commonly during the two or three nights before polling date, the contestants' henchmen dash from village to village in a last-minute bid to feed and, crucially, water their electors. From the middle distance, this may look like vulgar pork barrel politics: the buying of poor villagers' votes on the cheap. But this is not how the residents of Begun, including some of the fiercest local critics of corruption, see it. For them, the ability to provide is the politician's duty, and if you ask any child in a Rajasthani village about what politicians do, they will readily tell you: "They feed!" Politicians certainly complain that their opponents buy votes or addle voters' judgment with drink. But when they themselves feed and water their electors, they say that this is what the people want, that this is their political duty.

Voters are indeed disappointed when food and drink fail to arrive. But "feeding" is not really about putting food into people's mouths, but rather about generating bonds that last, bonds spun of the same moral substance as the ties that bind Kanjars and goddesses. Feeding—both the term and the performance—is the key moral idiom in which people evaluate politicians and conceive of the ways in which politicians relate, or ought to relate, to their constituents. It is as central to political bonds as it is to relations with patron deities. These are not transactional quid pro quo exchanges where payments are exchanged for votes. The feasts are not payments, but promises, and the election-time feeding frenzy is not a sale, but an exchange of vows, sealed with a customary exchange of food, much like the mutual feeding at weddings (see also Björkman 2014). This is how politicians publicly assume responsibility for their constituents, by showing off their willingness and ability to care for their people, to "do their voters' work."

As one farmer put it: *Who knows the meaning of their words, what will they do? People want what they can put in their mouths. When a politician puts bread in people's mouths, they know that he is their man, they trust him, and their heart rests with him.* Or, in the words of a young Gujar girl, *political leaders feed us from the heart* [man se]. Kalla said: *it is the duty* (dharm) *of politicians to feed us. If they feed us, we give them our votes.* Loyalties and their procurement are never certain, and voters cheat no less than do politicians. They may take freebies, but they never do so in public view. Although children hopped from feast to feast, gorging on cheap sweets and greasy curries, no self-respecting adult would feast promiscuously like that. Attending a feast is a public statement of loyalty to a party and a politician, and, unless you are sure, you won't go. So even while there, people were often reluctant about eating. They were deliberating, judging, choosing; they did not want to disclose their loyalties. *You can fill your belly today* (*by feasting with different candidates*), said one farmer, *but then you have to live in the village.* Those with a reputation for political promiscuity, those known for "eating from everyone's hands," lose their political integrity. *They cannot be trusted and no one will do business with them*, said Ramesh. Just as promiscuous feeders in other contexts become socially irrelevant, so do feast-hoppers become politically void. They lose credibility and with it their scope for pressing demands on politicians. Of course, people often hold cards close to their chest—an important tool in political negotiations—but this means avoiding public expressions of loyalty rather than making contradictory pledges to several candidates.

As politicians pursue electors' loyalties, they put on magnificent shows of largesse. At village feasts they dish out not only food but also crockery, blankets, clothing, bottles of alcohol, and promises of the much coveted "development" (*vikās*): hospitals, roads, jobs, electricity, shortcuts through the bureaucratic maze. Voters' expectations of provision express unambiguously the idea that politicians are big men whose duty it is to provide and protect—to care for their people. This sense is articulated in the honorifics, like *mā-i-bāp* (parents), *dādā* (grandpa or elder brother), *bāv-ji* (respected father), and *anndātā* (bread giver), commonly used to address politicians in rural North India, just as they are use to address royals and gods. Bonds between feeders and eaters run deep, and people describe those bonds in terms of trust and love, provision and protection or, in Kalla's formulation, as ties that transcend the give-and-take logic of reciprocity and give people leverage to press demands on politicians and lay claim to the goods of the state.

This cozy vision of moral bonds is a far cry from how politicians in fact perceive and pursue electoral competition: they see it as a race to win, by whatever means. Yet to advance their campaigns, they appeal, emphatically, to the pervasive moral logic of donor-doneeship. As one candidate put it, *these people are very simple, very innocent—if you feed them, they will give you their vote.* The villagers' "innocence" lies in their apparent preference for commensally meaningful feasts over financial profit. *They would rather fill their stomachs and drink their fill*, the candidate said, *than put shoes on their children's feet; but of course if they want me to act like their bread giver, I will*, he added emphatically. As another political boss reflected, *a politician must feed and care for his constituents, just like a father. We treat all these people here like our own children*, he said with a wink. *Who will feed them, if we do not?*

Politicians ceaselessly promise to "get things done" (*kām karnā*) for "their own people" (*āpane log*), to deliver exactly what they think voters want: not generalized policy, but concrete, targeted benefits, stopping just shy of promising richer harvests and heavier rains. But promises are not enough. Voters demand instantiations of the politicians' will and capacity to provide. During elections, candidates need to put on a show of largesse, to display their "bigness," as it were, which must nonetheless be carefully calibrated to display a proper balance of bigness and intimacy, which, as Ansell (2014) observed in Brazil, is pivotal to political patronage, to be grand but not too distant, an attitude one might describe as hierarchical populism. In the run-up to the elections, the choreography of this hierarchical populism is everywhere on display: the politicians' vague magnanimous nods of the head, their waves of the giving palm, or the superior's form of the *namaskar* greeting, in which the hands are not raised as high toward the forehead as they are by a subordinate, and the bystanders' genuflections, accompanied by the cries "*Anndātā!*" and "*Jay ho!*"

Not all giving is "moral." In Begun, gangs of young men often go door to door in the night on behalf of their political bosses. A row that ensued between Baiji's son and his wife during one such nocturnal visit is revealing:

> *I woke up in the middle of the night because I heard knocking at the front*
> *door. I opened it and saw two young boys. I recognized them, they were our*
> *neighbors. Nice boys, you know, one of them was that Brahman lawyer's*
> *son. So, I let them in and asked whether something had gone amiss. They*

came in and at first they didn't say anything. Then Suresh [her husband]
and my mother-in-law [Baiji] woke up. So I asked the boys to come in. They
sat down right here, on this couch, and one of them put down 1,000 rupees.
That's when I understood what they were up to. My husband asked what
the money was for, and they said the BJP. Our family has always voted for
Congress, so Suresh refused to take it. They didn't say much of anything
else. When I was showing them out, they threw the money into my hands
and ran away. Suresh saw this, and you will not believe the row we had that
night! He told me the money was dirty and that I should throw it away. This
money, he said, has the filth of politics [rājnīti kī gandhagī] on it. He said
this money will ruin us. But I thought: why should I throw it away? Politi-
cians have lots of money and they eat people's money, so why shouldn't I
take some too? I still voted for the Congress. We always vote for the Hand
[symbol of the Congress Party].

The domestic brawl provoked by the visit dramatized the moral tension that
riddles political competition. When the cynicism of the electoral game, the
hoarding of votes to win the race, is laid as bare as it was in this case, people
react with moral disgust or instrumental contempt. Financial accounts (no
doubt incomplete, but still revealing) of the local BJP caucus, which I was
shown by one of the party's senior members, suggest that the money allotted
to "individual donations" disappears quickly enough. Few occupy the moral
high ground taken up by Suresh, and most take the cash. And why should
they not? The shoving of cash into voters' pockets is blatantly not a gift, but a
"bribe" (*riśvat*) that obligates no one.

Although it may seem difficult to distinguish "gifts" from "bribes" in practice, villagers distinguish sharply between the two. Gifts are things donors
choose to give. They involve the exercise of personal will directed at others.
Or, as Humphrey (2012: 23) put it, they must be "initiatory, extra, ethical, and
gratuitous." Gifts have nothing to do with the giver's self-advancement or the
receiver's helpless necessity of privation. Bribes, by contrast, are made "out of
helpless compulsion" (*majbūrī se*). You can either reject or accept a bribe from
a candidate, but whichever you do, the giver does not deserve your vote. People
disagree about whether the same act constitutes a "gift" or a "bribe" (just as they
often disagree about what constitutes a "gift" or a "service"); while candidates

hope that voters will treat all donations as gifts and feel bound by them, the best way to ensure that donations secure electoral loyalties is to make a public display out of the act of giving itself. In Begun several senior party bosses from both the Congress and the BJP admitted that they know that clandestine giving convinces few. Indeed, there was agreement that because nocturnal donations are understood by many as attempts to "buy" votes, they may do more harm than good. The BJP, having spent nearly 150 million rupees on the campaign in Begun (almost twice what was spent that year by the Congress), two-thirds of which was distributed surreptitiously in cash, lost the election in 2008. The party caucus subsequently decided that funds for "individual donations" should be drastically culled and reallocated to "social charities," like weddings and birthday feasts—that is, to conspicuous giving.

Kanjar Big Men?

For Kanjars, involvement in the campaign held out the opportunity to obtain publicly recognized bonds with political patrons and a distant possibility of a political career for themselves. With the disintegration of the prior dominance of the BJP caucus, there was little certainty about the outcome of the 2008 elections or about the makeup of the power balance to come. The local chief of police thus could not safely ally with any one faction and did indeed, as the Rao said, hope instead to satisfy all parties. Given the limited manpower at hand, he was forced to draw on all available resources, including his "secret agents," Ramesh and his wife's cousin Ram Sukh (fig. 7.1). As we shall see, for them such involvement has marked their move into the publicly visible domain and the acquisition of the much coveted public recognition as men with patronal attachments, and ones of enviable importance. Ramesh joined a former district collector (chief of administration), who was contesting the elections as an independent, and Ram Sukh worked for the BJP. Their job was to "explain" (*samajhānā*), much as they do in their role as watchmen, the virtue of voting for their candidates. Kanjars employed as watchmen are particularly effective as advocates of candidacy because they are personally acquainted with a great number of people, have great rhetorical skills, and can, if rhetoric fails, threaten villagers into voting.

FIGURE 7.1 Ramesh (right) and Ram Sukh in 2020. Ramesh now has a Royal Enfield and a house in Begun, which he rents out. Photo by Serge Poliakov.

For Ram Sukh, who had been a successful police informer for some years, this was his second state assembly campaign, and for Ramesh, who had been working for the police for only four years, it was the first. For three weeks before the polling date, when campaigning was in full swing, Ramesh and Ram Sukh were run off their feet, from dusk till dawn. Both were employed in the election campaign, and I spent much of the weeks preceding the elections perched on the back of Ramesh's motorcycle, as he drove from one village to the next on his campaign rally, conveying the virtue of voting for "his" candidate to the villagers. Most villages that we visited were those in which Ramesh was employed as a watchman. They were an obvious port of call. Much work took place in the mornings and evenings, before the farmers went off to the fields. The process took quite a bit of time because, unlike most other campaigners, rather than organizing village-wide meetings, Ramesh visited individual households after dark, in the same way as he usually does the "explaining" as a watchman. His *jajmāns* were receptive, as ties of Ramesh's employment obliged them to pledge their allegiance to "his" candidate. Ramesh, however, took his job seriously. Not fooled by polite promises, he was intent on convincing his *jajmāns* properly. His arguments in favor of his candidate are telling of things he expected from a good MLA. A conversation Ramesh had with one Gujar householder went like this:

RAMESH: *So, have you met the District Collector Sahib?*

GUJAR: *No, but I heard he is a good man.*

RAMESH: *An excellent man! He is such a good old man, he spoke to us Kanjars just like a father.*

GUJAR: *Yes* [vaguely].

RAMESH: [after a pause] *He is not like the* [current MLA] *dog, who just feeds the Dhakars* [his own farmer caste]. . . *And these days he does not feed them, either. Have you heard how they are all crying against him? Collector Sahib left his job because of all the corruption in the administration. An honest man has no place in the administration. He is a good man. He will have a road built to your village and he will give you electricity.*

GUJAR: [interrupting] *Ah, brother, they all promise us roads and electricity. Why should this one be any different?*

RAMESH: *Look at the way* [the current MLA] *has eaten all government money, how fat he has grown! Let's see what this one can do. A new man needs a chance. And as a* [former] *government employee, he knows how to get government money.*

As ever, the conversation revolved around the MLAs' capacity, failure, and promise to provide. I have no way of telling whether by the end of this conversation, which went on for some time in a similar manner, Ramesh managed to convince his skeptical interlocutor. Yet I did see that while the two men differed in their enthusiasm about the particular candidate, they shared the same vision of a good politician as a resourceful provider.

Participation in the campaigns brings about a great transformation in the status of Kanjars. Ram Sukh has been a BJP henchman for years and in that time has acquired a visibly distinct standing from other Kanjars in Begun. He buys cloth from shopkeepers who otherwise refuse to do business with Kanjars. He smokes the most expensive of the cheap beedee cigarettes, and while most Kanjars huddle over their glasses of chai in the one stall, known locally as "little Mandawari," that serves Kanjars, he is free to drink chai (and even coffee, a chic drink) around town. When he hangs out in the court, as do most local men of importance, Ram Sukh does not squat in the corner of the courtyard with the rest of the Kanjars who have come for their "dates" (*tārīkhs*) in court, but sits on the benches with other farmers. Ram Sukh cuts an impressive figure against the background of the other Kanjars clad in dirty, tattered, and often ill-fitting trousers and shirts they have inherited from police patrons. Ram Sukh wears an impeccably laundered and pressed tunic and loincloth (*kurtā-dhotī*) ensemble, in the style of the politicians for whom he works, and farmers greet him with courtesy in the court and the marketplace, referring to him by his name rather than as "that Kanjar," as the rest are usually spoken of.

Ramesh was cultivating the same image. Soon after he was employed in the campaign, he busied himself with cultivating a proper look. He ordered a pair of trousers and two new shirts made from the same plain blue material that the candidate wore. Such sartorial references were, of course, signals that the candidate was his patron (recall discussions in chapter 6 and earlier in this chapter). And he assumed an air of importance. Whereas previously Ramesh was almost invariably home by the hour of dusk, waiting impatiently for the drinking to commence, he now came home late from his campaigning. One evening he even mentioned that he was thinking of drinking less, and on another he returned home with a newspaper he had bought in the town. Then, to our amazement, he opened it nonchalantly and started to read, instead of joining the drinking circle.

Such changes brought on a mixed reaction in the *bastī*. Ramesh, as his brothers observed, was becoming a "big man" (*baṛā ādmī*) in Begun with his new big *jajmān*, and that meant potential benefits for the community: political protection, greater public acceptance, and perhaps even jobs. Others worried that Ramesh would get above himself and become distanced from the community, and with good reason. Ram Sukh's rise in Begun has been accompanied by his rise above and away from the Kanjar community. Although, just like the other Kanjars, Ram Sukh lives in a Kanjar *bastī*, greets guests with a customary offering of liquor, and settles into a drinking circle on most evenings at sundown, he lives "separately" (*alag se*), as his caste mates point

out in hushed tones. Over the past five years, Ram Sukh has built for himself
a brightly painted, two-story house, which stands out in sharp contrast to the
other, rust-colored stone and adobe homes in the settlement. He has a color
TV and a very old ramshackle car, an unheard-of luxury among Kanjars. His
chai always has milk, and his guests always drink the most "clean" (fragrant,
undiluted) liquor. While most local Kanjar children leave school after four or
five years of schooling, both of Ram Sukh's sons were studying at a local college, one working on a bachelor's degree in English and another on a master's
degree in economics. In 2007, Ram Sukh bought a small plot of land on the
outskirts of Begun for 50,000 rupees, which he borrowed from a Brahman cloth
merchant through his BJP connections. He told his caste mates that he plans
either to resell the plot at a higher price or to build a house that he would rent
out. In a conversation he and I had, however, Ram Sukh mentioned that he
was thinking of moving into the house that he planned to build on the plot.
He said that he was tired of living amid the filth and ignorance of his settlement. Ram Sukh could not, of course, admit this sentiment to his caste mates,
for thinking in terms of "filth" or "ignorance" belongs to the gentile Kadza
realm—not Bhantu—thinking.

Such dramatic ascent in the public arena (whether through political connections, education, or work for the police) is a perilous affair for the standing
of "VIP" Kanjars within their own community. The Kanjar ethos of egalitarian
solidarity vis-à-vis gentiles assumes rigid adherence to one's caste, including
linguistic forms, dress, housing style, culinary habits, and so on. As we have
seen with Prem-ji, the lawyer, in the prologue, any departure from these norms
is understood as a betrayal of one's *khāndān,* and, if too flamboyant, the deviation may be construed as a move from within the caste to outside—from
being a Bhantu (insider) to being a Kadza (outsider). Wearing flashy clothes,
buying fancy china, building a pukka house, or eating more than one dish
for dinner constitutes an unacceptable separation from the community. And
Kanjars are quick to point out such digressions to their neighbors as "doing it
the Kadza way" or "becoming a Kadza." Community leaders who manage to
maintain their respectability are careful not to flash their wealth. And so the
village where Ram Sukh resides rumbles with mistrust at his show of difference: *Ram Sukh is a big man now*, said one woman, *too big for his own society*

[samāj]. *We don't like this. He has separated himself from his caste. He dresses and speaks like a Kadza.* Similar disapproval sounded in Mandawari at Ramesh's involvement in the campaign: *Soon he will be too big for his own kind, soon he will be talking and eating like a Kadza.* The trick lay in the balancing act between maintaining the visible markers of status and keeping one's appearances within the boundaries acceptable for a Kanjar. This balance is difficult to sustain because of the rigid structure of exclusion among Kanjars: one can be a Bhantu or a Kadza, but never both. For many upwardly mobile Kanjars, their newly acquired acceptance in mainstream society entails estrangement from their community. This happens to few, but it does happen. I knew three Kanjars (including Prem-ji) who had been ostracized in this way.

The perspicacious ones keep their head down, so that it is difficult to distinguish from appearance the rich from the poor among Kanjars. All wear similarly tattered clothes, all live in similarly unfinished shanty houses, and all have a monotonous diet. One elderly Kanjar in the neighboring district, who has been a successful moneylender for almost four decades and is not only one of the wealthiest Kanjars, but one of the wealthiest men in Begun, wears broken spectacles and broken shoes, and lives in a modest, one-story stacked-slab house. Ramesh's uncle, the man who owns the most land in the Mandawari *bastī* and is one of the wealthiest Kanjars in Begun, appears a "tramp" next to younger and less discerning men like Ramesh, men who like to show off. He has very good reasons to play down appearances. Displays of undue grandeur threatened not only unpleasant rumor, but ultimately very concrete exile from the community. One Kanjar I met in northern Rajasthan, whose grandfather was appointed the head of a criminal tribe colony, whose father became a policeman, and who himself has risen in local politics to become a member of the local *panchāyat* (village council) has had to move away from his native village, where his family were rejected as "Kadzas." In 1971 he bought land in northern Rajasthan and moved to establish his settlement there. Although originally from a thieving segment of the caste, no caste peer families give him their daughters in marriage, so that his and his brothers' families are now confined to marrying the lowest ranking Kanjars involved in prostitution, to procuring girls from poor Kanjar families or other closely related castes (Nats, Banchras, Guars) for exorbitant bride prices of up to 150,000 rupees (see table 6.1).

The ambitious Kanjars, those who wish to earn a respectable reputation outside their caste, are thus caught between the hierarchical structure of ambition and their own caste's egalitarian ethos that pulls them down. While patronal relations, and their absence, pull segments of the caste up or down, in the eyes of caste members, becoming a big man in one's own right is difficult. *That's the problem with our society*, said Ramesh, *every man thinks he is a king. There is no unity among Kanjars.*

A Setback for the Rao

Two weeks before the elections, I was having tea in Baiji's house when we heard what sounded like an artillery charge set to the sound of an amateur wedding band. We popped our heads out of the second-story window to see what was going on. The alleyway was crammed with a crowd moving rapidly toward the market square. First ran the children, banging steel plates together and blowing homemade horns; then came the youths on foot and in jeeps, shouting slogans and waving flags; then came the big men of the town, the businessmen, members of caste and village councils, political party members and fixers, advocates, and members of the municipal corporation. This was the Congress Party procession (*julūs*), during which the candidate, who had just been selected by the central party committee, would present himself to the town. As the crowd flowed past, I peered into the distance, waiting for the Rao to appear. Was he going to walk on foot or come by jeep? Was he going to sport the royal regalia or wear a plain shirt? Would he shake hands with the people, as I saw other candidates do, or would he keep a royal distance? I had plenty of time for speculation, as it took half an hour for the procession to reach its peak, when a snowstorm of flowers and confetti blocked our view. We could just about make out the candidate, who was not walking or riding in a jeep, or even on a horse, as many candidates do. Instead, he sat perched on a camel, almost high enough for us to touch, sporting an enormous turban and looking frightened of the animal.

He was not the Rao. In fact, I had never seen him before. This was "Sonia's candidate," explained Baiji, selected by the head of the Congress Party, Sonia Gandhi, very late in the day and parachuted into Begun. *The Congress Party* [*in*

Begun] has too much infighting, said Suresh, *they could not agree on a candidate and so Sonia-ji sent in her own man.*

> *But what about Rao Sahib?* I asked. *Why didn't he get the ticket?*
>
> *Rao-sa?!* Baiji laughed.
>
> *Yes, he told me he was sure he was going to get the Congress ticket.*
>
> *You see,* Suresh said with strained politeness, *this just shows how far he is from the people. Do you know how the Congress choose their candidates? The local committee will send the names of their top three or four men, and the president [of the local committee] will say which one he thinks is most likely to win. Then the All India Congress Committee conducts its own secret survey—they use a private company—to find out who is most likely to win, who connects to the people. They go around asking people in the bazaar whom they support, whom they will give their votes to. Rao-sa does not come down to the bazaar. Most people here have never even seen him. Why would they give him their vote?*

Suresh was getting excited, and Baiji took over to let him cool off:

> *Rao-sa has been away for too long. He thinks that in the thirty years that he's been gone things haven't changed in the town, that he can come back and people will hail him as the king.* [I remembered his comments on the "sleepy little town."] *Back then, when he won the elections, people had faith in the Rajputs* [Rajputõ ko mante the]. *They thought they were kings, they thought that now that the Britishers are gone, they will take responsibility for them. They will do their work. Some [Rajputs] did and some didn't. Rao Sahib was the king of Begun. Back then, he was the one people called "king," not the Mewar Maharana. If they saw his car in the bazaar, they would line up and fall to the ground in a heavy bow* [dhok]: *"The king has come! The king has come!" So he won the elections. Naturally.*

Next day, I was back at the citadel, bracing myself for the Rao's disappointment. But the Rao greeted me with his usual cheer, even though I thought I noticed a trace of angst on his face. *I am so sorry . . .* I started (how do you console an insulted king?), but he interrupted me at once. *Now, now, my dear, there is no need for concern. The Congress is a very muddled party, nah? You see how they don't know who is who and what is what. To bring a man from Delhi—such silliness!* Ajay, more visibly upset, added: *Papa-ji will run independently. He won as an independent before and he will win again. You don't need money when you have people's love.*

But love for the Rao was not what I sensed in the town. On my way to the fort, I was stopped by three policemen standing guard at the gate, which they defended, as they explained, from "intruders." It turned out that the Rao had secured a court order against a house extension that was being built by another, lesser Rajput family resident in the fort. By the time of my visit, the dispute was in full swing: the family had disobeyed the order, which the constables were summoned to enforce. They were supposed to see that no builders or building materials entered the fort.

It was a job they were doing halfheartedly, for their loyalties did not lie with the Rao. The citadel was not only the Rao's home, it also housed several dozen other families. These included lesser Rajputs who were related to the Rao as descendants of younger sons and concubines, or the family's hereditary servants like the Pathans who had joined the Rao's armies and stayed on as his retainers. When the Rao left Begun for Delhi, many of the royal servants passed under the patronage of these lesser Rajputs. After all, they had to have a patron. It was these people from whom Baiji and other royal servants now took customary gifts and small sums of cash on the occasion of festivals, deaths, births, and weddings. And it was they, even though they were not wealthy employers, who had many townspeople's loyalties. The constables were local men with relations to these families. In fact, one was from a Gujar (herder) family that once provided milk for the Rao's household, but which now worked for another Rajput family in the citadel. He was sent by his boss, the circle inspector, to guard the post, but, as he said to me over a beedee, he was not going to "go against the man from whose hand he eats."

Rao Sahib spent most of his life in Delhi. Now he wants to build a hotel, make money. He thinks he is a big boss, a great king, but the people here don't care for [mānte] him any more. The public is angry. Have you heard? They say he is not even a Rajput, that he has become a Baniya [merchant] who cares for money only, not people. He does not even have a mustache [as befits a Rajput].

The head of the local police station, who had sent the constables to guard the gates, was a different matter. He was not from Begun, where he had been posted for only three months. This was a "creamy post" (*malāī kī posting*), full of Kanjars and opium smugglers, and so full of lucrative opportunities, and he assisted the Rao *just in case*, as the constable put it, *just in case the Rao wins the election. He is afraid he'll get him transferred to "ice."*[4]

The Rao employed a small army of lawyers, but even they were reluctant in their work. *The Rao summons everyone to the fort, he does not want to come down to town at all, to mingle with the people*, said a local schoolteacher. *So, of course he does not have the people's good will. To keep people's faith, you need to show them you care. You need to be close to them. It's not enough to have the Rao's title.* The townspeople often spoke of this lack of care as a failure of generosity. "Stingy" (*kanjūs*) was the verdict issued again and again in the marketplace—a stinging criticism for a member of a ruling caste, whose social position is defined by generosity. *He has become a merchant* [baniyā]—a serious insult to any Rajput—*which is why he no longer drinks alcohol or eats meat.* Some builders from the town said that they had stopped working at the fort because the Rao failed to pay them sufficiently and on time; a painter told me that when he painted the Rao's name on his truck, he received 50 rupees for work that was worth 150; and a carpenter said he stopped working for the Rao because he hardly ever got paid. The meanness was experienced in ways other than poor pay. The citadel is also home to the temple of Dwarkadish, the town's patron deity, whom the townspeople were once free to worship. *Anyone from the town could go to the temple to pay their respects*, Baiji told me. But now Dwarkadish has been privatized. The temple was part of the Rao's palace complex, which he now treated as his private property, and to which townspeople no longer had access.

The Law of the Fishes

The disappointment that beset the Begun residents' relations with the Rao riddled the electoral field. For, despite talk of care and love, electoral spectacles of munificence were duplicitous, and they managed to fool few. More often than not, once ballots were cast, the rhetoric of "good governance" replaced promises of generosity. Ordinary people saw through this, deriding this rhetorical switch as "corruption" (*bhraṣṭachār*). The villagers are all too well aware of the contrast between politicians' prepolling promises and their postpolling failures to deliver on them. Most promises are empty, and many are in fact undeliverable, even if protagonists were inclined to try. The bread giver's role is impossible. One candidate lamented that when he was first elected MLA he kept his doors open, but was soon overwhelmed by requests for latrines, money, schools, jobs, and so on. He told me (in English):

> *People here have very primitive thinking. They do not understand politics and they do not understand my position—that I am a government servant only. Instead, they think I am a king or a god who can give them anything they may want. Their thinking is from the olden days of* rājās-mahārājās. *This backward thinking, madam, is the biggest problem in our India, which keeps our progress behind.*

When speaking to me, he was "code switching," or shuttling between different speech registers. He knew full well that "feeding and eating" was not *my* political idiom, not the way Oxford academics think about political duty. But with villagers he uses a very different language. Politicians' double-talk is not merely disappointing; it causes much more comprehensive moral upset. Villagers express the sense of betrayal through a nostalgic contrast between today's "hungry" (*bhūkā*) politicians and the apocryphal generous leaders who "feed from the heart." *Once upon a time,* said an elderly schoolteacher, pointing to a portrait of Gandhi that hung at a slight tilt on his office's crumbling wall, *our Indian politicians fed the poor and the poor belonged to them, but these days politicians just buy our votes: at elections they promise villagers all kinds of things. But when the votes are cast, they do not even open the windows of their cars when they drive through the bazaar, and nobody can even approach their office.*

Most people do not wax lyrical about imaginary Gandhian leaders, but denounce politicians as utterly corrupt, scoffing at the neglectful elected official as a *kamīn*, a "servant," or simply "the low." While the courts of law may prosecute politicians who throw electoral feasts for "bribery," the electorate, on the contrary, sees "corruption" in their *failure to feed.* When, instead of "feeding," politicians "eat," they not only reverse the transaction but turn the normative order of giving into the chaos of avarice. In the words of one farmer, *all politicians eat from everyone else. If you need any work done and you come into his office, he will take 50 rupees, 10 rupees, a bottle, anything he can eat from you—the dog!* As an elderly Brahman of my acquaintance explained, *this is how our degenerate age* [kaliyug] *is.* This age is subject to the "law of the fishes" (*matsya-nyāya*), when the big fish consume the small instead of feeding them (also Parry 1994: 112–15; Peabody 2003: chap. 1). *These days,* he continued,

> *instead of feeding the small people, the big people eat—this is today's dirty politics, child. Oh! At elections they only buy votes, but once they get them, they start filling their stomachs. Just look at our MLA. He is my friend's son, and I saw him when he was so small I could hardly see him. But his gut is full now* [after fifteen years in power], *and he does not even notice me anymore.*

This sense of "corruption" is not about the misuse of public office and funds for private gain, but about the corruption of a different moral ideal, which the villagers see as being under siege. By inverting the local order of mutual interdependence through a top-down flow of gifts, politicians' greed creates a moral horror reflected starkly in the image of ontological chaos when fish consume one another. The real "dirt" of politics lies in its mockery of the dearly held ideal, which candidates invoke only to pervert.

There is a further shift in the overturning of the rightful moral order. The politicians become even more cunning as they shift from the language of kingly largesse to the language of *sevā*, or "selfless service." Take this campaign speech by one of the candidates in Begun:

> *These are not the old raja-maharaja days. Everything is different now. The common man* [ām ādmī] *now rules. Before, the common man bowed down* [dhok diyā] *before politicians, but these days politicians must bow down before the common man. The "reign of the kings"* [rājõn kā rāj] *is gone; now the common man is king. He has the power of the vote-gift* [mat-dān] *and he has the right to demand service from the government. The politician now serves the citizen. This is our new India. Victory to the common man!*

The rhetoric of *sevā* is duplicitous, and the "common man" standing below the podium is not taken in by such sermons. Offstage, the same politicians who style themselves "people's servants" (*lok sevāks*) throw feasts and promise gifts, thereby still also fulfilling the role of patrons. In reality, everyone knows that politicians neither act nor see themselves as anyone's servants. Nor are they thought of as servants by anyone else. Their reputations, as we have seen, rely on the opposite image: a beneficent donor, placed conspicuously and unambiguously above the "servants." Talk of service is strategic, and politicians shape-shift into servants as and when it may suit. In the local idiom, "servant" means something very different from a "servant of the state." Servants are subordinates who can only receive, never give. So, when politicians say they are the people's servants, they relinquish responsibility and use a language that abnegates their duty to give. When politicians shuttle between the rhetoric of giving and serving, they deceive their voters in two distinct ways, lying both about what they *intend to do* and—worse still—about what they *can do*.

Many Begun thought it preposterous that a state representative should claim to be their "servant." The idea inverted the order of responsibility, sparing the politicians the burden that they, as superiors, bore. And many were indeed furious at the deception. *How can big politicians serve us, poor people* [garīb log]*?* said Kalla. *This talk is topsy-turvy* [ultā-shultā]. *And if we accept our politicians as our servants, how can we ask them for anything?* said her sister, putting her finger precisely on the fundamental contradiction. *They will say: I am your servant, you are the big man, so you give us money. But what can we, poor people, give?* Village voters do not see themselves as masters over politicians. Instead, they style themselves "poor men" (*garīb ādmī*), the title of inferiority and the term central to making demands on one's representatives. Everyone knows that when politicians speak of "serving the poor," they are speaking a foreign, and indeed menacingly duplicitous, "language of officialdom" (*sarkārī bolī*). As Ramesh's younger son, Lakshman, put it, *it is the politicians' business to rule* [rāj karna], *so they must rule and feed, not eat or serve.* As the schoolteacher quoted above pointed out, despite Gandhi's language of *sevā*, India's great political hero is locally seen as a donor and a great father figure, not a servant (which he often styled himself). Despite much talk of "service," when politicians try to woo voters, they boast, without fail, of generosity.[5]

A Rude Awakening

In early December 2008, a few days before I was due to leave, the election results were announced. The Congress candidate, the one who was parachuted in from Delhi and whom no one had seen before, won. *He didn't really win*, said Ramesh, *it's just that the others had lost. Serves them right. That Dhakar [the now-former MLA] has 700 cement turbine trucks, but where is all that money?* That day, in the afternoon, I returned to the Rao's castle to bid him goodbye. Ajay greeted me on the terrace, quick to forestall my sympathy: *Of course, we are disappointed, but we will fight again, and we will win.* There was much to be disappointed with. The Rao not only lost the election, but, as I later learned, received so few votes that he even lost his deposit.[6] As ever, he put on a brave face, but he could not hide his frustration:

> *You tell me, is this real democracy? Why did Sonia give this Gujar the* jagīr *[land grant]? Is he the choice of the people? Isn't that what democracy is supposed to be? Whoever has favor at the top gets the ticket? Now this Gujar thinks he is the Rao of Begun. It's preposterous. There is only one Rao in Begun: Hari Singh.*

He may well have been heir to the throne of Begun, but to be a lord he had to act like a lord. For now, as before in Indian polity, lordship was not a titular position, but rather an earned one; not an entitlement, but an honor granted by people for whom one assumed responsibility and who *became* "one's own." The Rao's electoral failure spoke plainly to this. And, despite his complaints about the top-down allocation of *jagīrs* in the party, the voters' choice was intensely democratic. As Old Shambhu put it, *the old days of the rajas-maharajas are gone now. In a democracy, anyone can be a king. If you do your people's work, you'll be king.*

While democracy has routinized the making and unmaking of "kings," which now follows regular electoral cycles, the idea that political authority has to be earned continually is far from new. As I have already discussed in chapter 1, that kingship is sustained by the act of giving is an idea as old as South Asia's political history itself. This idea still stands behind the dynamism of local political life. South Asian kings have never been monarchs, or absolute sovereigns of their states, for kingship was always open to those who could garner sufficient resources for royal largesse. As I noted in chapter 4, the long Rajput history is a story of upwardly mobile plunderers wrestling over resources necessary for kingly largesse to be lavished on subjects in bids to gain and retain thrones.

In this dynamic order, British imperial authorities often saw excess and disorder,[7] which they tried to "pacify" by fixing chiefs in their ranks, by regaling them with titles, honors, and gun salutes in a bid to install local kings as monarchs, or titular sovereigns of territorially fixed domains. Many Indian rulers, anxious to secure their ever vulnerable positions, welcomed these efforts. And from the early decades of the nineteenth century, the Raos of Begun collaborated with the British authorities, who settled the boundaries of their fief and negotiated a peace treaty with the Marathas, returning to them several dozen villages. This is why James Tod, the historian and British agent who led these efforts, is the Rao's hero. But in accepting British help, the Raos also surrendered their authority, passing over to them the right to adjudicate. Over time, not only did the Raos lose many of their fiscal and judicial rights, which formed the backbone of their capacity to provide and so their political authority, they also grew more distant from their subjects, often quite literally. Like many royals of his generation, the current Rao spent much of his childhood in a boarding school established by the British for the education of heirs to the princely states. He was schooled in English, took Oxford exams, studied ancient Greek and Roman history, and did things like drink lemon tea, unheard of in the town. So, before he even left to study in Udaipur and live in Jaipur as an MLA, he was already far from Begun, intellectually, culturally, and linguistically. While in Begun not a single person could converse in English, Hari Singh spoke a sophisticated, if a somewhat archaic, English after the fashion of British public schools. He has traveled around Europe and loved to chat about English literature and history. As his elder son, Maha, put it, *When you are brought up like that, you don't want to meet common people.*

As an MLA and a state minister, the Rao moved to Jaipur, returning less and less frequently to Begun. He "has not kept his relations" (*ristā nahī rakhā*), complained the people. But it was not only personal distance or snobbery, of which he was accused, that alienated him from the town. It was the Rao's practical incapacity to fulfill the role he was born to—to rule over and care for his people. In 1952, when the kingdom of Mewar acceded to the Indian Union, the

Raos lost their taxation rights and became, with the other Rajputs, pensioners of the new Indian state, from which they received privy purses. They also lost most of their ancestral properties; and after 1971, when the privy purse, too, was revoked, the remaining properties fell into disrepair, from lack of funds and eventually also from disuse. The loss of land and property, of their fiscal and judicial rights, and finally of the privy purse pensions— brought an end to the Raos' capacity to care for their people, and with it their position and power as chiefs. In 2008, the Rao was struggling to maintain his apartment, to say nothing of employing a large retinue or even a handful of servants. Only three servants now helped around the house, and the patron god Dwarkadish, who once had twenty-five priests in his attendance, now had only one. Besides, the Rao was being bled by interminable property disputes. Here again is the Rao's elder son, Maha:

> *When my grandmother was alive, people of all communities used to come to bow to her* [dhok dena]. *Every time you had to give them money. But to tell them now, "we have no revenue, so how can we give?" Any newborn child, especially Rajputs and near and dear communities, they would come and present their child to you. And you had to give a new pair of clothes and money to them. And they expect the same amount to be given to them these days. And how can he help people otherwise? Papa-ji has no power. What can he do? He can talk to the SDM* [subdivisional magistrate] *and the SDM will give him weird replies. And you don't like to be insulted every time. So, why bother? In the constitution you are just Mr. So and So. The only option is politics. When you join politics, you can show your power.*

But political office is not enough, for people expect from politicians personal, even intimate, involvement. They expect them to be there in times of need, which is why most career politicians hold daily audiences, known as *darbārs* (literally, "royal courts"). But the Rao was in Jaipur. *My father can deliver much more on the large*, said his elder son.

> *He cannot deliver small things. Now some people are compulsive liars: "Oh yes, I will talk to him." I have seen people dial up a number and give someone a mouthful in your presence, fire him on the phone, but he is talking blankly.*

Then he goes and has a laugh, "I have made a fool of him." That's all today's
politicians. He never indulges in all these things.

But, as far as the people were concerned, nor did he actually "do their work."
While the "large things" (statewide policy, programmatic initiatives) were invisible and hard to claim credit for, "small things," such as better roads, water
pumps, electrical wiring, funds for weddings and funerals, and jobs, were conspicuously absent from the Rao's record.

Across Rajasthan, and indeed across India, many Rajputs, especially those
who were at the top and so were more alienated from local affairs, lost much of
the local loyalty. If in the early decades after India's Independence people voted
for Rajputs, hoping that they would step up to their hereditary role, by the late
1970s a class of "new leaders" (Krishna 2002) took their place. These were en-
trepreneurial, effective, and often thuggish figures who promised to "get things
done," to protect and provide for their people (Piliavsky & Sbriccoli 2016). The
Dhakar MLA, who was ousted at this 2008 election, had been one of these new
"muscular" leaders, at that time becoming, as Ajay put it, *the new Rao of Begun.*

Ajay's New Beginnings

Not every Rajput landlord and chief lost his authority. Those who carried
on acting as chiefs retained people's favor. Some village chiefs (*thākurs*) and
chiefs of smaller estates who stayed put, and even some who moved to cities
but continued caring for their people, retained their people's loyalty. Several
thākurs in surrounding villages still adjudicated local disputes, endorsed political nominees, and supported large retinues of hereditary service families.
But for major nobles and royals, if there was to be any return to authority, the
road to it lay elsewhere. Their customary obligations were much greater, they
would have to patronize many more people, and this required the kind of
means that most did not have. For many, their wealth lay in their properties,
which since the 1970s they had been turning into hotels. In Rajasthan, this
has been the salvation of many Rajput fortunes and reputations; for some,
it has become the foundation of newly found political careers (Balzani 2003;
Henderson & Weisgrau 2007). This is what Ajay had in mind—to turn the
palace into a heritage hotel, and reclaim his forefathers' position as the lord
of Begun. *Take Samode, for example,* he said, *near Jaipur*:

It was winner of the award for the best heritage hotel in the country, for five
consecutive years, and was named the fifth best hotel in the world by the
Times *of London in 1999. The owner's father and grandfather graduated from*
Oxford. But the father separated from his wife and became a recluse. He used
to lock himself in his room and drink all day. They were selling their furniture
to antique dealers just for the bottles. He died drinking. When I was in univer-
sity, I visited Samode. There was just one old man, the retainer, standing at
the gate, who was a Rajput, but came as part of the first granny's dowry. The
second granny came from the royal family of Nepal. The family was living off
their old jewelry. A couple of movies were made there, so he hired out the place
for 5,000 rupees a month. One or two British films were there, and then he
made some money and converted five rooms into a hotel. So it has grown from
ten to twenty and thirty rooms. He was working on Saturdays and Sundays
because the bathrooms were being renovated in a rush because a group was
arriving. He had only seven or ten staff, one or two cooks. But now he bought
a house in Jaipur, and it is also like a mini-palace or Samode Haveli. He has
horse stables. Now they have close to 30 crores of rupees [approximately $4.5
million]. Once the Rajputs start earning money, political consciousness is tak-
ing place. An old family retainer from a Brahman family becomes a village
councilor [sarpanch] *because he has the backing of the Rao Sahib. All the*
villagers start coming for advice, and the villagers are now bowing to him.
He has employed more than 200 guys from the village, and through him they
are earning so much money. The tips are good and they are educating their
children. So, there is general prosperity.

Not every hotel-keeping venture had such a happy ending. Often, instead
of employing local people, Rajputs hired workers familiar with the "hospitality
industry": English- and French-speaking people from cities and seasonal tourist
industry migrants from Goa and Nepal. One such hotel was not far from Begun,
where the local Rao was mired in dozens of court cases, venturing into the town
only when taking hotel guests on jeep safaris. He complained that the hotel had
been burgled twice in the previous year, as had his fields, and that, despite "in-
ducements," the police were slow to cooperate: *they are in cahoots with the locals.*

Ajay understood that to run a successful business, and perhaps one day to
run for political office himself, he would have to reconnect with "the locals," he

would have to get them on his side. And he began doing so soon after he arrived, visiting the surrounding villages and the heads of local communities. The reconnection was no mean feat. Not only did Ajay have trouble understanding the local Mewari dialect and "the local mindset," as he put it, but everywhere he went he was expected, as the son of the Rao, to give. He once took me on a tour of villages that were settled by his ancestors, and the moment he arrived he was ambushed by people telling him about troubles they had with the police, about hospital bills, wedding expenses, houses that needed mending. They, too, were eager to renew the old bonds. And so he found himself in a quandary. He lacked the means, the requisite contacts, and the muscle power he would need to help them. But he could scarcely afford not to, if he wanted to regain authority in the town.

Faith in the old lords was dormant, but it was not dead. And it sprang to life at the first contact made by the Rao's family after several decades. The villagers had never before met Ajay, but you would have thought they had known him all their lives. If he played the part of a caring, generous patron, finding a way to satisfy people's expectations without going bankrupt, a political fortune stood there for the winning. Kailash-ji, a local lawyer and an astute political player, a "kingmaker," as he called himself, explained it this way:

> *The Rao is an old man. He has taken* sanyās [*deep retirement*]. *And, how do you say, he is a bit peculiar. You know, the Begun Raos are all a bit peculiar. Even Tod wrote that they were Benda Rajas [crazy kings]. But his son is clever. If he plays his cards well, hires local people, makes relations with them, he can be the king of Begun.*

Ajay could become what Kailash-ji called an "old-new leader" (*purānā-nayā netā*) with a political career spun out of old honors and new resources. When I asked him what he thought about the generation of "new leaders," Kailash-ji said that he thought there were no truly new leaders: *All leaders were old because anyone who becomes a politician has to do what people want, what they always want. He has to be king. That is why you will not see me in politics. It's a terrible job.* For, while the role and the obligations of the political leader may be old, *all leaders are always new,* said Kailash-ji. *They always have to woo people. No one stays king because his grandfather was a king, just so.*

Chapter 8

EVERY MAN A KING

I STARTED THIS BOOK with the question that haunted me with increasing intensity during my research in Rajasthan: why did I think (or rather feel) that hierarchy was a system of stasis antithetical to social dynamism and the freedom to hope? The people I lived with did not try to escape hierarchy; on the contrary, they looked to it to better their lives, to make them more secure and prosperous, respected and dignified. Their social hopes did not rest on visions of equality, but rather on unequal relations, through which they tried to live better lives. What left Kanjars beyond the social pale, and utterly vulnerable, was their failure to secure for themselves a place in such relations—to find a way *into* hierarchy, not out of it.

The logic of this was not difficult to understand, even if it took me some time to appreciate it, and more time still to convey it to others and get my understanding into print. My hosts thought that people's lives were never solitary endeavors. People were never self-made but were rather created inside relations. To live well, one had to relate well, to be inside caring, loyal, responsible relations that in every possible way generate and sustain life. In rural Rajasthan people often expressed the idea of such sociogenesis in the idiom of *khāndān*, or "social substance" generated inside socially procreative bonds, which people spoke about in the language of parenthood. These bonds were hierarchical, ontologically and morally: the fact of social precedence presupposed an asymmetry of obligation, making superiors responsible for those below. This is the crux of hierarchy as a moral theory: those who can do more, owe more. Power implies responsibility. *Noblesse oblige.* My hosts did not see inequalities of wealth, status, and power as social ills. Rather, these inequalities were a basic fact of life, which they did not wish to eradicate, but instead used to build a mutually beholden and socially generative life that was full of opportunity, that nourished social ambitions, and that gave structure to personal hope.

What initially blocked my understanding of this moral matrix were my egalitarian convictions that made nonsense of the idea of normative inequality. I saw every kind of inequality—wealth, gender, race, caste, or class—as inherently degrading, disabling for those with less. Having less money, less valuable skin color, less prestigious profession, less education, lower status, fewer political rights meant having fewer opportunities, less freedom to make the most of one's life. To me, socially prized possessions like wealth, rights, education, or social prestige were the building blocks of freedom and opportunity, of the capacity to act effectively on one's life. They were the necessary conditions of dreaming and acting on one's dreams. Disparity was intrinsically unfair and unjust; it enabled some while disabling others. It also allowed those with more to do as they pleased to those with less, to have power over others, the freedom to take advantage of them. My anthropological training had made me severely suspicious of analytical individualism, but it had done little to alert me to the analytical egalitarianism that is as inviolable in most contemporary anthropology as it is in the ambient ethos of popular liberal thought. My judgment of whether and to what extent people were able to improve their lives was egalonormative. And, as such, it was normatively commensurative: I compared them to others, assuming that those with more were able to *take* more rather than *give* more. I was judging through what I have termed "possessive value," applied to persons and to the things or attributes that they possess.

As I have tried to show in this book, this way of conceptualizing value as a quality of persons or things fails to capture much of the logic of my interlocutors' social judgment and the normative structure of their hope. Their attempts to live better lives were not guided by grudging comparisons or dreams of leveling their social world. They certainly perceived disparities, but what preoccupied them was not arithmetical imbalance, but rather what those with more did for those with less, and especially did for them. In fact, they wanted those who took proper care of them, those on whom they could depend—their "patrons"—to be as rich and powerful as possible, frequently bragging about their patrons' wealth and grandeur.

Liberal progressives will accuse me of advocating patrimonialism, an ethos of childlike dependence on all-powerful and all too often despotic big men. For they refuse to see dependence as opportunity and subordination as a path of ambition, as my Rajasthani interlocutors do. But are egalitarian advocates of level playing fields themselves so different in their own ambitions? In 1934, a year before he was shot, Huey Long, America's famous socialist politician, gave a speech in defense of equality. He said that the American government must make the richest citizens share their wealth with the poorest, and that extreme wealth should be capped, as should extreme poverty. He did not think that all American money should be divided equally, but he did set out what was, and still is, for America a drastic program of economic leveling. This is as socialist and egalitarian as American political rhetoric got: to each "a home, an automobile, and a radio" of their own. But his vision was far from egalitarian: a country not of equivalent people but of extraordinary ones, where, as he said, "every man was a king." The dispersal of wealth was not meant to establish parity, he insisted, but rather to ensure every individual citizen's *dignity*.

Now, the notion of dignity requires pause for thought. A linchpin of the current ideology of human rights, it refers to that special something that every human, regardless of race and rank, ought to have. Dignity is political modernity's ultimate moral good that signals the disavowal of any inherent or social distinctions. But, as philosopher Jeremy Waldron notes, things are not quite as they seem. We only need to turn to its history. In Roman usage, *dignitas* embodied the idea of honor, the privileges of office or rank, and the deference due to them, reflecting one's distinction in holding that rank or office. In England, nobles had gradations of dignity, in the order of duke, marquis, earl, viscount, baron (Waldron 2012: 30–31). Accordingly, the *OED* defines dignity as "the quality of being worthy or honourable; worthiness, worth, nobleness, excellence," "an honourable office, rank, or title; a high official or titular position," or "a person holding a high office or position; a dignitary." So, dignity, the idea absolutely fundamental to the discourse of human rights—global egalitarianism's contemporary lingua franca—is profoundly hierarchical, in its historical as much as contemporary usage. It encompasses notions of rank, status, privilege, deference, and distinction. The same is true of another "quint-essentially egalitarian" modern ideal—the idea of "respect." As Waldron points out, "the ordinary meaning of 'respect' has strong overtones of deference, and the idea of someone respecting another conveys some sense of deferring to her, making room for her, listening to her, allowing her will rather than one's own to prevail. 'Show some respect!' is a demand . . . that one should fall back or make room" (2007: 223). It is a demand for precedence. As the King James Bible says (Acts 10:34), "God is no respecter of persons," which is to say that He *does not* discriminate.

The notions of respect and dignity themselves imply no equivalence. On the contrary, they single people out as special, above-standing, or distinguished; to respect someone, or to treat them with dignity, is to commit thought-acts that are hierarchical in principle—to place them above or ahead of yourself, not as your equal. Equality comes only later: first every individual is endowed with dignity and respect, and then, insofar as each possesses these in equal measure, they become equals. Equality does not supersede hierarchy. It transvalues it by "levelling up everyone to something like the highest status that is consecrated in the older hierarchical conception" (Waldron 2012: 134). Hence the 1789 French *Declaration of the Rights of Man and of the Citizen*: "all citizens, being equal in the eyes of the law, are equally eligible to all dignities." This posits a universal entitlement to the privileges of high rank, as is the case with human rights (Waldron 2012). Every man can in principle be a king.

If dignity, respect, and rights are the necessary conditions of a good, egalitarian life, they are certainly not sufficient ones. They are there to safeguard each individual's opportunity for achievement, which is the chief value of any cultural system that we may think of as "individualist." And here I do not mean the ontology of free-floating monads, but a moral stance that prizes individual persons' hopeful pursuits. The very idea of personal achievement requires us to accept that people are different, as are their lives, and that even if they are guaranteed all kinds of legal, political, and economic equalities of opportunity, they will achieve different outcomes of status, power, and wealth.

We cannot place faith in the goodness of personal attainment and betterment without believing in hierarchy, which is to say, in nonequivalence as a social good. Within the formally egalitarian current ideology in Euro-America, neither the basic conditions for human flourishing nor its desired outcomes are egalitarian, in principle or in practice, making hierarchy both the necessary and the sufficient condition of good life.

What does get in the way of any aspiring individual is any attempt to level them with the others. That is to say that equivalence, egalitarianism's defining principle, is at odds with individualist morals. It may not be at variance with an individualist ontology, or a picture of atomized, equivalent humans, but it is certainly at odds with *moral* individualism, or the belief that every person has a right to advance themselves. It is in societies truly committed to the value of equality (small hunter-gatherer groups, monastic communities, the Soviet state in its stated ideals) that achievement is frowned upon and often actively blocked by elaborate mechanisms that prevent the recognition of merit, achievement, or accumulation of wealth. Take a well-known ethnography of the !Kung people, who refuse to recognize the hunters' merit, ascribing a kill to the spear's owner rather than the hunter (Lee 2012 [1984]). Or take the Siberian Yukaghir, who hold any kind of accumulation of property and its display in profound disdain (Willerslev 2007). In such societies, the guardian spirits that give animals to the hunter, or withhold them, make sure of this through supernatural sanctions. "Any hint of boasting or self-aggrandizement, and the slightest immodesty in speech, act or thought could lead to failure" (Vitebsky 2005: 269–70). Here, as elsewhere, the idea of equality is not an aspiring individual's friend. One cannot climb on a plateau.

The distaste for hierarchy among social scientists has obscured this rather obvious fact, and they continue to conjoin the values of individual achievement and social mobility with equality, as if equality was their precondition. Tocqueville's work was the major landmark (2000 [1835]), in which he described individualism as a consequence of America's "equality of conditions." Dumont also thought that egalitarianism and individualism were natural mates (although, *contra* Tocqueville, he believed egalitarianism to be a consequence of individualism, not *vice versa*). This conjoining persists despite the fact that anthropologists have already pointed out that individualism and egalitarianism need not go together (e.g., Béteille 1986; Robbins 1994). We continue to think of equality, individualism, and mobility as if they go together naturally.

It is not only that, as Dumont observed, wherever there is value, there is hierarchy (1981)—in other words, that one cannot make a judgment without value asymmetry. Movement in life, up or down, requires the recognition of differently ranked positions, whether or not we endorse them, or are even able to recognize them openly at all. So, wherever there is ambition, there is hierarchy. And to understand mobility, anywhere, we need to think about the structure of differentiation within which it occurs. In this book, while making sense of how a particular logic of relations works in one place, I also hope to have offered something of broader consequence in social analysis. I have suggested that instead of looking for different kinds of equality that may best assist people's ambitions, as moral and political philosophers invariably and social scientists normally do, we should turn our attention to the ideas that structure different paths of ambition, the world over—and so to different logics of hierarchy. I have suggested that we come to grips with the fact that purposefulness of hopeful action need not be at odds with dependence and subordination, but on the contrary often relies on them. Kanjars and their neighbors are not the only ones who strive for, achieve, or fail to achieve distinction and to live better lives through social asymmetry. Should the reader, whoever she may be, look around, she will find this is also true of her life. I end this book where such a discussion can only begin. Or such, at least, is my hope.

Prologue

1. The 2011 Census of India (http://www.censusindia.gov.in/2011census/PCA/ SC.html) registered 206,467 people who self-identified as Kanjars in the north Indian states of Chhattisgarh, Bihar, Delhi, Uttar Pradesh, Jharkhand, Madhya Pradesh, Rajasthan, Uttarakhand, and West Bengal. Kanjars also live in Pakistan and Bangladesh, but most reside in Uttar Pradesh (115,968), Madhya Pradesh (18,216), and Rajasthan (53,816).

2. See Dumont (1957), Dirks (1987), and Pandian (2013).

3. In the later days of the Raj, all kinds of other (nonrobber) nomadic communities were criminalized under the Criminal Tribes Act of 1871 (Nigam 1990a; 1990b; Radhakrishna 1989; 2001; Singha 1998), but originally Criminal Tribe legislation was aimed at the robber castes as pivotal players in local politics (Piliavsky 2013b).

4. Kanjars are frequently murdered by furious neighbors. In the two decades since the Mandawari pogrom, twenty have been killed in the Begun administrative block alone.

5. This is true right across South Asia, where "vagrants" (as opposed to nomads) like Kanjars, Sansis, or Kallars (see chapter 4) are much more drastically marginalized than the ritually "polluted" peoples.

6. Mandawari is divided into three sections that house two extended families from a single patriclan (got). In 2008, there were 50 households and 170 people living there (see map 0.1). Most Kanjars in Mandawari have fields of their own, and some even hire laborers for their cultivation, although in 2008 most of their income still came from the sale of country liquor, cattle rustling, and burglary.

7. Most Kanjars speak the local Mewari and their own Kanjari languages. I spoke Hindi at the start of my research and later learned Mewari and Kanjari.

8. Villages have become such unpopular research locations that a recent Companion to the Anthropology of India (Clark-Decès 2011) does not include a single chapter that focuses on village affairs or is even based on research substantially conducted in rural areas. There are, of course, exceptions: D. Mines (2005), Berger (2015), Gold (2017), Vitebsky (2017), Sbriccoli (2016), Tilche and Simpson (2017).

9. Here "aspiration" is routinely treated as the exclusive preserve of the educated middle class: as in, "Millions of Indian voters are no longer poor and illiterate but middle class and aspirational" (Indian Express, 16 June 2019).

10. Even anthropologists intent on studying nonactivist matters, usually end up in NGOs. Take B. Singh (2015) who, while researching a tribal community's relations with its neighbors and gods, lived in the office of an NGO (to which he dedicated his book), not in the village, as he would almost certainly have done three decades back.

11. In Rajasthan, there are fifty-nine Scheduled Castes, which constitute the majority of the population, making reservations in education and public service accessible only to the most educated and well-off in their midst. The only social category that has any reservation value in Rajasthan is the category of the Schedule Tribe, of which there are only a dozen. This is why the Gujar protests in 2007 contested the privileges received by the Meena tribe, demanding for themselves tribal status. Despite the colonial label of "criminal tribe," the Kanjars are listed as a "caste" in the current schedule of reservations.

12. Nor did Kanjars mobilize their social hopes through the category of "Dalit," which is not a term Kanjars use to describe themselves and one that is only rarely in circulation in local everyday speech.

13. See Moodie's (2015: 13–14) critique of this ladder-like conception of "social mobility."

14. On this, see Megan Moodie's helpful discussion (2015: 13–16). Naveeda Khan's (2012) vision of social aspiration in Pakistan also amounts to the pursuit of equivalence: here everyone wants to be a good Muslim, she writes. This may well be true of Pakistan (although see A. Khan 2016; 2018), but in India no single identity or aspiration is the beacon of virtue.

15. However, they are only notionally horizontal, because often, on closer inspection, collectivities like the Yadav super-caste, and even "egalitarian" Naxalite formations, often turn out to be organized and recruited not through (egalitarian) appeals to shared ethnic or ideological attachments, but hierarchically: through patronal networks, via connections to patron-gods and leaders styled as lords or bosses (Michelutti 2008; Price & Ruud 2010; Berenschot 2012; Kamra & Chandra 2017).

16. It would be important to understand the interplay of egalitarian and hierarchical value in India's social activism and political mobilization. But such an analysis is precluded by the analysts' egalo-normative convictions (but see Hansen 2001; Michelutti 2008; Subrahmanian 2009; Roy 2016; 2018). For South Asia, there is nothing like James Ferguson's (2013) or Jason Hickel's (2015) work on the value of hierarchical attachments among the subaltern classes of Africa. No work discusses whether and to what extent the egalitarian ideology espoused by activists has actually transformed their everyday relations or broken down the hierar-

chical structuring of family, village, and neighborhood life. For a recent exception, see Evans (2019).

17. This was true of people I spent time with not only in rural Rajasthan, but also in rural Madhya Pradesh (Piliavsky & Sbriccoli 2016) and rural Uttar Pradesh, where I also conducted field research. This is despite Rajasthan being far from peculiarly immune to self-respect movements or upliftment schemes, which, in fact, abound in the state (e.g., Bhatia 2006; P. Bhargava 2007; Moodie 2015).

18. While fewer and fewer ethnographers now stray beyond the activist circuit, or indeed beyond cities (see note 8 on p. 175), this gulf of values is richly attested in ethnographies of village life from Tamil Nadu (Mines 2005) to Orissa (Berger 2015), Nagaland (Wouters 2015), Gujarat (Tilche & Simpson 2017), and Madhya Pradesh (Sbriccoli 2016). There are, of course, historical and regional variations. But the task for a sociologist is to grasp the theme on which these variations are played. By taking egalitarianism as the universal normative theme, we make ourselves tone deaf to much of India's historical and social experience.

19. It is precisely because contemporary social scientists tend to mistake *langue* for *parole* that Dumont's description of conceptual coherence in the Brahmanical vision of caste has been so often misconstrued as an account of social stasis, harmony, and consensus.

20. I am referring, respectively, to Robbins (1994; 2004) and Haynes (2017a; 2017b), Kapferer (2011), Ansell (2014), Robbins and Siikkala (2014), Barraud (2015), Ferguson (2013), Peacock (2016).

21. E.g., Robbins (2004; 2013b; 2015), Robbins and Siikala (2014), or Haynes (2017b).

22. Social scientists used to speak of "Eurocentrism," a term that has tellingly fallen out of use since the turn of the millennium (see Google Ngram), as the privileging of European perceptions in the study of the wider world. By "metropolitan" I mean something more precise than that. I mean the treatment of a progressive, left-liberal ideology as the universal norm, which in so doing installs the normative apperception of a particular global class of university-educated commentators on society (whether they are employed in academia, development organizations, the media, or anywhere else) as the intellectual metropolis from which the entire world can be understood and judged. This discourse is neither confined to Europe (or Euro-America or "the West"), nor is it representative of how most people (Europeans or Euro-Americans or Westerners) think.

Chapter 1

1. For some recent writings on hierarchy as a social good, see Ferguson (2013), Iteanu (2013), Peacock (2013), Ansell (2014), King (2014), Hickel (2015), Fumanti (2016), Haynes and Hickel (2016), Keeler (2017).

2. See De Reuck and Knight (1967) for an early comparative debate arising out of *Homo Hierarchicus*. Other symposia dedicated to the book include *Contributions to Indian Sociology* (December 1971), *Journal of Asian Studies* (August 1976), and Allen (1978). In his preface to the second English edition of *Homo Hierarchicus*, Dumont gives a lengthy account of his early critics (1980: xi–xliii).

3. The literature on the flattening (or "substantialization" or "ethnicization") of caste is very large. For helpful overviews, see Gupta (2005) and Manor (2010).

4. Shifts in this direction in the social sciences were already apparent in the 1950s, when M. N. Srinivas remarked that in the United States "'pure' . . . sociology . . . which has as its aim the making of intellectually significant statements about the nature of human social relationships," was being displaced by studies of social problems, for which there was plentiful funding (1952b).

5. The Preamble to the Indian Constitution echoes the American: "We, the people of India, having solemnly resolved to constitute India into a sovereign socialist secular democratic republic and to secure to all its citizens: justice, social, economic and political; liberty of thought, expression, belief, faith and worship; equality of status and of opportunity; and to promote among them all fraternity assuring the dignity of the individual and the unity and integrity of the Nation."

6. See Deleuze and Guattari (1980); Strathern (1988), and R. Wagner (1991); Callon (1986), Law (1986), and Latour (2005).

7. On the follies of empiricism, see Leach (1957), Ardener (1989), Dresch and James (2000), Kapferer (2005), Dresch (2012), or Dresch and Scheele (2015). Lots was also written about it in the *Journal of the Anthropological Society of Oxford* throughout the 1970s. For an approving early account of this shift, see Ortner (1984). The recent anthropology of ethics (e.g., Lambek 2010; Pandian & Ali 2010; Laidlaw 2013) and the anthropology of law (Rosen 2006; Dresch & Skoda 2012; Pirie & Scheele 2014; Dresch & Scheele 2015) still emphasize thought.

8. In 2007, Latour was the tenth most cited social scientist and the only "anthropologist" in the top ten (THE 2009, 26 March: https://www.timeshighereducation.com/news/most-cited-authors-of-books-in-the-humanities-2007/405956.article?storyCode=405956&sectioncode=26).

9. For critiques of this approach, with special reference to Barth, see Asad (1972), W. James (1973), and Dumont (1980).

10. On the other side of the Atlantic, sociologists were developing their own ideas of primitive egalitarianism. Ferdinand Tönnies (1957 [1887]) posited two types of sociality: Gemeinschaft, or simple, primitive "community" based on shared sentiments and experiences, and Gesellschaft, or complex, modern "society" bound by contract. Both presupposed a basic equivalence of one or another kind, either of sentiment or of contract. Durkheim, following Tönnies, advanced

his own conception of primitive solidarity as a union of parities: his "mechanical solidarity through likeness," or the union of "collective conscience" (Durkheim 1893: bk. 1, chap. 2). Organic solidarity is, of course, based on difference, not equivalence, but it is only the evolutionary fruit of more advanced, complex societies. Mechanical solidarity remains the historical and logical base.

11. It is not that anthropologists have paid no attention to hierarchical social forms. On the contrary, these have played a major role in anthropology, from Frazer's explorations in divine kingship (1913) to Hocart's work on kings (1927; 1936) and the voluminous Africanist literature on kingship, chieftaincy, and descent (for an overview, see Feeley-Harnik 1985), and studies of stratification in Southeast Asia (Sahlins 1958; Geertz 1980). But it never amounted to a cogent comparative debate about hierarchical principles, of the sort that Dumont tried to start. Sahlins's early work (1958) and his more recent writings (1983; 2008; 2015; 2017) focus on hierarchy, but it is telling that his best known essay, "The Original Affluent Society" (1972), should be about egalitarian groups.

12. Where "chiefs and chieftainship" is the biggest single index entry.

13. For more on the hierarchical foundations of so-called egalitarian societies, see Flanagan (1989).

14. For some fine ethnographies of societies united by "otherness," see Munn (1992), Viveiros de Castro (1992), Keane (1997), Stasch (2009), or Vilaça (2010).

15. But see Bouglé (1925), Woodburn (1982), Gullestad (1986), Flanagan and Rayner (1988), Flanagan (1989), Robbins (1994), Sather (2006), and Rio (2014).

16. On freedom (e.g., Englund 2006; Mahmood 2011; Ferguson 2013); on individuals (e.g., Lukes 1973; Macfarlane 1978; Carrithers et al. 1985; Dumont 1986).

17. "The concept of moral equality forms the horizon within which we debate about what is morally right and what is just. Debate, both within philosophy and outside, focuses on what the best conception of moral equality is . . . rather than whether it is in fact a good thing for the concept of equality to play such a central role in our moral and political thinking" (J. Wilson 2007: 21–22). "Every plausible political theory today has the same ultimate value of equality. . . . The notion of equality is found in Nozick's libertarianism as much as in Marx's communism." They all occupy the "egalitarian plateau" (Kymlicka 2002: 3–5). As Jeremy Waldron remarked, "philosophers ask whether we should be aiming for equality of wealth, equality of income, equality of happiness, or equality of opportunity . . . [but] there is precious little . . . on the background idea that we humans are, fundamentally, one another's equal"; for the modern philosopher is as certain of "basic equality" as that the sun will rise again tomorrow (2002: 1–2, 4). Although those few philosophers who do turn a critical eye to equality recognize that it is one of their discipline's most intractable problems (Arneson 1999; Steinhoff 2015).

18. Tocqueville thought otherwise: "Individualism is democratic in origin and threatens to grow as conditions get more equal" (2000 [1835]: 507). Anthropologists too have shown that the two need not go together (e.g., Kapferer 1989; Robbins 2004).

19. On this, see also Béteille (1986: 123) and Macfarlane (1993: 17). Dumont was so singularly focused on the category of the individual that he, oddly enough, inspired individualist ruminations among post-1968 French liberals, including Rosanvallon and Gauchet (Collins 2015).

20. Most recent theoretical work on hierarchy is animated by Dumont's ideas: Mosko and Jolly (1994), Rio and Smedal (2009), Robbins and Siikala (2014), Houseman (2015 [1984]), Peacock (2015), Haynes and Hickel (2016), Keeler (2017).

21. See Parry (1998) for the most up-to-date overview of Dumont's South Asianist critics. They haven't bothered with him much since then.

22. As Sahlins observed, "Durkheimian sociology, British structural-functionalism, French structuralism, White's and Steward's evolutionisms, Marxism of base and superstructure, cultural ecology, cultural materialism, and even poststructuralist epistemes, discourses, and subjectivities: all these paradigms assumed that the cultural forms, relations, or configurations they were explicating were within a more or less coherent order" (2010: 102). Critics of the idea have been as different as Barth (1969), Appadurai (1988), Strathern (1992), Dresch (1998), and Sahlins (2010).

23. This is a variant of linguistic markedness theory (e.g., Jakobson 1984 [1932]; Greenberg 1966; Waugh 1982), which tells us that in opposed categories the general category (the "unmarked" one) stands for the whole and encompasses the specific (or "marked"): as an unmarked category, "man" refers to "human," but to "the male," when used as a marked category.

24. It still survives in Catholic dignitary teaching (Waldron 2008: 71).

25. The Christian spirit is most explicit in Hegel (2019 [1807]). On the decisive, if often unremarked, influence of Hegel on modern sociology, and especially on Weber and Durkheim, see Knapp (1986).

26. But see Robbins (2013) and Robbins and Siikala (2014) for an alternative reading of Dumont's value monism as a model for social change.

27. The word was first used by Pseudo-Dionysius in the sixth century CE to describe the order of celestial intelligences (angels, archangels, and the like). In the High Middle Ages, its sense was extended to the ecclesiastical hierarchy and in the seventeenth century to the whole of creation.

28. "Hierarchy is not," writes Dumont, "a chain of superimposed commands, nor even a chain of beings of decreasing dignity, nor yet a taxonomic tree, but a relation that can succinctly be called 'the encompassing of the contrary'" (1980: 239). This idea of hierarchical encompassment, however, is an afterthought to *Homo Hierarchicus*, where it appears only in the postface to the revised 1980 English edition

and draws more on the work of his Africanist student, Raymond Apthorpe (1956), than Dumont's own analysis of Indian life, which describes an order of asymmetrical, ranked precedence, not than encompassment (on this, see Acciaioli 2009; Macfarlane 1993; Graeber 1997).

29. Dumont followed Hegel's vision of India, a country that Hegel never visited but described as static and antithetical to dialectical thought (Rathore & Mohapatra 2017).

30. The army of Dumont's South Asianist critics is vast and their writings too numerous to name pieces individually. For prominent examples, see David (1977), Appadurai (1986; 1988), Dirks (1987), Raheja (1988a; 1988b), and Inden (1990). For a summary, see Parry (1998).

31. On valor, honor, and strength, see S. Sinha (1962), R. Fox (1971), and van der Veer (1993: 34–35); on urbane wealth and economic autonomy among merchants, M. Mines (1994), Hardiman (1996), or Babb (2004). Others have noted that the values of power and purity in combination anchor the structure of caste (Burkhart 1978; Das 1982; Lerche 1993) or that multiple values (Brahmanical purity, kingly strength, merchant wealth, and so on) are invoked differentially in different contexts as sources of social worth (Burghart 1978; Malamoud 1982; Gupta 2000; Cort 2004).

32. Although central to Marx's own analysis, value is conspicuously absent from Marxist analyses that have prevailed in South Asian studies.

33. See Haynes and Hickel (2016) for a recent call to prise hierarchy and holism apart.

34. In the ancient Brahmanical theory of human society, it takes the form of a cosmic man (*puruṣa*), with each social class (*varṇa*) derived from one part of his body.

35. Dumont, notably, avoids the nation-state in his *Essays on Individualism* (1986), although he makes preliminary remarks on Indian nationalism in an appendix to *Homo Hierarchicus* (1980).

36. For a selection of good vintage examples, see Wiser (1936), Pocock (1955), Carstairs (1957), Mayer (1960), Cohn (1961), Babb (1973), Khare (1976a; 1976b), Marriott (1978), Raheja (1988b), and Parry (1994).

37. E.g., Inden (1985; 1986), Dirks (1987), Raheja (1988a; 1988b; 1989), and Quigley (1993; 2005).

38. Following Hocart, Dirks insisted that "ritual and political forms were fundamentally the same" (1987: 5), and Quigley argued that "those who rule must be pure" (1993: 169).

39. Inden wrote, for example, that the "hierarchy of ritual offices centered on a king (or local lord)" and that castes "were themselves offices of the state" (1986: 436).

40. If Raheja's concept of "auspiciousness," as opposed to purity, put a twist in Hocart's model (see Parry 1991), other neo-Hocartians followed him more closely, treating the order of service and gift as a continual purification of patrons (e.g., Dirks 1987; Quigley 1993). Raheja's dominant caste is at the "conceptual center," rather than at the top: it embodies the all-important value of auspiciousness, serves as the role model for others, and is the source of well-being for "the village as a whole" (1988a: 148, 244). But her substitution of horizontal "centrality" for the vertical metaphor of hierarchy makes no difference to her model's conceptual monism.

41. The giver's superiority in India was, of course, noted by Mauss long ago (2002 [1925]).

42. All this is premised on Marriott's theory of relational personhood. Transactions, he argued, were the source of Indian persons, or "dividuals," which were composed of "bio-moral particles" that mingled and mixed during exchange (1976; also Daniel 1984). Today anthropologists associate the concept of the "dividual" with the work of Marilyn Strathern (1988), who borrowed it from Marriott.

43. Apparently, he even invented a board game to show how this works (Vitebsky, personal communication).

44. For an account of his changes of mind, amid broader shifts in South Asian anthropology, see Berger (2012).

45. Nor, of course, are Euro-American families, although here people tend to be surprised when you point out this fact. I try this on undergraduate students all the time, and the result, almost invariably, ranges from denial to surprise.

46. A point also made by Marriott (1978). For parallel observations in other settings, see Hickel (2015) and Malara and Boylston (2016).

47. Even if he sees such social precedence as necessarily degrading and exploitative to those below.

48. See Clark-Decès (2018) for the parent-child language of hierarchical relations in Tamil Nadu.

49. For broad-ranging discussions of this, see Stein (1980) and Dirks (1987).

50. On hospitality as a form of control, see Pitt-Rivers (1968) and Shryock (2004).

51. Several authors have already argued that the desirability of gifts in India depends on who is giving and taking them. On the positive value of *dān*, see Laidlaw (2000). Indeed, the moral ambiguity of gifts is implied in Parry's own analysis, if read more broadly: gifts transfer the donors' substance (good or bad, desirable or not). If gifts from ordinary sinners imperil the receiver, gifts from princes or saints transfer the donors' morally desirable qualities (see Copeman 2011: 1057). The transfer of a revered teacher's saliva is "a source of grace and power" for its recipients (S. Bayly 1989: 52), as are gifts from patron-gods (*prasāda*) (Appadurai 1981: 287).

52. The notion that Indian gifts, most paradigmatically food, carry something of the giver to the recipient has been discussed in detail by ethnographers of India (for overviews, see Heim [2004] and Copeman [2011]). It was they who perceived that Mauss's idea of the "spirit of the gift" was no spurious mystification, but the key to his conception of the substantively binding nature of gifts (Parry 1986; Raheja 1988a; 1988b). It was they, too, who developed Mauss's idea of self-transfer into a full-fledged theory of relational consubstantiation (e.g., Marriott & Inden 1973; 1977).

53. In his *Dictionary of Urdu, Classical Hindi and English* (1884), still the most detailed and historically rich, John Platts writes that khāndān derives from "??āna-dān" and refers to "family, household; race, lineage, descent, house (of a prince, &c.)." In Himachal Pradesh, it refers to a "group of agnates" (Parry 1979: 137). Historically, the word is of Persian derivation and has nothing to do with gifts or food as ascribed to it by current Hindi folk etymology registered by Platts.

54. In rural Rajasthan, these gradations still matter today, even if the drummers in question have not drummed for some time. As former royal servants, Baiji's family enjoys special respect in Begun, much above other drummers, and they certainly do not marry people who have historically drummed for Gujars. This is also attested in the *jajmānī* literature (pp. 45–50), which shows that each "caste" can occupy almost every status and is by no means the horizontal community we habitually think it to be.

55. The idea that social being, or personhood, is a matter of dependence on others, and thus something that people pursue, is widespread and has been especially richly documented in Africa (e.g., Radcliffe-Brown 1965; LaFontaine 1985; Fortes 1987; Kopytoff 1987; Englund 1996; Ferguson 2013; Hickel 2015).

56. The Mahabrahman funeral priests are moral "cess-pits" who "see themselves as endlessly accumulating the sin they accept with the gifts of the pilgrims and mourners who visit the city, and . . . liken themselves to a sewer through which the moral filth of their patrons is passed" (Parry 1986: 460). While Parry argued that it is the pollution of death that pulls them down, I see this as a problem of patronal disarray, of having an endlessly large and varied range of donors.

57. As Norbert Peabody (1991b) showed for the Rajasthani kingdom of Kota, purohits could, and frequently did, quite literally remove their kings' patron deities by taking away their murtis (embodiment images), and so putting the kings' legitimacy into serious peril. Without a patron, a king, just as a Kanjar, ceased in crucial ways to exist. On Peabody's own reading, kings lost authority because they lost divinity, not patronage. But should that have been the case, kings could have found substitute gods, for divinity is not in deficit in India. It is the fact that the gods were patron gods that made them irreplaceable, for much of the point of patronage is in the patron's personal specificity.

58. Raheja and Parry distinguished among a number of different kinds of gifts, showing that only gifts conventionally glossed as *dāna* or *dān* were "poisonous" (Raheja 1998b: chap. 5; Parry 1994: 140–41). (See Copeman [2011] for an overview of reflections on the multivocality of Indian gifting.) Nevertheless, in their work, the toxic *dān* remains the most important socially connective prestation and, as such, most crucially informs their analysis.

59. In classical Latin, *generositas*, from *gens* or "clan," meant "good breeding" or "nobility of stock," and was linked to the Greek verb for "becoming" and the Latin for "generate." This sense passed into medieval usage across European languages. In Middle English "generosity" meant "nobility" or "excellence of breed," eventually acquiring the sense of conduct and character befitting good breeding, and ultimately the modern meaning of status-independent moral virtues, such as courage, forgiveness, magnanimity, willingness to give.

60. As Susan Bayly noted some time ago, the "politically structured system of honor and patronage" that underpinned caste involved Hindus, Christians, and Muslims alike (1989: 37–38).

61. Which is what Srinivas, unsurprisingly, thought it was (1968: 7).

62. Historians of Rajputization have not made this point explicitly, but it emerges clearly from their empirical work.

63. See Singer (1972), M. Mines (1988; 1992; 1994), M. Mines and Gourishankar (1990).

64. I use the word in a sense very different from that of Bourdieu (1984 [1979]), who saw in distinction a matter of possessive value, of difference between valued attitudes and attributes that people possess. In contrast, I see distinction as a quality of relations, not people.

Chapter 2

1. Muslims, many of them the descendants of Pathans who over the centuries found employment in the Begun Raos' armies, are a sizeable minority in the town, constituting about 20 percent of its population.

2. Compare the South Indian kingdom of Pudukkottai, made famous by Nicholas Dirks (1987), which had only 377 revenue villages.

3. The English word "family," which now connotes blood relations, derives from the Latin word *famulus*, meaning "servant or slave." The Roman familia, or the household (domus) of a paterfamilias, included relatives as much as servants and slaves (Saller 1984).

4. Traditionally, there were twelve core *kamīn* castes: genealogists, panegyrists, family priests, sweepers, milkmaids, drummers, washermen, gardeners/florists, farmers, potters, barbers, and dancing girls. They were both "workers" (*kamīns*) and

"priests" (*purohits*), undifferentiated, as in Parry's Kangra (1979: 59–63); *jajmān* was a generic patron, not only the patron of priests.

5. Mourning was the prerogative of family priests (*purohits*), whose women would cut their hair and wail for twelve days after a death in the family of their *jajmān*. The old *purohit* women in Begun, who once received gifts for their mourning, still do this today in a ghostly echo of a relationship that, as we shall see, is no more.

6. *Jajmānī* is a highly Sanskritic word, rarely used in popular speech, though people do speak of *jajmān* patrons. The word normally used is *birat*, which I shall use when discussing the ethnographic situation (for a detailed discussion, see chapter 6), while sticking perforce with *jajmānī* when discussing the scholarly literature.

7. E.g., Wiser (1936), Kolenda (1963), Mandelbaum (1970: 161–62), Benson (1976), Dumont (1980: 98–101).

8. For recent reflections on *jajmānī* studies and their critics, see Piliavsky (2014c) and Krishnamurthy (2018).

9. He did see these changes as the disintegration of a perfect, ancient order, but there is of course no evidence, as his critics have already shown, that it was ever so.

10. I make no claims for India's civilizational unity. I shall merely point out that much of what Wiser described in Uttar Pradesh in the 1930s has also been observed by ethnographers in Tamil Nadu and Rajasthan, and by historians of medieval, early modern, and modern kingship in Karnataka, Rajasthan, Andhra Pradesh, and Tamil Nadu (e.g., Stein 1980; Dirks 1989; Price 1989; Ikegame 2013).

11. Dumont, who wrote a fair amount about *jajmānī* relations, overlooked this fact (1980). Wiser himself described it as a "Hindu" system despite the fact that the exchanges he observed in Karimpur involved Muslims and Christians.

12. Wiser records protests by barbers and leathersmiths (1936: 98), but there are many other examples of contest and insubordination in the *jajmānī* literature, despite critics' claims that they were studies of frozen life.

13. We shall see these changes throughout this book, especially in relation to the waning of the bardic trade (chapter 6), but also in relation to others (chapter 8). On the decline of *jajmānī* relations, see, for instance, Harriss (1991), Breman (1993), Mendelsohn (1993), Harriss-White (1996), Jeffery and Jeffery (1997), or Gupta (1998).

14. Fuller (1977), for instance, argued that historically people made *jajmānī* offerings to village patrons as much as to supra-local military elites, and that it is only colonial meddling with the local political and economic structures that truncated *jajmānī* exchange, leaving anthropologists with the artifact of a village-bound, "caste-based economic system" (Fuller 1977: 107–9; 1989; also Wolf 1966: 47–57;

Karanth 1987: 2217). Good showed that prestations that have been conventionally treated as exclusive to customary exchange between service castes and their
jajmānī were also part of exchange within castes at various rites of passage (Good
1982: 26; also Raheja 1988b).

15. The Political Resident in Mewar wrote that the kingdom "is becoming a hot
bed of lawlessness. Seditionist emissaries were teaching people that all men are
equal. The land belongs to the peasants and not the state or landlords. It is significant that the people are being urged to use the vernacular equivalent to the
word 'comrade' instead of the customary honorific styles of address. His Highness
[Maharana of Mewar] is said to have been threatened to be meted the fate of the
'Czar'. The Movement is mainly anti-Maharana, but it might soon become anti-
British and spread to adjoining British area (NAI, 1923, Report on Disturbances in
the Begun Estate in May 1921, Foreign & Political (Secret), File No. 428-P).

16. In 1864, Rao Megh Singh III was sentenced to nine months of imprisonment
and fined 5,000 rupees by British authorities as punishment for *sātī* committed by
a woman on his land (RSAB, Rajputana Agency Record, 1868, [Sati], No. 74).

17. NAI, 1923, Fortnightly Memorandum No. 45 for the period ending 31 May 1921,
Foreign & Political (Secret), File No. 428-P. The farmers in Begun (mostly Dhakaṛs)
appealed to the Maharana, refusing, once their pleas were left unheard, to pay land
revenue. A staging of one meeting in protest in the village of Mandawari resulted
in the arrest and injury of a number of farmers (NAI, 1923, Report on Disturbances
in the Begun Estate in May 1921, Foreign & Political (Secret), File No. 428-P). In 1921,
Rao Anop Singh imprisoned a few protesters and staged public floggings and beat-
ings with shoes (*Rajasthan Kesari*, 29 May 1921).

18. NAI, 1923, Fortnightly Memorandum No. 48 for the Period Ending 15 July 1921,
Foreign & Political (Secret), File No. 428-P.

19. This was common practice across the subcontinent (Dumont 1956; Shulman
1980; Gordon 1994; Mayaram 2003; Piliavsky 2013b), and several neighboring chiefs
also employed robber castes, including Moghias, Sansis, and Kanjars, to keep the
peasants in check (Pande 1974; Surana 1983; Ram 1986).

20. NAI, 1923, Foreign & Political (Secret), File No. 428-P.

21. Veiling is a gesture of family belonging in India, where one veils from agnates
in the conjugal household or the clan (Jacobson 1974; U. Sharma 1978; 1980; Raheja
& Gold 1994: 114). Kanjar women veil from the Rao and his family because they see
him as the head of their extended service family. The same is also true more widely
in Begun, where women from the Rao's hereditary *kamīn* families still veil from
him, as they do from their fathers-in-law and husbands' elder brothers.

22. This was not the first time that the British colonial presence in India directed
attention to thieving communities patronized by the landed chiefs. As early as

1793, Regulation XXII of the East India Company government under Lord Corn-wallis empowered magistrates in Bengal to exercise summary penal powers over certain tribes identified as dacoits, recidivists, and vagrants (R. Guha 1963). In the first half of the nineteenth century special administrative, judicial, policing, and penal measures were already introduced for the suppression of thuggee (Gordon 1969; Freitag 1998; K. Wagner 2007).

23. On the creation and implementation of the act, see Yang (1985), Nigam (1990a; 1990b), Freitag (1985; 1991; 1998), Radhakrishna (1992; 2001), and Singha (1993). By the turn of the twentieth century, there were already a dozen such settlements established in princely states across Central and Western India. These housed Bhils, Minas, Bagris, Badhaks, Moghias, Nats, Sansis, and Kanjars. The biggest colonies included those at Mirkabad in Gwalior; at Bani and Bodhanpur in Rajgarh; at Mughalkheri, Kurarwar, and Kalkheri in Narsinghgarh; at Dhamana in Kachhi-Baroda; at Kularas in Maksudangarh; at Chamari, Bhawangaon, and Bichpuri in Khilchipur; and at Nowgong in Bundelkhand, Bharatpur (*Imperial Gazetteer of India* 1908–31: 9:384; Mayaram 2003: 139).

24. Encyclopaedia of Social Work in India 1987: 377.

25. Census of India, 1961 1962: i, 8, 12, 26. The same was true across Rajasthan, where many robber caste settlements created originally by the landlords were later targeted by the criminal tribe legislation. In Mewar, all four of the criminal tribe settlements were established on land given to such communities by the Raos (Gautam 1983: 18–22; *Village Survey Monographs: Ramnagar Kanjar Colony* 1967: 5–6). This further supports my argument that the criminal tribe legislation was initially aimed at agents of local rule, not nomadic communities.

26. BRFPA, Chechi and Mandawari roll-call registers, 1930–33.

27. These could include land, buffaloes, agricultural tools, and money for building homes, all of which were provided as part of the "reclamation" efforts by agricultural development schemes in the settlements (*Village Survey Monographs: Ramnagar Kanjar Colony* 1967: 10–12).

28. Chakravarti's (1975) study suggests that such liaisons between criminal tribesmen and their overseers were commonplace after the Independence. In 1945 one Rajput village leader in Jaipur district was accused of hiring the thieving services of local Minas in order to force his neighbors to agree with his decisions in the *panchāyat* (village council). Chakravarti writes that prior to Independence the Rajput's father had been deputed by the police to take a roll call at night of all the village Minas. After his father's death the register was maintained by the Rajput headman. It was alleged that he "permitted two Meenas . . . to go out and steal. Through them he also developed contacts with other Meenas . . . [some of whom became his] dharm brothers . . . [The Rajputs'] association with Meenas provided

them with an additional means of coercing their opponents" (Chakravarti 1975: 73). For more on such "corruption" in the administration of criminal tribe colonies in Rajputana, see B. Bhargava (1949: 111) and *Village Survey Monographs: Ramnagar Kanjar Colony* (1967: xx).

29. Such arrangements, where the inmates were not allowed to leave their settlement for more than three or four weeks, nonetheless restricted their movements. Whereas prior to Independence the Kanjars of a nearby village used to go as far as Lahore and Bombay on their thieving raids, the range of the Chechi Kanjars was now largely restricted to nearby territories within an approximately 200 kilometer radius (for more on this territorial shrinking, see chapter 6).

Chapter 3

1. Kanjars are "ex-criminal" or "denotified" because in 1952 the Criminal Tribes Act was repealed, and in 1956 it was replaced with the new Habitual Offenders Act, the provisions of which closely mimicked those of its predecessor. Today names of members of former "criminal tribes" crowd the lists of "habitual offenders" and in the Begun police station twenty-four of the twenty-nine listed "habitual offenders" are members of "denotified tribes," twenty-two of them Kanjars.

2. For a sampling of these monographs, see B. Bhargava (1949), Kapadia (1952), Garg (1965), or Shah (1967).

3. The Compendium is compiled and updated by the district police office staff by the order of the district superintendent of police. It combines information collected from Kanjar informers by officers designated as "Kanjar experts" (to be discussed) and "people's knowledge" (*logõ kī jānakārī*), or hearsay about Kanjars gathered by more junior officers.

4. The use of "secret languages" is common among professional communities across South Asia. Charan genealogists use a specialist language called Dingal to make their records (Shah & Shroff 1958; Smith 1975; Ziegler 1976); merchants employ special terms to conceal conversation from buyers; and each rank grade in the police has its own argot used to keep things from outsiders and officers of different rank. David Washbrook (1991) pointed out that Sanskrit, too, functioned as a Brahman argot. For a more general discussion of the Indian uses of secret languages, see Mehrotra (1977).

5. By the end of my field research, I realized that a number of other non-Kanjars who frequented Kanjar villages, whether to drink or to make deals with them, also had a basic grasp of the Kanjar argot, although they did not often advertise the fact. Most "Kanjar experts" and other police officers knew these languages.

6. In South Asia, eighty-four is a conventional number of parts that make up a whole. Various other castes, from merchants to Gujar herders, Brahmans, and

Thugs have held that their caste comprises eighty-four clans or tribes (Tod 1920 [1829–32]: 1:120; Elliott 1859: 2:58–60; K. Wagner 2007: chap. 4). Ramesh also claimed that each Kanjar family had a treasure hidden in the jungle. I never learned the location of any such treasure, and neither, I believe, did my Kanjar friends.

7. Classical governance treatises (*nītiśāstras*) give a sense of the extent of involvement of secret agents in the Indian political sphere (e.g., Kamandaki 1896 [c. 400–600 CE]). Kautilya (1967 [fourth century BCE]), the author of the best known text of the sort, devotes much of his *Arthaśāstra* to the description of spies, secret agents, and the methods they are to employ in helping the king.

8. South Asia is not the only home to such "invisible" people who negotiate the social backstage. In the Middle East there is a whole class of "invisible" go-betweens (*dalāls*) who run errands, deliver messages, and act as mediators for respectable people (Dresch 1989: chap. 4; 1998). In Amazonia, the nomadic Makú have a similar relationship with the Tukanoan-speaking settled peoples (Stephen Hugh-Jones, personal communication). And vagrants played a similar role in medieval and early modern Europe (Beier 1985).

9. For more on this, see Freed and Freed (1964: 153) or Mandelbaum (1970: 1:64–65). To my naive question as to why the Gujar could not raise the issue with her directly, my host explained, with some exasperation, She is his younger brother's wife [*chhoṭī bhābhī*]! How could he speak to her?"

10. It is precisely on this prohibition that the younger brother and his wife attempted to capitalize, the husband deputing his wife to steal the goats and thus depriving the plaintiff of any obvious response.

11. *Samajhānā* means literally "to make someone understand," "explain," or appeal to reason thought to be blurred by passion. On the didactic significance of the term, see Carstairs (1957: 47).

12. The use of robbery in warfare and governance on the subcontinent can be traced beyond the turn of the Common Era. Kautilya (c. fourth century BCE) tells us that "by proclaiming war, [the king] can carry off, by force, the grains, cattle and gold of his enemy" (Kautilya 1967: 7.4). For more on the history of plunder politics, see chapter 4, pp. 90–96.

13. Although watchmen receive regular payments (at the time of research, each household made semiannual payments of 100 rupees), when their services are required for a particular job, gifts (often alcohol) are often brought to negotiations so as to underscore the donor role of the *jajmān* and the *chaukīdār's* obligation to service.

14. Debt repayment is one of the most common causes of confrontations that involve the aid of Kanjars. Of the fourteen cases of Kanjar-facilitated mediation, of which I was aware during my fieldwork in 2007 and 2008, nine were concerned

with debt repayment. As most loans are made informally within circles of kith and kin, their repayment cannot be enforced through official means.

15. More recently thieving has been put to a different use to "ruin" opponents by planting illegal opium poppies and their derivative drugs ("brown sugar," heroin) into opponents' homes and then informing the police of their possession. The law regarding possession of opium and its derivatives is punished by a minimum of ten years' imprisonment with no bail and virtually no possibility of bribing one's way out.

16. Thus, in the course of the past twenty years, twenty-two Kanjars in and around Begun have been murdered by nearby villagers suspecting them of thieving under their rivals' aegis. Many more Kanjars suffer nonlethal assaults.

17. Not all conflicts are so easily resolved, and some raiding contests may carry on for months or even years.

18. For more on Kanjars' relations with the police and the way these have shaped relations among Kanjars, see chapter 6 and Piliavsky (2013a).

19. Policemen frequently throw Kanjars in jail without warrant or trial, often to extract a "bail" sum for their release. Such temporary incarcerations are left unrecorded, provided that the head jailer is willing to accept a small fee, usually a small fraction of what the Kanjar families pay to the police. Because there were virtually no inspections of prisons, jailers and police officers had little fear of being caught.

Chapter 4

1. Although William Crooke, the great scholar of South Asian folklore, speculated that the word "Kanjar" derived from the Sanskrit *kānana-cāra*, or "wanderer in the jungle" (1896a: 3:136), it is more likely that the name comes from *khānjarī*, a small tambourine played in the Mughal courts (Wise 1883: 253; Hunter 2010: 6, 8), or from khanjar, a dagger used in dance performances. Several other entertainer castes, such as Lulis, Hurukhis, Domnis, Kamachanis, and Natwas, also derive their names from the instruments or the type of dance or performance they were known for (Abu'l Fazl 1873–94 [c. 1590]: 3:272; Bhakkāri 1961–74: 2:191).

2. From the Hindi kānchan for "gold," "gilt," or a yellow pigment used by women to decorate their skin (Yule et al. 1903: 280). Historically, Indian "dancing girls" were divided into temple servants (like *devadāsī, ceṭī,* and *kanīz*) and those who engaged in more ordinary erotic trade, which often combined sex and entertainment (J. Forbes 1834 [1813]: 1:61).

3. Numerous colonial accounts suggest that Kanjars were known to be involved in the erotic trade throughout the late nineteenth and early twentieth centuries (Plowden 1883 1:316; Eastwick 1883: 88; Ibbetson 1916 [1883]: 263, 288–89; Rose 1908:

411; Rose et al. 1911: 454–55, 474–75; Gayer 1909: 55; Baines 1912: 106–7; Russell 1916: 1:76, 2:223; Blunt 1931: 150–51).

4. Bernier remarked that the Kanchanis "danced in the principal open places in the city" (1891 [c. 1660]: 274), and Manucci described their marketplace shows, which were staged, "beginning at six o'clock in the evening and going on till nine, lighted by many torches, and from this dancing they earn a good deal of money" (1907 [1708]: 1:196).

5. Their use of portable instruments, such as the lute, the barrel drum, and the hand cymbals, suggests their itinerancy (Wade 1998). The inscription beneath the eighteenth-century painting of a Kanchani performing for a hill state raja mentions a previous visit, suggesting that Kanchans visited courts periodically (Goswamy 1997: 88).

6. In his nineteenth-century translation of Abu'l-Fazl's Ain-I-Akbari, Henry Jarrett noted that "Kanchan" was an honorific and "Kanjar" was a term of abuse, "synonymous with 'Greek' in the lowest sense of this word" (Abu'l-Fazl 1873–94 [c. 1590]: 3:257n), which is to say, "a cheat, a roisterer, or a loose person" (OED: ad loc). Jarrett's was a nineteenth-century distinction, not invoked by Abu'l-Fazl himself. The distinction between Kanjar and Kancan is still invoked in the red-light district of Lahore, where "Kanjari" is a word for a common prostitute and "Kanchani" a designation for a respectable dancing girl (Brown 2006: 415).

7. This fate was not limited to the Kanjars. Many entertainers lost patronage and with it their standing during the austere reign of Aurangzeb (1658–1707), who largely did away with the courtly arts, which his father, Shah Jahan, had done so much to support (Wheeler 1867–81: 4:pt. 2:325; Trivedi 2002). Courtly patronage of the arts suffered further blows after the 1857 rebellion, when the powers of many royal patrons were substantially reduced (Trivedi 1999: 104–5). Many performers lost employment and social standing. Itinerant entertainers were the first to lose patronage and were driven to seek new sources of livelihood.

8. In Mewar Kanjars say that the rope was stretched across the Khari River by the raja of Deogarh, a major fiefdom. Local Rajputs have their own version of the narrative, known as "the dancer's curse." In their telling, it is a king's loyal nobleman rather than his wife who cuts the rope. When Rajputs tell the story, they like to say that the king was both drunken and debauched, and made the offer in jest. Kanjars, however, treat this promise as a solemn pledge. In some versions of the narrative it is the raja himself who cuts the rope in fear of losing half of his kingdom to a dancing girl.

9. On the relation of the Bhantu word *kadzā* and the Rom *gadjo*, see Fraser (1992) and Saul & Tebutt (2004). This supports the unfashionable old theory of

Roma descent from India's itinerant castes (Rüdinger 1990 [1782]; Turner 1926; Hancock 1998: 378–79; Matras 2004: 57–65).

10. The name Bagri, for instance, derives from Bagar, a town in northern Rajasthan (*Gazetteer of the Bombay Presidency* 1873–1901: 9:pt. 1:510); Sansi from Sansmal, the name of a Rajput lord; and names like Kanjar, Dhadi or Hurukiya from the instruments of one or another itinerant trade (Abu'l Fazl 1873–94 [c. 1590]: 3:271).

11. Sleeman (1849: 253), Wise (1883: 218), Rose et al. (1911: 1:475), *Gazetteer of the Bombay Presidency* (1873–1901: 9:pt. 1:510), Williams (1889), Gayer (1909: 55), Russell (1916: 1:374), Blunt (1931: 149).

12. As far back as 1766 the Punjabi poet Waris Shah wrote that in Western Punjab Kingars (a Punjabi pronunciation of Kanjars) were hawkers of small articles of earthenware (Shah 1966 [1766]: 112). Later on, Kanjars have been described as itinerant snake charmers (Williamson 1808: 2:173–74; 1810: 2:181; Sleeman 1849: 391; Crooke 1896a: 3:138); mat weavers (Williamson 1810: 2:39; Sherring 1872: 389; Crooke 1896a: 3:137–38; Russell 1916: 1:76); vegetable, dairy, and fish sellers (H. Wilson 1855: 333; Carnegy 1868: 16–17; Waterfield 1875: 28; Plowden 1883: 1:301, 305; Wise 1883: 73, 86); makers of ropes and strings (Sherring 1872: 389; Plowden 1883: 1:305; Ibbetson 1916 [1883]: 289; Balfour 1885: 2:236; Gayer 1909: 56; Russell 1916: 1:76); weaver's comb makers (Sherring 1872: 1:389; Ibbetson 1916 [1883]: 289; Crooke 1896a: 3:137; Russell 1916: 1:76); hunters and trappers (Plowden 1883: 1:305; Crooke 1896a: 3:137); hat and glove knitters (Gunthorpe 1882: 81); iguana catchers (Ibbetson 1916 [1883]: 289; Nesfield 1883: 968; Crooke 1896a: 3:137; Rose et al.1911: 3:474); stone cutters (Nesfield 1883: 968; Crooke 1896a: 3:137); makers of clay pipe bowls (Ibbetson 1916 [1883]: 290); palmists and medicine men (Ibbetson 1916 [1883]: 289; Russell 1916: 1:76); executioners (Ibbetson 1916 [1883]: 289; Crooke 1896a: 3:137); weavers of baskets (Balfour 1885: 2:497; Baines 1912: 106–7, 150; Russell 1916: 1:76); makers of toys (Berland 1982); sieve and comb makers; woodcutters; as well as occasional dealers in oxen and camels (Crooke 1896a: 3:137–38).

13. Respectively, Crooke (1896b: 136), Ibbetson (1916 [1883]: 289), Rose et al. (1911: 3:475), Russell (1916: 3:331), and Baines (1912: 106–7).

14. Although long-distance travel, and especially overseas voyages, has long been a source of anxiety for high ranking Hindus, who feared crossing *kālā pānī*, literally "black or murky water," which imperiled their social standing by severing their bonds (Bass 2012: 27). Several ancient and medieval texts prohibit overseas travel as a grave sin (e.g., Baudhayana II.1.2.2) or prescribe rigorous penance and purification rituals for reentry into society on return (Kane 1993 [1930–62]: 933–37). The Hindu reluctance to travel overseas was noted repeatedly by Portuguese sailors during the Age of Discovery (Gabaccia & Hoerder 2011: 84–86), and the East India Company did not require its upper-caste Indian soldiers to serve overseas (Metcalf

& Metcalf 2006: 61). In 1824, anxieties about *kālā pānī* even prompted a mutiny at Barrackpore, when Indian soldiers fighting in the first Anglo-Burmese War refused to be transported to Chittagong by sea (Walpole 1980: 279). The globe-trotting, upper-caste Indians are presumably no longer subject to the *kālā pānī* taboo, but it would be interesting to have ethnographic work on any residues of this tradition.

15. A thirteenth-century Gujarati tale of one Rathor Rajput, who in vain sought the hand of a high-ranking princess, tells us that "the entrenched Rajput dynasties of the desert considered Rathors socially inferior and indeed not even Rajputs because they did not have, as is customary with Rajputs, their Charans [eulogists]." The unhappy suitor was told that for a Rajput, forging a proper relationship with bards was indeed "more important than founding a kingdom" (Ujwal n.d.: 36).

16. From the sixteenth century onward , the active production of genealogies among Rajputs in Western India did not only help to consolidate Rajput political identity in opposition to Mughal rule (Kolff 1990: 73), but also elevated the status of Rajput lineages in the eyes of the Mughals (Tessitori 1917: 25; Henige 1974: 202).

17. See S. Sinha (1962), Chambard (1963), R. Sinha (1992: 242–43), Kothari (1991: xi); Snodgrass (2006).

18. As Tessitori (1917) points out, even the high-ranking royal Charans were once lowly wandering minstrels descended from itinerant herdsmen.

19. Such as the Gujars described by Raheja (1988) or the Kolis in Shah and Shroff's study (1958: 264–68).

20. Across India, chroniclers and panegyrists are known by a much wider variety of function-, region-, and community-specific names, including Atit, Devalvakiya, Bhand, Kapdi, Lavaniya, Magan, Nagari, Palimaga, Ranimaga, Turi, Jaga, Raval, Barva, Rav, Barot, Vahivanca, Mir, Mirasi, Dhadhi, Kattiyakaran, or Bhattu, among others (Shah & Shroff 1958: 248; Chambard 1963; Waghorne 1985: 9–24).

21. Colonial accounts observed that itinerant communities commonly served as bards for people other than Rajputs. Nomadic Banjara traders have been the Bhats of Charans (ul Hassan 1920: 17–21); the Doms, Beriyas, and Sansis, of the Jaṭs, Gujars, and other low-ranking communities (on Doms, see Williams 1889: 125; Baines 1893: 200; Risley 1908: xxviii; on Beriyas, Williams 1889: 44–45, 55; Agrawal 2004: 223n5; on Sansis, Sleeman 1849: 253; Griffin 1865: 1:219; Gunthorpe 1882: 78; Williams 1889: 42; Baines 1912: 109), the Dhadhi drummers, of the Jats (Bor 1987: 62; Vaudeville 1996: 292); the Langa and Manganiyar musicians, of the merchants and lesser Rajputs (Kothari 1994); the Nat acrobats, of the leather workers (Richardson 1803; Snodgrass 2006); and the Jogi-Kalbeliya snake charmers, of the Bhils. Just as the clan names of the high-raking bards often derive from their patrons' clan or case names (Shah & Shroff 1958), the clan names of many low-ranking Bhats come from the clan or caste names of their patrons (Williams 1889: 40–43). Manu rec-

ommends that an unemployed Śūdra (servitor) should take to genealogical writing (in Baines 1893: 204), and the engagement of various low-standing itinerant groups as genealogists may be a very old practice. Kanjars figure prominently in colonial accounts of low-caste bards, a number of which are described as the bards of upwardly mobile Gujar, Mina, Bhil, Koli, and Jaṭ clans (see Richardson 1803: 470; Sleeman 1849: 265, 404; Gunthorpe 1882: 78, 81, 87; Crooke 1896a: 2:25; Gayer 1909: 55–56; Gajrani 2004: 136).

22. On various ceremonial occasions in Rajasthan, Charans received a bowl of sweetened water mixed with opium before the Rajputs (Vidal 1997: 97) and at royal assemblies, the highest ranking Rajput present rose whenever a Charan entered or left, as an expression of utmost deference. The royal bards ate and smoked huqqas together with Rajputs (Russell 1916: 2:339) and had "their seats of the hide of the lion, tiger, panther, or black antelope" (that is, on the throne) beside the ruler. They bore honorific titles of *mahārājās* ("great princes") (Tod 1920 [1829–32]: 1:342) and *pol paṭs* ("gatekeepers"), and at weddings received generous sums (*tyāg*) before all others (Qanungo 1960: 93). Tod tells us that a bardic tradition holds that in the eighth century King Ram Parmar gave the whole province of Kutch to his Charans (1920 [1829–32]: 1:110n1). In the early twentieth century, for instance, in Merwara "in most of larger estates there are villages held by Charans" (*Imperial Gazetteer* 1904–9: 1a:91).

23. Tod wrote that in Rajasthan, "the Rajput has always, until recent times, favoured the Bhāt or bard more than the Brāhman" (Tod 1920 [1829–32]: 1:xxxiii) and that "the Rajpoot slays buffaloes, hunts, and eats the boar and deer, and shoots ducks, and wild fowl [cookru]; he worships the horse, his sword, and the sun, and attends more to the martial song of the bard than to the litany of the Brahmin" (ibid: 1:57). In the early nineteenth century Maharaja of Jodhpur Man Singh (r. 1803–4) proclaimed in his verses of praise for the Charans that they "excel the Rajput in four things, namely brains, education, purity of heart and religious piety" (Ujwal n.d.: 24–25, in Tambs-Lyche 1997: 196). Colonial presence changed this order. While Brahman paṇḍits were incorporated into the colonial administration and ultimately fixed at the apex of Indian society (Derrett 1968; Dirks 1987), by the late nineteenth century, royal Charan and Bhats, who were important legal, diplomatic, and scholarly authorities (Tod 1920 [1829–32]: 1:xxxiii, 2:500; Bayley 1916 [1894]: 46, 11, 25), and whose functions colonial officials sought to replace with state institutions, were removed from their position of prominence in local courts, and society (Vidal 1997).

24. The Charan women had long been thought of as the sacred embodiments of the goddess (Enthoven 1975 [1920–22]: 1:283). Since it was believed that anyone who shed the blood of a sacred Charan would meet with ruin, Charans and Bhats

employed "threats of suicide" (*trāga, trāgu, tāga, chāndnī,* or *dhārnā*) to press their claims (Tod 1920 [1829–32]: 2:814–16). Tod narrates a suicide of eighty Bhamuniya Bhats before the king of Mewar, who confiscated their lands (1920 [1829–32]: 2:815) and Forbes gives a picturesque account of the self-immolation of a Charan who contested a claim against one Gujarati chief. The headless ghost of the Charan later injured the chief's wife, threw stones at the palace, killed a servant girl, and finally possessed the chief himself, bringing his kingdom to near ruin (A. Forbes 1856: 2:387), a story much alive in Gujarat today (Singhji 1994: 254). Today the Rajasthani and Gujarati countryside is dotted with stone memorials (*pāliyas*) to bards who performed *trāga* suicide in defense of herds or village communities (Tod 1920 [1829–32]: 2:1700; Shah & Shroff 1958: 251; also A. Forbes 1856: 691; Enthoven 1975 [1920–22]: 1:284n2). The British began treating *trāga* as murder in 1808, although the full punishment for murder was not awarded until 1872 (Gazetteer of the Bombay Presidency 1899: 9:pt. 1:212; Vashishta 1982; 1985). Their impunity had Charans and Bhats employed as messengers, carriers of goods, caravan escorts, and village guards, as well as guarantors for agreements and revenue collection (Tod 1920 [1829–32]: 2:813–15; A. Forbes 1856: 1:447, 466; Shah & Shroff 1958: 250–51; Vidal 1997: 94–97); their homes were often used as sanctuaries by Rajput rebels (A. Forbes 1856: 1:435; Vidal 1997: chap. 4).

25. The same applies not only to royal bards, but also, for instance, to royal priests (*rāj purohits*), who have likewise enjoyed the repute of ancient and exclusive attachment to kings, the repute that has placed them at the top of the status scale, alongside the royal bards.

26. Early modern sources are peppered with references to elaborate networks of messengers, informers, and spies maintained by the Mughal and Rajput statesmen. Manucci, for instance, writes that "the best means that kings possess for the good regulation of their kingdom is through trusty spies. These report to the prince what goes on in the realm, chiefly amongst the officials. And with truth it may be said that the Mogul country is behind none other in having that kind of person, from whom may be learnt all that passes. But throughout his reign Aurangzeb had such good spies that they knew (if it may be so said) even men's very thoughts. Nor did anything go on anywhere in the realm, above all in the city of Dihlī [Delhi], without his being informed" (1907 [1708]: 2:18).

27. As custodians of words and history with a special license to gather and relay the truth, bards have been thought of as particularly reliable informers, messengers, and negotiators (Vidal 1997: chap. 4). In Rajasthan, bards often performed the tasks of matchmakers, who found appropriate matches, kept up communication between the families of bride and groom, and ensured that agreements were maintained on both sides (Suri 1977: 87). In times of revolt, Charans were employed by their Rajput patrons to communicate with the ruler, and by kings to send mes-

sages to the tribal regions (Vidal 1997: 94). In the popular Marwari tale of the lovers Bhola and Maru, the traitor Umar-Sumara, representing an ancient Rajput tribe, has a Charan for his emissary and spy (Vaudeville 1996: 292). In a similar fashion, the royal Bhats served as negotiators and messengers "between kings and some of the groups from whom they drew their allies and military recruits, including the so-called Tribal Populations" (Snodgrass 2006: 68).

28. Indeed, one of the innovations of Akbar's governance were the Dak-Mewras (Meo posts) "who were stationed at every place" (Abu'l-Fazl 1873–94 [c. 1590]: 1:252n2).

29. Compare *Gazetteer of the Bombay Presidency* (1883: 16:318), Census of India (1962: 32), G.N. Sharma (1970: 166), Westphal-Hellbusch (1975: 126), Gordon (1985), and Skaria (1998). In Rajasthani tales about the legendary ruler of Mewar, Rana Pratap, Bhils repeatedly appear as the king's informers, escorts, and messengers.

30. According to his grandson, Mahendra Singh Mewar.

31. *Chor chorõ kā jānatā*, literally "a thief knows thieves."

32. See Gordon (1969) on similar arrangements with various kinds of "marauders" in eighteenth-century Western India.

33. NAI, 1877, T. H. Thornton, "Report on the Moghias of Mewar," Foreign (Political-A), January 1877, Proceedings, 190–94.

34. One colonial official was so impressed with the work of such thieving castes that he wrote that in Rajasthan and Central India they possessed, "a perfect system of intelligence" and that, "they knew everything that is going on in the country side" (NAI, 1877, W. J. W. Muir, Report on the Moghias of Hadoti and Tonk, Foreign (Political-A), January 1877, Proceedings, 190–94.

35. In the late nineteenth century, families employed as watchmen (*chaukīdārs*) in Western Rajput and Maratha states were known to receive monthly salaries of 3 rupees and sometimes 3–4 *bīghās* (1 *bīghā* equals roughly five-eighths of an acre) of tax-free land. Their office sometimes became a hereditary right. In 1879 the political agent in Gwalior wrote that in the state "as a vacancy occurs among the Moghia chowkidars, it is always filled up by the appointment of a Moghia, even though a boy of five or six years old may be the only one available. I saw a child about that age in Nikum, who is in receipt of his Rs. 3 a month" (NAI, J. R. Fitzgerald, 25 February 1879, Letter [No. 76A] including his Report on the Control of Moghias in Central India and Rajputana to T. Cadell, political agent in Mewar, Foreign [Political-A], October 1879, Proceedings, 36–48; NAI, 1877, W. J. W. Muir, Report on the Moghias of Hadoti and Tonk, Foreign [Political-A], January 1877, Proceedings, 190–94). For more general descriptions of Indian systems of village watch and ward, see Elphinstone (1884), Indian Police Commission (1913), Matthai (1915: especially chap. 4), Griffiths (1971), and Arnold (1976; 1986).

36. For more on the peregrinations of robber watchmen, see Piliavsky (2013b: 759–60).

37. On tribal chiefs, see Kolff (1990: 17), S. Guha (1996; 1999) and Skaria (1999: especially chap. 9); on Mughal raids, Gommans (2002: especially chap. 2); on Marathas, Gordon (1993; 1994); on southern "bandit kings," Dumont (1957), Blackburn (1978: 44), Richards and Rao (1980), Shulman (1980), and Bes (2001); and on the Rajput politics of plunder, Fox (1971: chap. 3), Humes (1995), Kasturi (1999; 2002) and Vidal (1997).

38. Employment of robbers for warfare and protection is mentioned in some of the oldest available legal and statecraft texts. In his *Arthaśāstra*, Kautilya recommends that thieves be employed to "destroy the flock of the enemy's cattle or merchandise in the vicinity of wild tracts" (Kautilya 1967 [c. fourth century BCE]: 13.3; also 7.14), and that "when a king finds that as his enemy's subjects are ill-treated, impoverished and greedy and are ever being oppressed by the inroads of the army, thieves, and wild tribes, they can be made through intrigue to join his side" (7.4). He also advises that "brave thieves, and wild tribes who make no distinction between a friend and a foe" be employed for negotiations with other kings (13.3). The legal commentator Bhraspati sets down the rules for sharing the spoils of raids with hired robbers: "When everything has been brought from a hostile country by freebooters, with the permission of their lord they shall give a sixth part to the king and share (the remainder) in due proportion" (Jolly 1889: 241). The raider-king is a common protagonist of the broader Indo-European narrative tradition, where "raiding is presented as a heroic action, sanctioned by divine approval, hedged with ritual, and open in its use of force to regain that which rightfully belongs to the Indo-European warrior and/or his people" (Lincoln 1991: 11; also Dumézil 1969).

39. British authorities on the subcontinent were duly unnerved by such practices. In 1774 Warren Hastings lamented that the *zamīndārs* of Bengal were the "nursing mothers" of thieving groups (O'Malley 1925: 305–6), and Sleeman later observed that "a Rajput chief, next to leading a gang of his own on great enterprise, delights in nothing so much as having a gang or two, under his patronage, for little ones. There is hardly a single chief, of the Hindoo military class, in the Bundelcund, or Gwalior territories, who does not keep a gang of robbers of some kind or other, and consider it as a very valuable and legitimate source of revenue" (Sleeman 1844: 1:188). On relations between Rajput landlords and Thugs, see Sleeman (1840) and K. Wagner (2007).

40. India's landed population has long been known to take to roadside banditry at times of need, whether to earn or to rebel (Guha 1983; Kolff 1990; Gordon 1994; Vidal 1997). The structure and substance of this vast "military labor market" (Kolff 1990), from which the politics of raiding and protection drew its force (and which

embraced, by Kolff's estimation, at least 10 percent of active male population in pre-British India [1990: 3]), as well as the origins, identities, and social organization of plundering entrepreneurs, have attracted a good deal of historians' attention. See, among others, R. Fox (1971), Kolff (1971; 1990), Lorenzen (1978), Shulman (1980), Gordon (1994), Levi (1994), Gommans (2002: 42-43), and Pinch (2006).

41. On Minas see Chakravarti (1975: 73).

42. The Gauri drama, for instance, performed by Bhils and Minas in Mewar today, celebrates their robbery of the Gangaur festival in Jaipur (Erdman 1985: 169–71). In Gold and Gujar's description of a village in central Rajasthan, the popular history of Minas is a story of banditry (2002: 6067). In the same way, the prominent part recently played by Gujars in the famous Chambal River Valley gangs is widely understood as a natural continuation of their ancestral business of banditry.

43. By 1806, in the district of Jahazpur (southeastern Rajasthan) alone, there were twenty-four Mina towns and villages (Broughton 1892 [1809]: 105). Four decades later, Sleeman observed that most Minas were employed as watchmen, occupying fifty-nine villages across northern Rajasthan and around Delhi (1849: 331).

44. Sleeman, too, noted that the employment of hillsmen as thieves was on the decline (1849: 331).

45. From the early nineteenth century, many such hill-country robber bands of Western and Central India became increasingly patronized by the British. Colonial army officers employed Bhil robber bands in military parties (the first such Bhil Corps was formed in 1825 in Khandesh) and assumed, just like Rajputs, formal patronage over them through gifts of food and land (Russell 1911: 2:375). For more on the history of British "reclamation" of hillsmen in Western India, see, for instance, Unnithan-Kumar (1997), S. Guha (1999), and Skaria (1999).

46. Such a shift was gradual and incomplete. While by the end of the eighteenth century many vagrant communities were increasingly involved in plunder, some settled tribal groups persisted in the business of theft well into the late nineteenth and twentieth centuries.

47. One of Sleeman's Baori informers told him that his gang was hired by the Maharana of Mewar (at the monthly rate of 6 rupees per man) to defend the kingdom from Bhils. "My father, Zalim Sing, and Gyanah Naek," insisted the informer, "were the chiefs of one party of one hundred men, which was stationed in attendance of the Rana himself, at the city of Oodeypoor; and I have now in my possession, a certificate shewing that rent-free lands were given to him by the Durbar [ruler], in consideration of services rendered to the State" (Sleeman 1849: 377).

48. Sleeman is not the only source on this rising "brotherhood" of professional thieves. His contemporary John Malcolm, for instance, noted that certain Baoris

protected by Marwari aristocrats were hired in the late eighteenth century to aid in the prison break of Jai Singh, the young prince of Jodhpur (1832: 1:469).

49. Sleeman's Delhi-based informers, for instance, used the name "Kanjar" interchangeably with "wanderer," describing Kanjars as "vagrants about the great city [Delhi]" who "followed armies and lived in the suburbs of cities, and in the wild wastes" (Sleeman 1836: 162, 144).

50. Itinerant bards were so commonly employed in military operations that the very name "Bhat," used for all mobile, low-status bards, derives from the Hindustani *bhaṭ*, or "combatant" (Platts 1884: ad loc.), a title often adopted by warriors, such as the Bhatta Rajputs (B. Walker 1968: 2:119). Just like Rajput *jāgīrdārs* (landholders), royal bards (both Charans and Bhats) performed military service and gathered mercenary forces, for which they received land grants (Singhji 1994: 249n).

51. *Badnām bevkufõ kī barbādī aur hośiyārõ kā kuṛā hai.*

52. This is precisely why, in the context of *jajmānī* relations, courtly ritual, or devotional practice, the exchange of gifts for services has always been necessarily a public exhibition (see chapter 6 for more on the politics of display in such relations).

Chapter 5

1. In South Asian lore, raids and robberies often appear in the repertoire of royal heroics, alongside battles and hunts (Shulman 1980; 1985). The raider-king is a common protagonist of the broader Indo-European narrative tradition, where "raiding is presented as a heroic action, sanctioned by divine approval, hedged with ritual, and open in its use of force to regain that which rightfully belongs to the Indo-European warrior and/or his people" (Lincoln 1991: 11; also Dumézil 1969).

2. These are not the *birādarī* factions I discuss in chapter 2.

3. Because most Kanjars live in single-moiety villages, this means that they conveniently have at least two villages as their base of operations.

4. In southeastern Rajasthan, the Gudarawat clan has acquired the repute of a "fallen clan" (*girā huyā got*) or a "half clan" (*ādhī-got*) "with no brothers" (*koi bhāī nahĩ hai*). It seems someone from the clan was a police informer, and now members of other clans avoid eating with and marrying them. It is also said that this clan "has no goddess" (*mātā-jī nahĩ hai*).

5. For more on Navaratri, see Fuller and Logan (1985).

6. The Kanjars' vision of sacrifice as a community generating process echoes the old conception of sacrifice as a cosmogonic act, which we find in Brahmanic texts (e.g., Biardeau 1976).

7. The vegetarian offerings made to such goddesses befit their vulnerable char-

acter, reflecting the general equation between "weakness" (the moral and corporal weariness attributed to the "grass eating" Brahmans and merchants) and vegetarian diet.

8. Out of eleven children born during my stay in the Kanjar *bastī*, three died at birth and one did not live to the haircutting ceremony.

9. Family goddesses can be represented either with an anthropomorphic image (*mūrat*) or with vermilion marks on the walls of the house.

10. Sometimes, instead of moving the household goddesses to the village altar, Kanjars set up a larger image of the deity (see figure 5.4).

11. The offerings normally include spirits, incense, oil lamps, grain, rice pudding, jaggery, vermilion, turmeric, and henna, as well as the burnt offerings of cow dung, coconut, and ghee.

12. See also Evans-Pritchard (1956), Campbell (1964: 33), and Herzfeld (1990) on the relation between segmentary social systems and the order of "refracted" divinities in Africa and Greece.

13. The sequence of events follows the classical structure of Hindu sacrifice (Biardeau 1976: 138–53).

14. E.g., Whitehead (1921: 55, 68–73, 99) and Moffatt (1979: chap. 6).

15. Most Kanjars slaughter the animals with the conventional Hindu *jhaṭkā* ("jerk") of the sword meant to sever the head of the animal in a single stroke. This is true of all but three Kanjar clans (Bamanawat, Nannawat, and Gudarawat), who perform sacrifice in the Muslim *halāl* manner, with a bloodletting cut on the neck.

16. Appadurai has argued that alimentary relations between Hindus and their gods are normally about "feeding the gods and eating their leftovers (*prasādam*)" (1981: 496). See also Babb (1975: chap. 2), Dumont (1959 [1953]; 1957), Fuller (1988), and Moffatt (1979: 261–64).

17. The Ashapal Kanjars, conversely, avoid the gallbladder of their goat during the festival and daily meals.

18. The senior clansmen boil the meat and roast the entrails without using spices or grease required for a *pakkā* (cooked) preparation, and the flatbreads are also half-baked with oil.

19. The idea of food preparation as "service" (offered to husbands by wives or by devotees to deities) is widespread in South Asia, even if it has received little attention from anthropologists, apart from brief discussions by Khare (1976a) and Appadurai (1981).

Chapter 6

1. Although in principle Kanjar bards, thieves, and prostitutes can still (just about) eat together and marry, in practice, they rarely do.

2. Essentially every daily or ceremonial activity can thus be subcontracted, means permitting, to a servant. In Northern India, Rajputs (and Rajputizing castes) have traditionally patronized at least twelve formal servant (*kamīn*) castes for twelve tasks (recall chapter 2). And the highest ranking Rajputs patronized many more, so that every ritualized practicality, all the way down to the most intimate life proceedings, from breastfeeding to mourning, has been historically delegated to servants. This practice was so important to the standing of a community that even the lowliest castes, such as leather workers (Bhambhis), have endeavored to patronize servants of their own (Snodgrass 2006).

3. The bards may also attend their patrons' weddings or other life-cycle ceremonies. The annual visits, in whose course the relation is played out in full, however, remains its necessary focus.

4. As one *jajmān* said to Komal Kothari, Rajasthan's great ethnographer, the bards "carry the weight of our genealogy on [their] heads." Although the importance of bards and genealogies has waned, in rural North India their absence still jeopardizes a family's marriage prospects and may indeed risk them being ostracized by the caste (Bharucha 2003: 220–21).

5. On the reliance of political authority on public displays of largesse in precolonial India, see Dirks (1987) or Peabody (2003).

6. Kanjars are aware of such public nature of their work. As the man seen donning the turban in figure 6.1 explained, the size of their donations is relative to the size of the village in which their patrons reside. While the residents of large, multicaste villages, who can exhibit their generosity before their neighbors, tend to give more, fearing the loss of their pedigree, the dwellers of single-household hamlets often refuse to pay at all. For similar reasons, many Charan genealogists of lower-than-Rajput communities, who make their genealogical entries in the privacy of their patrons' homes, have lost their patrons, who, having no audience for their donorship, mostly offer them no more than a customary cup of chai. This suggests that the significance of patronal display takes precedence over genealogy as such.

7. Most local villagers could name a traveling band of bards who still worked for Gujars, Minas, and Bhils.

8. An old Indian adage tells us that a complete human being resides in five articles of clothes (turban, shirt or overcoat, trousers, shawl, and handkerchief, making up a full suit of clothes) and can, accordingly, be referred to as "five pieces of clothing" (*panchõ kapṛe*). Although modern anthropologists have given little attention to clothing, it has been observed that in India clothing and communal identity are intimately entwined. M. N. Srinivas, for instance, remarked that when a Nayar man puts on his office job uniform—the shirt—he literally "takes off his caste,"

and when he takes off the shirt in the evening, he puts his caste back on (1968: 123). For a discussion of the social significance of clothing in India, see also Tarlo (1996).

9. On the importance of turban exchange in Rajasthan, see Peabody (1991a) or Sahai (2006: 131).

10. The sartorial union of servants and patrons is most obvious among Rajputs' servants, who are entitled to wear clothing like that of their *jajmāns* (recall chapter 2). Colonial ethnographers often noted with surprise that low-caste people often wore fine clothes like their rank superiors' (e.g., Enthoven 1975 [1920–22]: 1343). Wiser likewise noted that *jajmāns* often passed down clothing to their *karnewāles*, who entertained "a smug satisfaction in that the clothes which were formerly worn by one of the Twice-Born, may bring them special protection" rather than fear that "someone see them wearing second hand clothes" (1936: 104).

11. This proverb is echoed in a Punjabi saying: "*Zamīn ba yak sāl banjar shawad, / Gujar be yak nukta Kanjar shawad* (In one year land becomes waste, / By one dot [meaning syllable] 'Gujar' becomes 'Kanjar')" (Rose et al. 1911: 3:351).

12. In his study of low-caste bards, Snodgrass has likewise argued that "Bhats insult their Bhambhi [leather worker] patrons . . . primarily by drawing attention to their stinginess." He documented several means for bards to disgrace stingy patrons, for example, by poking poetic insults at tightfisted patrons (Snodgrass 2006: chaps. 3 and 5). "If not properly rewarded for services rendered, I was told, my informants parade a skinny, pitiful-looking human figure of wood and cloth around the village . . . Bhats, shouting abuses, yell, 'Look at this poor, skinny man! Thanks to his patrons, he is starving! Look at how they take care of him!'" The Kanjar bards I observed were said to have paraded a dog around the village with a rope around its neck, shouting ironically, "Look what our generous patrons have given us!"

13. Such abuse is increasingly ineffective, because *jajmāns*, as Snodgrass (2006) points out, are increasingly drawing on other sources of status and authority. Insofar as Rajputs, the ultimate donors, occupy the apex of social hierarchy in Rajasthan, the bards' *jajmāns* are encouraged to be, and ought to act as, generous benefactors. Common imagery presents the Brahman as approaching the Rajput with his palms turned up, as a gift's recipient, and the Rajput approaching the Brahman with his palms turned down in a giving gesture (Harlan 1992: 122).

14. The drummer families employed by the Begun Rajputs may deploy family members who cannot drum, or drum badly, to the weddings and other festivities hosted by their *jajmāns*, where they receive (irrespectively of their musical skill) customary payments of food, clothing, and cash. Three Brahman families once employed by the Begun Raos have abandoned their priestly profession for the business of law. Now employed as advocates, they are locally known as "Rao-ji's Brahmans" and are invited by the Rao to life-cycle events and festival celebra-

tions. Failure to invitate them will certainly prompt offense. Kothari also observed that among the Manganiyar musicians in Western Rajasthan performers who sing badly or cannot sing at all still receive a customary sum of cash (*nēg*) from their patrons (Bharucha 2003: 222). Similarly, Wiser (1936) noted that *jajmāns* are often stuck with poorly skilled servants.

15. Such entitlements may include patrons' protection in local council and in court; invitations to weddings, funerary feasts, and festival celebrations; and token customary gifts.

16. When *jajmāns* are no longer able or willing to pay their servants, they can withdraw patronage by accusing their servants publicly of infidelity. I watched one Gujar family that no longer wished to employ their Kanjar bards chase their clients away by shouting: "You eat from everyone! Where is your *birat*? Where is our *birat*? Go! We will no longer feed you." A number of Gujars around Begun, who have abandoned their *jajmānī* obligations toward the bards, have likewise told me that they have done so because their bards started to "eat from everyone's hands." The erosion of such relationships has more to do with pedigree losing its significance as a marker of status or with the inability of *jajmāns* to continually sponsor their Bhats. It is important, however, that the rhetoric of infidelity is invoked as a legitimate reason to break the ties.

17. Here is the full text of the letter.

In the year of Holy Rām 938 [881 CE] I vow by my Bhojrāj and by Bajorī and Dev Nārāyaṇ and by the Bagrāwats of Cagalyā, by Rāṇ Bajorī and the forty million progeny of the Rāṇ Chōchu Bhāṭ and by the drops of Bhojrāj's winemakers. Sārū Dev, king of Citrakoṭ [Chittaurgarh], Udaipur and Makhand of Mewāṛ and of Nokoṭi [Jodhpur], Marwāṛ, chased away nine hundred and ninety-nine [Gujar] clans, sending them to Ajmer. If you don't believe me, I give you the oath of Dev Darbār [Nārāyaṇ]. I give you the oath of Sāḍū Mātā and Bhoj Rāj. This copper letter was made. Bajorī was already alive when Ajmer City was settled. Ferāyo jī's Bajorī was already alive when Rāṇ City was settled and filled the sight of a half-opened eye. If you don't believe me, I give you Bābā Rūp Nāth jī's oath. Bajorī was already alive when Bhināī City was settled and when the king Karam Singh jī came. And all the villages in Bhināy were then filled with Gujars. If you don't believe me, I give you Dev Nārāyaṇ's oath. And Kheṛā was filled with the sons and grandsons of Jāsī Nāth Kajoḍ, and then this copper letter was made by Manomathī Mārapat from Surajmāl. Bajori was already alive when Bhīnāth's daughter Kadam Surāmā jī came. The king Śahī Singh settled Śahī Bhālā Śāhapurā, Śāhapurā in Jorāsī. As many villages as there were, as many Gujar copper letters were made. If you don't believe me, I give you Dev Darbār's oath. There are copper letters for 290 villages. All hundred are true. The Gujars come from Makhand of Mewāṛ, Nokoṭī of

Marwār, Sigalorī, Madāriyā, Kharī River, Ajmer, Bajāgī, Sālne, Panārā, Bāwal, Bundī, near Bālī in the Baīsā district. For those who do not believe me, there is an oath of nine hundred and ninety nine [Gujar] clans. I give you the oath of Sawāī Bhoj. Norang has settled Bundī and that is when Hāḍā Bār's Bajorī is. It is written above that this is a true copper letter. See this copper letter as the order of Kalco Kalā's Pacā's. [The copper letter] is from the ancient days. Bajorī is the hundred truths of the king of Koṭā.

Clan elders' signatures: Posawān's son Ratan jī from the village of Bhināy. Signature: Moṭar's son Kalyāṇ jī from the village of Cudrā. Signature: Cāṛ's daughter Ūgmā jī from the village of Sar. Signature: Kajoṛ jī's son Choṭu jī. Signature: Māl Suti's son Rām from the village of Śāhipurā. Of the village of Bāṛlī. Signature: Lārawā Bhotī from Sīgawal. Mābatā's. Ḍudī's Bāgu jī and Nīlā jī from the village of Bādawārā. Signature: Cauhan's son Pahat from Satā Wāḍiyā. Signature: Khatāṇā's Gujar from Ekal Sigā. Signature: Rām Paṭel's Kamarāw from Dātolāī. Signature: Gadaṛ Puwal's from Kanecaṇ and Odā's from Anopurā. Kiśan jī Moṭar's. Greetings to all! If you don't believe me, I give you the oath of 999 [Gujar] clans. All 999 clans own the villages in Ajmer where this copper letter was made. These nephews have the face of the Goddess's progeny. As long as the lamp burns, Bajorī Kanjarī lives. It is written above that this is a true copper letter. Signature: Nīlā jī Ghāvoṛ's. Signature: Bhurā jī Kālas's. Signature: Amarā jī Bhāmar's. Signature: Ghulī jī Maṛā's. Signature: Ghukal jī who sired Devā jī. Lakāe's Chogā jī Kāroliyā. Banerā in the Bhīlwārā district and Ḍurḍā Gejolī Nīlud. Jīwan jī who has settled in Khārās. For the names of these Gujars I give vow with the oath of Dev Nārāyaṇ. Signature: The elder Āgocā's. Signature: Mādu jī's from Taṛvā. Signature: Gāgā jī's from Litarīwa. Mādu from Kāṭundā. Signature: Sewātā jī from Kuśac Nabāb.

18. With the market value of goods and services being typically much higher than what servants receive for their work from their *jajmāns*, and hereditary patronage altogether dwindling these days, many people are keen to make a few extra rupees on the side. A study of *birat* exchange at the Krishna temple in Nathdwara (western Mewar) shows that the market price for pottery was often fifty times higher than what craftsmen received from their patron priests. And yet the potters did not abandon their traditional ties of service (Jindel 1976: 129–30).

19. The bards told me that Gujars, whose generosity I describe, constituted one of only three patron communities that still pay appropriate (*khāndānī*) amounts. When patrons refuse to give, the bards usually continue to come for another few years, each time cajoling or castigating their patrons into generosity. If their trips continue to be futile, they eventually give up, and the bond is thus lost. Near Begun I met a family of Kanjar Bhats from western Madhya Pradesh, who had been coming to the area and leaving empty-handed for the fourth year. They said this was the

last year that they would come to Begun. The young Bhats from Gopalpura did not think that their *jajmāni* work would last more than three years.

20. See Snodgrass (2006) for various new kinds of work that bards now find for themselves in the tourist industry.

21. Serving as entertainers, rather than bards, Kanjars sing a mixture of local and popular Bollywood tunes, dance, and occasionally give a ropewalking performance.

22. Equaling at the time approximately $350.

23. Kanjars maintain commensal superiority over sweepers: they give them food, but do not accept it from them.

24. I include in this count marriages between Kanjar Bhats from Gopalpura who are married, but whose children, having been married as children, do not yet live with their spouses. As village elders insist, before the coming of British rule (*angrejõ kā rāj*), the Kanjars of Gopalpura "did nothing but steal," taking up the profession of bards over the course of the past century. The village started as a temporary encampment of one (Dasawat clan) family, whose men became genealogists to some local Gujars in the late nineteenth century, when demand for the production of pedigrees among actively Rajputizing communities was at its peak. Thus, in the late nineteenth and early twentieth centuries, Kanjar Bhats acquired a growing number of *jajmāns*. According to village elders, by the time of the Independence, they worked for so many Gujar villages that they could no longer service them all, passing on some of them to a family of another (Singhawat) clan, with whom they had marriage relations. Today's residents of Gopalpura are descendants of these two families, which were, in the wake of the Independence, permanently settled, along with another (Udawat clan) family of Kanjar bards (who were employed by Minas).

25. When Ramesh and I visited Gopalpura, he was served food separately from the rest, in recognition of his superior standing that did not allow commensal relations with them.

26. At home Ramesh's young son, Lakshman, always devoured chocolates that I, as his "aunt," gave him, but when we were out in public, he refused to accept them, thus signaling his refusal to "eat from everyone's hand."

27. Here prostitution is a family business, and every member of a household, not just the sex workers alone, participates in the trade. While heads of households, both senior women and men, manage the business, men in subordinate positions (the prostitutes' sons, brothers, and husbands) take over their working wives' duties; they cook and clean, and look after children. For a description of a similar arrangement among a related Bediya community in Jaipur, see Agrawal (2002; 2004); and Brown (2006) on Kanjars in the sex trade in Lahore.

28. "Bhat" and "Nat" are both names used for low-caste bards, such as Kanjars, who are often called Nat Bhats. As a title used in reference to elite bards, Bhat is a

more respectable name than Nat, which is commonly used for low-ranking street performers. Thus, Snodgrass observes that when the low-caste bards he worked with in Udaipur split into two sections, one which served higher ranking Bhambhis, and another that served lower ranking Raigars, the first came to be known as Bhats and the second as Nats (2006: 70).

29. Girls from the thieving and bardic segments of the community are, occasionally, married to Kanjar Nats, who, ever in search of housewives and prospective working girls, offer exorbitant bride prices (some reaching 150,000–200,000 rupees, equaling approximately $2,500–$3,500). If a girl from a Kanjar thief family is married to a Kanjar Nat (to pay off a debt, build a house, or to cover legal fees), it will be said that her parents have "sold" (*bech diyā*) her, not "married" (*byāv kiyā*) her, a tragic transaction that renders her lost to her kin, as if she had married a Kadza (non-Kanjar). I eventually learned that two girls from Mandawari were recently "sold" to the Nats. They were not included, however, in the lists of village kin relations, which my hosts helped me prepare. The girls were no longer kin.

30. Among Kanjars, regulations of sexual intercourse apply only to relations with other Kanjars, who are subject to the caste council (*jāti panchāyat*). Kanjar men are allowed to have casual relations with women of other castes, but Kanjar women risk banishment, should they have an affair with a Kadza.

31. Other markers of superior status include rules of comportment, communication, and eating precedence.

32. This has been exploited both by Kanjar prostitutes to gain access to women and by higher ranking Kanjars to obtain large bride wealth, which other Kanjars in their communities deride as the dishonorable "sale" of girls (see note 30, above).

33. While most Kanjar households in Mandawari owned no more than 10 *bīghās* of land, the descendants of five adopted families owned as many as 150 *bīghās*. Adopted families still dominate village politics, as most elders (*panches*) are drawn from their ranks.

34. Such localization of thieving beats has placed increasing economic pressure on local farmers, who are already hard pressed to make ends meet by the dwindling water supply and the steady population growth. Tensions between Kanjars and their land-tilling neighbors have led to an increasing incidence of violence against Kanjars. Over the past two decades, twenty-four men of the brotherhood have been murdered by their farmer neighbors.

35. Although field officers are not supposed to stay in one posting for more than two years, many remain there for many decades, often for the duration of their careers. The system of promotions is fiercely competitive and the salary raises minimal, so that there is hardly any movement up the ranks among field officers. While the Rajasthan Police Rules prescribe posting outside one's native "judicial

circle," most low-ranking officers actually find employment near their home villages. These days such administrative favors on the part of the posting authorities are simply considered part of the "deal" in the routine purchase of such positions. For more on the inner workings of the Indian police, see Jauregui (2016).

36. In Rajasthan this trend is particularly prominent in the Rajput and Mina communities.

37. Of the sixteen constables, head constables, and assistant subinspectors in the local police station, twelve had been well acquainted with the local Kanjars for more than ten years and four had multigenerational relationships (two of these going back three generations) with them.

38. At the time, this was equal to approximately $1,800, a substantial sum for someone of their background.

39. While locals often blame policemen for their greed (*bhūk*, literally "hunger"), and international observers and upper-echelon officers are quick to describe such activity as "corrupt," the dire underpayment of field officers makes such collusion virtually inevitable. At the time of fieldwork, constables earned a monthly wage of 3,005 rupees during the first five years in service, less than half of an average government schoolteacher's salary of 8,000 rupees. The career success of senior officers, on the contrary, relied more heavily on their satisfaction of target quotas, or the percentage of reported cases investigated and resolved and offenders apprehended, rather than on the relatively measly sums of cash that they can procure from Kanjars.

40. That is, unlike in most cases of appeal by Kanjar (and other poor) villagers, an intracommunal complaint reported by the *sardārs* is likely to be filed and investigated.

41. Rules of comportment that apply to interactions with Rajput superiors apply likewise to patrons in the police. When receiving instructions, informers stand erect with hands folded in front and eyes lowered before the officers, responding with a *hukum* (Sir), traditionally used in reference to Rajput patrons.

42. Territorial divisions have been an essential feature of Indian police since its establishment in the 1860s (i.e., Arnold 1986; Chattopadhyay 2000). Today, if an officer observes a crime just beyond the boundary of his own station, he is not held responsible for its pursuit. And, vice the versa, the jurisdictions of police stations are virtually impermeable to officers from other jurisdictions. In Western and Central India, such territorial agonism in the police is attested by the extensive colonial archive of correspondence about police extradition (Madhya Pradesh State Archives [Bhopal], Police and Judicial files). Much of the discussion, from the nineteenth century onward, has been preoccupied with the difficulty of apprehending offenders across the boundaries of police jurisdictions, habitually treated by officers as

their own exclusive domains. In Rajasthan, even if in "hot pursuit," officers must obtain permission for it from the local police station, making tracking down offenders across police jurisdictions effectively impossible. Kanjars make good use of this.

Chapter 7

1. In 2013 the Election Commission cracked down on feasting, which went undercover, but in 2008 electoral feasts were still held in the open.

2. Electoral feasting is a pan-Indian tradition that dates back to India's first elections, held in 1952, and they remain an indispensable feature of electoral politics, from the shores of Kerala (Subha 1997: 77–81) to the Thar Desert (Vij 2010), from the hills of Nagaland (Wouters 2015) to Arunachal and Himachal Pradesh (Rana 2006: 158; *Times of India* 2012).

3. The term *qatal kī rāt* was originally adopted from the celebrations of the Muslim festival of Muharram, in which the vigil commemorating the martyrdom of Hussein is held on the ninth evening, known as the "Night of the Long Knives." The phrase can also be used to describe eves of major transitional events, whether before a wedding or before the announcement of the Indian Administrative Service examination results. In the electoral context, the reference alludes to this being the final, murderous battle.

4. A posting with few opportunities for extra income.

5. This vision of food and cash distribution as a matter of generosity and "hospitality" is reflected in some early post-Independence reflections on the practice of feeding voters: "Yet there may be mere ordinary hospitality [in voter feeding] with no corrupt intention and to dub even such hospitality as a corrupt practice may be too severe" (G. Srivastava 1957: 328).

6. Which candidates must submit in order to run for elections and which they forfeit, if they receive less than one-sixth of the total vote.

7. The long history of European polities is of course equally tumultuous (see Shakespeare's history plays).

Record Collections Consulted

Begun Police Station Records

BRFPA—Begun Royal Family Private Archive

CDSPO—Records of the Chittorgarh District Superintendent of Police Office

Chittorgarh District Collectorate Records

NAI—National Archives of India

RSAB—Rajasthan State Archives in Bundi

West Bengal State Archives

References

Abu'l-Fazl ibn Mubarak. 1873–94 [c. 1590]. *The Ain-i-Akbari by Abul Fazl 'Allami.* Ed. and trans. Heinrich F. Blochmann and H. S. Jarrett. 3 vols. Calcutta: Asiatic Society of Bengal.

———. 1897–1921 [c. 1590]. *The Akbarnāma of Abu-l-Faẓl.* Trans. Henry Beveridge. 3 vols. Calcutta: Asiatic Society of Bengal.

Acciaioli, Greg. 2009. "Distinguishing Hierarchy and Precedence: Comparing Status Distinctions in South Asia and the Austronesian world, with special reference to South Sulawesi." In *Precedence: Social Differentiation in the Austronesian World*, ed. M. P. Vischer. Canberra: Australian National University Press, 51–90.

Agrawal, Anuja. 2002. "Kinship, Economy and Female Sexuality: A Case Study of Prostitution among the Bedias." PhD diss., Jawaharlal Nehru University.

———. 2004. "'The Bedias are Rajputs': Caste Consciousness of a Marginal Community." *Contributions to Indian Sociology* (n.s.) 38/1: 221–46.

Anderson, Elizabeth. 1999. "What Is the Point of Equality?" *Ethics* 109: 287–337.

Angle, Stephen C., et al. 2017. "In Defence of Hierarchy." *Aeon.* https://aeon.co/essays/hierarchies-have-a-place-even-in-societies-built-on-equality.

Anjaria, Jonathan S. 2012. "The Politics of Illegality: Mumbai Hawkers, Public Space and the Everyday Life of the Law." In *Street Vendors in the global Urban Economy*, ed. Sharit Bhowmik. Delhi: Routledge, 91–108.

Ansell, Aaron. 2014. *Zero Hunger: Political Culture and Antipoverty Policy in Northeast Brazil*. Chapel Hill: University of North Carolina Press.

Appadurai, Arjun. 1981. "Gastro-Politics in Hindu South Asia." *American Ethnologist* 8/3: 494–511.

———. 1986. "Is Homo Hierarchicus?" *American Ethnologist* 13/4: 745–61.

———. 1988. "Putting Hierarchy in Its Place." *Cultural Anthropology* 3/1: 36–49.

———. 2004. "The Capacity to Aspire: Culture and the Terms of Recognition." In *Culture and Public Action*, ed. Vijayendra Rao and Michael Walton. Stanford, CA: Stanford University Press, 59–84.

Appadurai, Arjun, and Carol Appadurai Breckenridge. 1976. "The South Indian Temple: Authority, Honour and Redistribution." *Contributions to Indian Sociology* (n.s.) 10/2: 187–211.

Apthorpe, Raymond. 1956. "Social Change: An Empirical and Theoretical Study." PhD diss., University of Oxford.

Ardener, Edwin. 1989. *The Voice of Prophecy and Other Essays*. Oxford: Berghahn Books.

Arneson, Richard. 1999. "What, If Anything, Renders All Humans Morally Equal?" In *Singer and His Critics*, ed. D. Jamieson. Oxford: Blackwell, 103–28.

Arnold, David. 1976. "The Police and Colonial Control in South India." *Social Scientist* 4/12: 3–16.

———. 1986. *Police Power and Colonial Rule: Madras, 1859–1947*. Delhi: Oxford University Press.

Asad, Talal. 1972. "Market Model, Class Structure and Consent: A Reconsideration of Swat Political Organisation." *Man* 7/1: 74–94.

Babb, Lawrence A. 1973. "Heat and Control in Chhattisgarhi Ritual." *Eastern Anthropologist* 26: 11–28.

———. 1975. *The Divine Hierarchy: Popular Hinduism in Central India*. New York: Columbia University Press.

———. 2004. *Alchemies of Violence: Myths of Identity and the Life of Trade in Western India*. London: Sage.

Baines, Jervoise A. 1893. *General Report on the Census of India, 1891*. London: Her Majesty's Stationery Office.

———. 1912. *Ethnography (Castes and Tribes)*. Strasbourg: Trübner.

Balfour, Edward G. 1885. *The Cyclopaedia of India and of Eastern and Southern Asia, Commercial, Industrial, and Scientific; Products of the Mineral, Vegetable, and Animal Kingdoms, Useful Arts and Manufacturers. 3d ed. 3 vols.* London: Bernard Quaritch.

Balzani, Marzia. 2003. *Modern Indian Kingship: Tradition, Legitimacy and Power in Rajasthan*. Oxford: James Currey.

Barraud, Cécile. 2015. "Kinship, Equality, and Hierarchy: Sex Distinction and Values in Comparative Perspective." *HAU: Journal of Ethnographic Theory* 5/1: 227–50.

Barth, Fredrik. 1959. *Political Leadership among Swat Pathans.* London: Athlone Press.

———. 1969. *Ethnic Groups and Boundaries: The Social Organization of Culture Difference.* Boston: Little, Brown.

———. 1992. "Towards Greater Naturalism in Conceptualizing Societies." In *Conceptualizing Society*, ed. Adam Kuper. London: Routledge, 17–33.

Bass, Daniel. 2012. *Everyday Ethnicity in Sri Lanka: Up-Country Tamil Identity Politics.* London: Routledge.

Baudhāyana Śrauta Sūtra. 1904–24. Trans. and ed. Willem Caland. 3 vols. Calcutta: Bibliotheca Indica.

Bayley, Charles S. 1916 [1894]. *Chiefs and Leading Families of Rājputāna.* Calcutta: Office of the Superintendent of Government Printing.

Bayly, Chris A. 1996. *Empire and Information: Intelligence Gathering and Social Communication in India, 1780–1870.* Cambridge: Cambridge University Press.

Bayly, Susan. 1989. *Saints, Goddesses and Kings: Muslims and Christians in South Indian Society, 1700–1900.* Cambridge: Cambridge University Press.

Bejan, Teresa. 2011. "'The Bond of Civility': Roger Williams on Toleration and Its Limits." *History of European Ideas* 37/4: 409–20.

Beier, A. L. 1985. *Masterless Men: The Vagrancy Problem in England 1560–1640.* London: Methuen.

Bellwood, Peter. 2006. "Hierarchy, Founder Ideology and Austronesian Expansion." In *Origins, Ancestry and Alliance: Explorations in Austronesian Ethnography*, ed. James J. Fox and Clifford Sather. Canberra: Australian National University Press, 19–42.

Berger, Peter. 2012. "Theory and Ethnography in the Modern Anthropology of India." *HAU: Journal of Ethnographic Theory* 2/2: 325–57.

———. 2015. *Feeding, Sharing, and Devouring: Ritual and Society in Highland Odisha, India.* Berlin: de Gruyter.

Berland, Joseph C. 1982. *No Five Fingers Are Alike: Cognitive Amplifiers in Social Context.* Cambridge, MA: Harvard University Press.

Bernier, François. 1891 [c. 1660]. *Travels in the Mogul Empire, AD 1656–1668.* Trans. Irving Brock. Westminster, UK: Archibald Constable.

Berreman, Gerald D. 1971. "On the Nature of Caste in India: A Review Symposium on Louis Dumont's *Homo Hierarchicus*: The Brahmanical View of Caste." *Contributions to Indian Sociology* 5/1: 16–23.

———. 1972. *Hindus of the Himalayas.* Berkeley: University of California Press.

Bes, Lennart. 2001. "The Setupatis, the Dutch, and Other Bandits in Eighteenth-Century Ramnad (South India)." *Journal of the Economic and Social History of the Orient* 44/4: 540–74.

Béteille, André. 1986. "Individualism and Equality." *Current Anthropology* 27/2: 121–28.

Bhakkāri, Farīd. 1961–74. *Zakhirat ul Khwanin.* Ed. S. Moinul Haq. 3 vols. Karachi.

Bhandarkar, D. R., and R. G. Bhandarkar. 2000. *Aśoka.* Delhi: Asian Educational Services.

Bhargava, Bhawani S. 1949. *The Criminal Tribes: A Socio-Economic Study of the Principal Criminal Tribes and Castes in Northern India.* Lucknow: Universal Publishers.

Bhargava, Pradeep. 2007. "Civil Society in Rajasthan." In *Rajasthan: The Quest for Sustainable Development,* ed. Vijay S. Vyas et al. New Delhi: Academic Foundation, 257–81.

Bharucha, Rustom. 2003. *Rajasthan: An Oral History: Conversations with Komal Kothari.* New Delhi: Penguin Books.

Bhatia, B. 2006. "Dalit Rebellion against Untouchability in Chakwada, Rajasthan." *Contributions to Indian Sociology* 40/1: 29–61.

Biardeau, Madeleine. 1976. "Le Sacrifice dans l'hindouisme." In *Le Sacrifice dans l'Inde ancienne,* ed. Madeleine Biardeau and Charles Malamoud. Paris: Presses Universitaires de France, 7–154.

Björkman, Lisa. 2014. "'You can't buy a vote': Meanings of Money in a Mumbai Election." *American Ethnologist* 41/4: 617–34.

Blackburn, Stuart H. 1978. "The Kallars: A Tamil 'Criminal Tribe' Reconsidered." *South Asia: Journal of South Asian Studies* 1/1: 38–51.

Blunt, Edward A. H. 1931. *The Caste System of Northern India: With Special Reference to the United Provinces of Agra and Oudh.* London: Oxford University Press.

Boas, Franz. 1911. *The Mind of the Primitive Man: A Course of Lectures Delivered before the Lowell Institute.* New York: Macmillan.

Boehm, Christopher. 2009. *Hierarchy in the Forest: The Evolution of Egalitarian Behavior.* Cambridge, MA: Harvard University Press.

Booth, F. S. G. D. L. 1916. *Criminocurology; Or, The Indian Criminal and What to Do with Him: Being a Review of the Work of the Salvation Army among the Prisoners, Habituals and Criminal Tribes of India.* London: Liddell's Printing Works.

Bor, Joep. 1987. "The Voice of the Sarangi." *Quarterly Journal of the National Centre for the Performing Arts* 15–16: 6–178.

Bouglé, Célestin. 1925. *Les idées égalitaires: Étude sociologique.* Paris: Librairie Félix Alcan.

Bourdieu, Pierre. 1984 [1979]. *Distinction: A Social Critique of the Judgment of Taste.* Trans. Richard Nice. Cambridge, MA: Harvard University Press.

Breman, Jan. 1993. *Patronage and Exploitation.* Delhi: Oxford University Press.

Bṛhaspati. 1998. *Bārhaspatya Sūtam: Aphorisms of Bṛhaspati on Indian Polity.* Ed. and trans. Balram Srivastava. Delhi: Pratibha Prakashan.

Broughton, Thomas B. 1892 [1809]. *Letters Written in a Mahratta Camp during the Year 1809: Descriptive of the Character, Manners, Domestic Habits and Religious Ceremonies of the Mahrattas*. London: Archibald Constable & Co.

Brown, Louise T. 2006. *The Dancing Girls of Lahore: Selling Love and Saving Dreams in Pakistan's Pleasure District*. New York: Harper Collins.

Burghart, Richard. 1978. "Hierarchical Models of the Hindu Social System." *Man* 13/4: 519–36.

Burkhart, Geoffrey. 1978. "Marriage Alliance and the Local Circle among Some Udayars of South India." In *American Studies in the Anthropology of India*, ed. Sylvia Vatuk. New Delhi: Manohar Publications, 171–210.

Burridge, Kenelm. 1975. "The Melanesian Manager." In *Studies in Social Anthropology: Essays in Memory of E. E. Evans-Pritchard by His Former Oxford Colleagues*, ed. J. H. M. Beattie and R. G. Lienhardt. Oxford: Clarendon Press, 86–104.

Caldwell, Bruce. 1991. *The Jajmani System: An Investigation*. Delhi: Hindustan Publishing.

Callon, Michael. 1986. "The Sociology of an Actor-Network: The Case of the Electric Vehicle." In *Mapping the Dynamics of Science and Technology: Sociology of Science in the Real World*, ed. Michael Callon et al. London: Palgrave Macmillan, 19–34.

Campbell, John K. 1964. *Honour, Family, and Patronage: A Study of Institution and Moral Values in a Greek Mountain Community*. Oxford: Clarendon Press.

Carnegy, Patrick. 1868. *Notes on the Races, Tribes and Castes Inhabiting the Province of Avadh*. Lucknow: Oudh Government Press.

Carrithers, Michael, Steven Collins, and Steven Lukes, eds. 1985. *The Category of the Person: Anthropology, Philosophy, History*. Cambridge: Cambridge University Press.

Carstairs, G. Morris. 1957. *The Twice-Born*. London: Hogarth Press.

Cashdan, Elizabeth. 1980. Egalitarianism among Hunters and Gatherers. *American Anthropologist* 82/1: 116–20.

Census of India, 1901: Ajmer-Merwara. 1901. Delhi: Government of India Press.

Census of India, 1961. 1962. Delhi: India Office of the Registrar General.

Census of India, 2001. http://www.censusindia.net/.

Census of India, 2011. http://www.censusindia.gov.in.

Chadwick, H. Munro. 1926. *The Heroic Age*. Cambridge: Cambridge University Press.

Chakravarti, Anand. 1975. *Contradiction and Change: Emerging Patterns of Authority in a Rajasthan Village*. Delhi: Oxford University Press.

Chambard, Jean-Luc. 1963. "La Pothī du Jagā, ou Le Registre secret d'un généalogiste de village en Inde centrale." *L'Homme* 3/1: 5–85.

Chandra, Kanchan. 2004. *Why Ethnic Parties Succeed: Patronage and Ethnic Head Counts in India*. Cambridge: Cambridge University Press.

Chatterjee, Partha. 1998. "Community in the East." *Economic and Political Weekly* 33: 227–82.

———. 2004. *The Politics of the Governed: Reflections on Popular Politics in Most of the World*. New York: Columbia University Press.

Chattopadhyay, Basudev. 2000. *Crime and Control in Early Colonial Bengal, 1770–1860*. Calcutta: K. P. Bagchi.

Chechi and Mandawari registers of roll call. 1928–33. Begun Royal Family Private Archive.

Clark-Decès, Isabelle, ed. 2011. *A Companion to the Anthropology of India*. London: Blackwell.

———. 2018. "Toward an Anthropology of Exchange in Tamil Nadu." *International Journal of Hindu Studies* 22: 197–215.

Clastres, Pierre. 1977. *Society against the State*. Ed. and trans. P. Hurley and A. Stein. Oxford: Blackwell.

Cohen, Gerald A. 1989. "On the Currency of Egalitarian Justice." *Ethics* 99/4: 906–44.

Cohn, Bernard. 1959. "Notes on Law and Change in North India." *Economic Development and Cultural Change* 8/1: 79–93.

———. 1961. "The Pasts of an Indian Village." *Comparative Studies in Society and History* 3: 241–49.

Collins, Jacob. 2015. "French Liberalism's 'Indian Detour': Louis Dumont, the Individual, and Liberal Political Thought in Post-1968 France." *Modern Intellectual History* 12/3: 685–710.

"Compendium concerning Kanjar Gangs Resident in Chittorgarh District" [*jīlā chittaugaṛh meiñ rahane wāle kanjar gaing sambandhī kampendiyam*]. Chittorgarh District Collectorate.

Copeman, Jacob. 2011. "The Gift and Its Forms of Life in Contemporary India." *Modern Asian Studies* 45/5: 1051–94.

Cort, John E. 2004. "Jains, Caste and Hierarchy in North Gujarat." *Contributions to Indian Sociology* (n.s.) 23/1–2: 73–112.

Crooke, William. 1896a. *The Tribes and Castes of the North-Western Provinces and Oudh*. 4 vols. Calcutta: Office of the Superintendent of Government Printing Press.

———. 1896b. *The Popular Religion and Folk-lore of Northern India*. 2 vols. Westminster, UK: Archibald Constable.

Dalrymple, William. 2006. *The Last Mughal: The Fall of a Dynasty, Delhi, 1857*. Delhi: Penguin.

Daniel, Valentine. 1984. *Fluid Signs: Being a Person the Tamil Way*. Berkeley: University of California Press.

Das, Veena. 1982. *Structure and Cognition: Aspects of Hindu Caste and Ritual. 2d ed.* Delhi: Oxford University Press.

———. 2006. *Life and Words: Violence and the Descent into the Ordinary*. Berkeley: University of California Press.

Deleuze, Gilles, and Félix Guattari. 1980. *Mille plateaux*. Paris: Les Éditions de Minuit.

De Neve, Geert. 2000. "Patronage and 'Community': The Role of a Tamil 'Village' Festival in the Integration of a Town." *Journal of the Royal Anthropological Institute* 6/3: 501–19.

De Reuck, Anthony, and Julie Knight, eds. 1967. *Caste and Race: Comparative Approaches*. London: Ciba Foundation/Churchill.

Derrett, J. Duncan M. 1968. *Religion, Law and the State in India*. New York: Free Press.

Dharampal-Frick, Gita, et al. 2015. *Key Concepts in Modern Indian Studies*. New York: New York University Press.

Dirks, Nicholas B. 1987. *The Hollow Crown: The Ethnohistory of an Indian Kingdom*. Cambridge: Cambridge University Press.

Dresch, Paul. 1989. *Tribes, Government and History in Yemen*. Oxford: Clarendon Press.

———. 1998. "Mutual Deception: Totality, Exchange and Islam in the Middle East." In *Marcel Mauss: A Centenary Tribute*, ed. Wendy James and Nicholas J. Allen. Oxford: Berghahn Books, 111–33.

———. 2000. "'A Wilderness of Mirrors': Truth and Vulnerability in Middle Eastern Fieldwork." In *Anthropologists in a Wider World: Essays on Field Research*, ed. Paul Dresch, Wendy James, and David Parkin. Oxford: Berghahn Books, 109–27.

———. 2012. "Introduction: Legalism, Anthropology, and History: A View from Part of Anthropology." In *Legalism: Anthropology and History*, ed. Paul Dresch and Hannah Skoda. Oxford: Oxford University Press, 1–37.

Dresch, Paul, and Wendy James. 2000. "Fieldwork and the Passage of Time." In *Anthropologists in a Wider World: Essays on Field Research*, ed. Paul Dresch, Wendy James, and David Parkin. Oxford: Berghahn Books, 1–26.

Dresch, Paul, and Judith Scheele. 2015. "Rules and Categories: An Overview." In *Legalism: Anthropology and History*, ed. Paul Dresch and Judith Scheele. Oxford: Oxford University Press, 1–27.

Dresch, Paul, and Hannah Skoda, eds. 2012. *Legalism: Anthropology and History*. Oxford: Oxford University Press.

Duarte, Luiz Fernando Dias. 2017. "O Valor dos valores: Louis Dumont na antropologia contemporanea." *Sociologia & Antropologia* 7/3: 735–72.

Dumézil, Georges. 1969. *Heur et Malheur du Guerrier*. Paris: Presses Universitaires de France.

———. 1973. *The Fate of a King*. Trans. Alf Hiltebeitel. Chicago: University of Chicago Press.

Dumont, Louis. 1957. *Une sous-caste de l'Inde du Sud: Organisation sociale et religion des Pramalai Kallar*. Paris: Mouton.

———. 1959 [1953]. "A Structural Definition of a Folk Deity of Tamil Nad: Aiyanar the Lord." *Contributions to Indian Sociology* 3: 75–87.

———. 1966. "Marriage in India, the Present State of the Question: III. North India in Relation to South India." *Contributions to Indian Sociology* 9: 90–114.

———. 1966. *Homo hierarchicus: Le système des castes et ses implications*. Paris: Gallimard.

———. 1970. *Homo Hierarchicus: The Caste System and Its Implications*. London: Weidenfeld & Nicolson.

———. 1977. Homo aequalis: *Genèse et épanouissement de l'idéologie économique*. Paris: Gallimard. (English translation as *From Mandeville to Marx*, 1977.)

———. 1980. *Homo Hierarchicus: The Caste System and Its Implications*. 2d ed., expanded. Chicago: University of Chicago Press.

———. 1981. "On Value: Radcliffe-Brown Lecture in Social Anthropology, read on 22 October 1980." *Proceedings of the British Academy*: 207–41.

———. 1986. *Essays on Individualism: Modern Ideology in Anthropological Perspective*. Chicago: University of Chicago Press.

———. 1994. *German Ideology: From France to Germany and Back*. Chicago: University of Chicago Press.

Dunn, John. 1978. "Practising History and Social Science on 'Realist' Assumptions." In *Action and Interpretation: Studies in the Philosophy of the Social Sciences*, ed. Christopher Hookway and Philip Petit. Cambridge: Cambridge University Press, 145–75.

Durkheim, Émile. 1893. *De la division du travail social*. Paris: F. Alcan.

———. 1895. *Les Règles de la méthode sociologique*. Paris: F. Alcan.

Durkheim, Émile, and Marcel Mauss. 1963 [1903]. *Primitive Classification*. Trans. and introd. Rodney Needham. London: Cohen & West.

Dworkin, Ronald. 1977. *Taking Rights Seriously*. London: Duckworth.

Eastwick, Edward B. 1883. *Handbook of the Panjāb, Western Rajpūtānā, Kashmīr, and Upper Sindh*. London: John Murray.

Elphinstone, Mountstuart. 1884. *Selections from the Minutes and Other Official Writings of the Honourable Mountstuart Elphinstone, Governor of Bombay*. London: Richard Bentley & Son.

Encyclopaedia of Social Work in India, Vol. 3. 1987. New Delhi: India Ministry of Welfare.

Engels, Frederick. 1902 [1884]. *The Origin of the Family, Private Property and the State, in the Light of the Researches of Lewis H. Morgan.* Trans. E. Untermann. Chicago: Charles H. Kerr.

Englund, Harri. 1996. "Witchcraft, Modernity and the Person: The Morality of Accumulation in Central Malawi." *Critique of Anthropology* 16/3: 257–79.

———. 2006. *Prisoners of Freedom: Human Rights and the African Poor.* Berkeley: University of California Press.

Enthoven, Reginald E. 1975 [1920–22]. *The Tribes and Castes of Bombay.* 3 vols. Delhi: Cosmo Publications.

Erdman, Joan L. 1985. *Patrons and Performers in Rajasthan: The Subtle Tradition.* Delhi: Chanakya Publications.

Eriksen, Thomas H. 2002. *Ethnicity and Nationalism.* 2d ed. London: Pluto Press.

Erndl, Kathleen M. 1993. *Victory to the Mother: The Hindu Goddess of Northwest India in Myth, Ritual and Symbol.* Oxford: Oxford University Press.

Evans, Nicholas. 2019. *Far from the Caliph's Gaze: Being Ahmadi Muslim in the Holy City of Qadian.* Ithaca, NY: Cornell University Press.

Evans-Pritchard, E. E. 1940. *The Nuer: A Description of the Modes of Livelihood and Political Institutions of a Nilotic People.* Oxford: Clarendon Press.

———. 1956. *Nuer Religion.* Oxford: Clarendon Press.

Feeley-Harnik, Gillian. 1985. "Issues in Divine Kingship." *Annual Review of Anthropology* 14/1: 273–313.

Ferguson, James. 2013. "Declarations of Dependence: Labour, Personhood, and Welfare in Southern Africa." *Journal of the Royal Anthropological Institute* 19/2: 223–42.

Fernandes, Leela, and Patrick Heller. 2006. "Hegemonic Aspirations: New Middle-Class Politics and India's Democracy in Comparative Perspective." *Critical Asian Studies* 38/4: 495–522.

Flanagan, James G. 1989. "Hierarchy in Simple 'Egalitarian' Societies." *Annual Review of Anthropology* 18: 245–66.

Flanagan, James G., and Steve Rayner. 1988. *Rules, Decisions, and Inequality in Egalitarian Societies.* Aldershot, UK: Avebury.

Forbes, Alexander K. 1856. *Rās Mālā; or Hindoo Annals of the Province of Goozerat, in Western India.* 2 vols. London: Richardson Brothers.

Forbes, Duncan. 1857. *A Dictionary, Hindustani and English: Accompanied by a Reversed Dictionary, English and Hindustani.* London: Sampson Low, Marston & Co.

Forbes, James. 1834 [1813]. *Oriental Memoirs.* 2d ed. 2 vols. London: Richard Bentley.

Fortes, Meyer. 1987. "The Concept of the Person." In *Religion, Morality and the Person: Essays on Tallensi Religion*, ed. Jack Goody. Cambridge: Cambridge University Press, 247–86.

Fortes, Meyer, and E. E. Evans-Pritchard. 1940. *African Political Systems*. Oxford: Oxford University Press.

Fox, James J. 1988. "Origin, Descent and Precedence in the Study of Austronesian Societies." Public lecture in connection with De Wisseleerstoel Indonesische Studien, Leiden University, 17 March.

———. 1994. "Reflections on 'Hierarchy' and 'Precedence.'" In *Transformations of Hierarchy: Structure, History and Horizon in the Austronesian World*, ed. Margaret Jolly and Mark S. Mosko, *History and Anthropology* (special issue) 7: 87–108.

———. 2009. "Precedence in Perspective." In *Precedence: Social Differentiation in the Austronesian World*, ed. Michael P. Vischer. Canberra: Australian National University Press, 1–12.

Fox, James J., and Clifford Sather, eds. 1996. *Origins, Ancestry and Alliance: Explorations in Austronesian Ethnography*. Canberra: Research School of Pacific and Asian Studies, Australian National University.

Fox, Richard G. 1971. *Kin, Clan, Raja, and Rule: State-Hinterland Relations in Preindustrial India*. Berkeley: University of California Press.

Fraser, Angus M. 1992. *The Gypsies*. Oxford: Blackwell.

Freed, Ruth S., and Stanley A. Freed. 1964. "Spirit Possession as Illness in a North Indian Village." *Ethnology* 3/2: 152–71.

Freitag, Sandria B. 1985. "Collective Crime and Authority in North India." In *Crime and Criminality in British India*, ed. Anand A. Yang. Tucson: University of Arizona Press, 140–61.

———. 1991. "Crime in the Social Order of Colonial North India." *Modern Asian Studies* 25/2: 27–61.

———. 1998. "Sansiahs and the State: The Changing Nature of 'Crime' and 'Justice' in Nineteenth-Century British India." In *Changing Concepts of Rights and Justice in South Asia*, ed. Michael Anderson and Sumit Guha. Delhi: Oxford University Press, 82–113.

Fukuzawa, Hiroshi. 1972. "Rural Servants in the 18th-century Maharashtrian Village—Demiurgic or Jajmani System?" *Hitotsubashi Journal of Economics* 12/3: 14–40.

Fuller, Chris J. 1977. "British India or Traditional India? An Anthropological Problem." *Ethnos* 42: 95–121.

———. 1988. "The Hindu Pantheon and the Legitimation of Hierarchy." *Man* (n.s.) 23/1: 19–39.

———. 1989. "Misconceiving the Grain Heap: A Critique of the Concept of the Indian Jajmani System." In *Money and the Morality of Exchange*, ed. Jonathan Parry and Maurice Bloch. Cambridge: Cambridge University Press, 33–63.

Fuller, Chris J., and Penny Logan. 1985. "The Navarātri Festival in Madurai." *Bulletin of the School of Oriental and African Studies, University of London* 48/1: 79–105.

Fumanti, Mattia. 2016. *The Politics of Distinction: African Elites from Colonialism to Liberation in a Namibian Frontier Town*. Canon Pyon, Herefordshire, UK: Sean Kingston.

Gabaccia, Donna, and Dirk Hoerder, eds. 2011. *Connecting Seas and Connected Ocean Rims: Indian, Atlantic and Pacific Oceans and China Seas Migrations from the 1830s to the 1930s*. Leiden: Brill.

Gajrani, Shiv. 2004. *History, Religion and Culture of India*. 6 vols. Delhi: Isha Books.

Garg, R. P. 1965. *Dacoit Problem in Chambal Valley: A Sociological Study*. Varanasi: Gandhian Institute of Studies.

Gautam, Mohan K. 1983. "Itinerant Camping Life to Settled Basti Alliances: The Mechanism of Ethnic Maintenance and Social Organization of the Kanjars of North India." *Eastern Anthropologist* 36/1: 15–29.

Gayer, George W. 1909. *Lectures on Some Criminal Tribes of India and Religious Mendicants*. Nagpur: SN.

Gazetteer of the Bombay Presidency. 1873–1901. Ed. James M. Campbell and Reginald E. Enthoven. Bombay: Government Central Press.

Geertz, Clifford. 1973. *The Interpretation of Cultures: Selected Essays*. New York: Basic Books.

———. 1980. *Negara: The Theatre State in Nineteenth Century Bali*. Princeton, NJ: Princeton University Press.

Gilmartin, David. 2014. "The Paradox of Patronage and the People's Sovereignty." In *Patronage as Politics in South Asia*, ed. Anastasia Piliavsky. Cambridge: Cambridge University Press, 125–53.

Gold, Ann G. 2017. *Shiptown: Between Rural and Urban North India*. Philadelphia: University of Pennsylvania Press.

Gold, Ann G., and Bhoju R. Gujar. 2002. *In the Time of Trees and Sorrows: Nature, Power, and Memory in Rajasthan*. New Delhi: Oxford University Press.

Gommans, Jos. 2002. *Mughal Warfare: Indian Frontiers and High Roads to Empire, 1500–1700*. London: Routledge.

Good, Anthony. 1982. "The Actor and the Act: Categories of Prestation in South India." *Man* (n.s.) 17/1: 23–41.

———. 1985. "The Annual Goddess Festival in a South Indian Village." *South Asian Social Science* 1/1: 19–67.

Gordon, Stewart. 1969. "Scarf and Sword: Thugs, Marauders and State Formation in Eighteenth Century Malwa." *Indian Economic and Social History Review* 6/4: 416–29.

———. 1985. "Bhils and the Idea of a Criminal Tribe in Nineteenth-Century India."

In *Crime and Criminality in British India*, ed. Anand Yang. Tucson: University of Arizona Press, 128–39.

———. 1993. *The Marathas, 1600–1818*. Cambridge: Cambridge University Press.

———. 1994. *Marathas, Marauders, and State Formation in Eighteenth-century India*. Delhi: Oxford University Press.

Goswamy, B. N. 1997. "Nainsukh of Guler: A Great Painter from a Small Hill-State." *Artibus Asiae, Supplementum* 41: 5–304.

Graeber, David. 1997. "Manners, Deference, and Private Property in Early Modern Europe." *Comparative Studies in Society and History* 39/4: 694–728.

Greenberg, Joseph. 1966. *Language Universals: With Special Reference to Feature Hierarchies*. The Hague: Mouton.

Gregory, Chris. 2014. "Unequal Egalitarianism: Reflections on Forge's Paradox." *Asia Pacific Journal of Anthropology* 15/3: 197–217.

Griffin, Lepel H. 1865. *The Panjab Chiefs: Historical and Biographical Notices of the Principal Families in the Territories under the Panjab Government*. Lahore: T. C. McCarthy.

Griffiths, Percival J. 1971. *To Guard My People: The History of the Indian Police*. London: Benn.

Guha, Ranajit. 1963. *A Rule of Property for Bengal: An Essay on the Idea of Permanent Settlement*. Paris: Mouton.

Guha, Sumit. 1996. "Forest Polities and Agrarian Empires: The Khandesh Bhils, c. 1700–1850." *Indian Economic and Social History Review* 33/2: 133–53.

———. 1999. *Environment and Ethnicity in India, 1200–1991*. Cambridge: Cambridge University Press.

———. 2016. *Beyond Caste: Identity and Power in South Asia, Past and Present*. Leiden: Brill.

Gullestad, Marianne. 1986. "Equality and Marital Love: The Norwegian Case as an Illustration of a General Western Dilemma." *Social Analysis* 19 (August): 40–53.

Gunthorpe, Edward J. 1882. *Notes on Criminal Tribes Residing in or Frequenting the Bombay Presidency, Berar, and the Central Provinces*. Bombay: Times of India Steam Press.

Gupta, Dipankar. 1997. *Rivalry and Brotherhood: Politics in the Life of Farmers in Northern India*. Delhi: Oxford University Press.

———. 2000. *Interrogating Caste: Understanding Hierarchy and Difference in Indian Society*. New Delhi: Penguin Books.

———. 2004. *Caste in Question: Identity Or Hierarchy?* London: Sage.

———. 2005. "Caste and Politics: Identity over System." *Annual Review of Anthropology* 34: 409–27.

Gupta, R. K., and S. R. Bakshi, eds. 2008. *Rajasthan through the Ages, Vol. 5: Marwar and British Administration*. New Delhi: Sarup & Sons.

Haekel, Josef. 1963. "Some Aspects of the Social Life of the Bhilala in Central India." *Ethnology* 2/2: 190–206.

Hancock, Ian F. 1998. "Romani." In *Encyclopedia of the Languages of Europe*, ed. Glanville Price. Oxford: Blackwell, 378–82.

Hansen, Thomas B. 2001. *Wages of Violence: Naming and Identity in Postcolonial Bombay*. Princeton, NJ: Princeton University Press.

Hardiman, David. 1987. *The Coming of the Devi: Adivasi Assertion in Western India*. Delhi: Oxford University Press.

———. 1996. "Usury, Dearth and Famine in Western India." *Past & Present* 152: 113–56.

Harlan, Lindsey. 1992. *Religion and Rajput Women: The Ethic of Protection in Contemporary Narratives*. Berkeley: University of California Press.

Haynes, Naomi. 2013. "On the Potential and Problems of Pentecostal Exchange." *American Anthropologist* 115/1: 85–95.

———. 2017a. "Contemporary Africa through the Theory of Louis Dumont." *Sociologia & Antropologia* 7/3: 715–34.

———. 2017b. *Moving by the Spirit: Pentecostal Social Life on the Zambian Copperbelt*. Berkeley: University of California Press.

Haynes, Naomi, and Jason Hickel. 2016. "Hierarchy, Value, and the Value of Hierarchy." *Social Analysis* 60/4: 1–20.

Hegel, Georg W. F. 2019 [1807]. *The Phenomenology of Spirit*. Ed. and trans. Terry Pinkard. Cambridge: Cambridge University Press.

Heim, Maria. 2004. *Theories of the Gift in South Asia: Hindu, Buddhist, and Jain Reflections of Dana*. London: Routledge.

Henderson, Carol, and Maxine Weisgrau, eds. 2007. *Raj Rhapsodies: Tourism, Heritage and the Seduction of History*. London: Ashgate.

Henige, David P. 1974. *The Chronology of Oral Tradition: Quest for a Chimera*. Oxford: Clarendon Press.

Hertz, Robert. 1960. *Death and the Right Hand*. Trans. R. and C. Needham. Aberdeen: Cohen & West.

Herzfeld, Michael. 1990. "Icons and Identity: Religious Orthodoxy and Social Practice in Rural Crete." *Anthropological Quarterly* 63/3: 109–21.

Hickel, Jason. 2015. *Democracy as Death: The Moral Order of Anti-Liberal Politics in South Africa*. Berkeley: University of California Press.

Hocart, Arthur M. 1927. *Kingship*. London: Oxford University Press.

———. 1970 [1936]. *Kings and Councillors: An Essay in the Comparative Anatomy of Human Society*. Cairo: Printing Office Paul Barbey.

———. 1950. *Caste: A Comparative Study*. London: Methuen.

Hoekstra, Kinch. 2013. "Hobbesian Equality." In *Hobbes Today: Insights for the 21st Century*, ed. S. A. Lloyd. Cambridge: Cambridge University Press, 76–112.

Houseman, Michael. 2015 [1984]. "The Hierarchical Relation: A Particular Ideology or a General Model?" *HAU: Journal of Ethnographic Theory* 5/1: 251–69. (Translation of "La Relation hiérarchique: Idéologie particulière ou modèle général?" In *Différences, valeurs, hiérarchie: Textes présentés à Louis Dumont*, ed. Jean-Claude Galey. Paris: Éditions de l'École des Hautes Études en Sciences Sociales, 299–318.)

Huizinga, Johan. 1955 [1919]. *The Waning of the Middle Ages: A Study of the Forms of Life, Thought and Art in France and the Netherlands in the Fourteenth and Fifteenth Centuries*. London: E. Arnold.

Humes, Cynthia A. 1995. "Rājās, Thugs, and Mafiosos: Religion and Politics in the Worship of Vidhyavāsinī." In *Render Unto Caesar: The Religious Sphere in World Politics*, ed. Sabrina P. Ramet and Donald W. Treadgold. Washington, DC: American University Press, 219–47.

Humphrey, Caroline. 2012. "Inequality." In *A Companion to Moral Anthropology*, ed. Didier Fassin. London: Wiley Blackwell, 302–19.

Hunter, Thomas M. 2010. "The *Saṅgīt-Sāra* on the Art of Instrumental Music: Translation and Commentary on the *Vādya* Section of a Manuscript Attributed to Tānsen." Unpublished manuscript.

Ibbetson, Denzil. 1916 [1883]. *Panjab Castes: Being a Reprint of the Chapter on "The Races, Castes and Tribes of the People" in the Report on the Census of the Panjab*. Lahore: Superintendent Government Printing, Punjab.

Iglesias, Teresa. 2001. "Bedrock Truths and the Dignity of the Individual." *Logos* 4/1: 114–34.

Ikegame, Aya. 2013. *Princely India Re-Imagined: A Historical Anthropology of Mysore from 1799 to the Present*. London: Routledge.

Imperial Gazetteer of India. 1908–31. Ed. William S. Meyer et al. 26 vols. Oxford: Clarendon Press.

Inden, Ronald B. 1985. "Lordship and Caste in Hindu Discourse." In *Indian Religion*, ed. R. Burghart and A. Cantlie. London: Curzon Press, 159–77.

———. 1986. "Orientalist Constructions of India." *Modern Asian Studies* 20/3: 401–46.

———. 1990. *Imagining India*. Oxford: Oxford University Press.

Indian Police Commission. 1913. *History of Police Organization in India and Indian Village Police, Being Select Chapters of the Indian Police Commission, 1902–1903*. Calcutta: University of Calcutta Press.

Iteanu, André. 1990. "The Concept of the Person and the Ritual System: An Orokaiva View." *Man* 25/1: 35–53.

———. 2013. "The Two Conceptions of Value." *HAU: Journal of Ethnographic Theory* 3/1: 155–71.

Jacobson, Doranne. 1974. "The Women of North and Central India: Goddesses and

Wives." In *Many Sisters: Women in Cross-Cultural Perspective*, ed. Carolyn J. Matthiasson. New York: Free Press, 17–112.

James, Susan. 1984. *The Content of Social Explanation*. Cambridge: Cambridge University Press.

James, Wendy. 1973. "Illusions of Freedom: A Comment on Barth's Individuals." *Journal of the Anthropological Society of Oxford* 4/3: 155–67.

Jauregui, Beatrice A. 2016. *Provisional Authority: Order, Police, and Security in India*. Chicago: University of Chicago Press.

Jeffrey, Craig. 2009. "Fixing Futures: Educated Unemployment through a North Indian Lens." *Comparative Studies in Society and History* 51/1: 182–211.

Jeffrey, Craig, and John Harriss. 2014. *Keywords for Modern India*. Oxford: Oxford University Press.

Jindel, Rajendra. 1976. *Culture of a Sacred Town: A Sociological Study of Nathdwara*. Bombay: Popular Prakashan.

Jodhka, Surinder. 2012. *Caste: Oxford India Short Introductions*. New Delhi: Oxford University Press.

Jolly, Julius. 1889. *The Minor Law-Books. Part I. Nārada and Brihaspati*. Sacred Books of the East 33. Oxford: Clarendon Press.

Kāmandaki. 1896 [c. 400–600 CE]. *Kamandakiya Nitisara, or The Elements of Polity*. Ed. and trans. Manmatha Nath Dutt. Calcutta: Elysium Press.

Kamra, Lipika, and Uday Chandra. 2017. "Maoism and the Masses: Critical Reflections on Revolutionary Praxis and Subaltern Agency." In *Revolutionary Violence versus Democracy: Narratives from India*, ed. Ajay Gudavathy. Delhi: SAGE Publishing India, 191–215.

Kane, Pandurang V. 1993 [1930–62]. *History of Dharmaśāstra (Ancient and Medieval Religious and Civil Law)*. 3d ed. Poona: Bhandarkar Oriental Research Institute.

Kapadia, K. M. 1952. *The Criminal Tribes of India. Sociological Bulletin* 1.

Kapferer, Bruce. 1989. "Nationalist Ideology and a Comparative Anthropology." *Ethnos* 54/3–4: 161–99.

———, ed. 2005. *The Retreat of the Social: The Rise and Rise of Reductionism*. New York: Berghahn Books.

———. 2011. *Legends of People, Myths of State: Violence, Intolerance, and Political Culture in Sri Lanka and Australia*. London: Berghahn Books.

Karanth, G. K. 1987. "New Technology and Traditional Rural Institutions: Case of 'Jajmani' Relations in Karnataka." *Economic and Political Weekly* 22/51: 2217–19, 2221–24.

Kautilya. 1967 [c. fourth to third centuries BCE]. *The Kauṭilīya Arthaśāstra*. Trans. and ed. Rudrapatna Sharma Sastri. Mysore: Mysore Printing & Publishing House.

Keane, Webb. 1997. *Signs of Recognition: Powers and Hazards of Representation in an Indonesian Society*. Berkeley: University of California Press.

Keeler, Ward. 2017. *The Traffic in Hierarchy: Masculinity and Its Others in Buddhist Burma*. Honolulu: University of Hawaii Press.

Khan, Arsalan. 2016. "Islam and Pious Sociality: The Ethics of Hierarchy in the Tablighi Jamaat in Pakistan." *Social Analysis* 60/4: 96–113.

———. 2018. "Pious Masculinity, Ethical Reflexivity, and Moral Order in an Islamic Piety Movement in Pakistan." *Anthropological Quarterly* 91/1: 53–82.

Khan, Naveeda. 2012. *Muslim Becoming: Aspiration and Skepticism in Pakistan*. Durham, NC: Duke University Press.

Khare, Ravindra S. 1976a. *The Hindu Hearth and Home*. Durham, NC: Carolina Academic Press.

———. 1976b. *Culture and Reality: Essays on the Hindu System of Managing Foods*. Simla: Indian Institute of Advanced Study.

King, Diane E. 2014. *Kurdistan on the Global Stage: Kinship, Land, and Community in Iraq*. New Brunswick, NJ: Rutgers University Press.

Kipling, Rudyard. 1901. *Kim*. London: Macmillan.

Knapp, Peter. 1986. "Hegel's Universals in Marx, Durkheim and Weber: The Role of Hegelian Ideas in the Origin of Sociology." *Sociological Forum* 1/4: 586–609.

Kolenda, Pauline. 1963. "Toward a Model of the Hindu Jajmani system." *Human Organization* 22/1: 11–31.

Kolff, Dirk H. A. 1971. "Sannyasi Trader-Soldiers." *Indian Economic and Social History Review* 8/2: 213–18.

———. 1990. *Naukar, Rajput and Sepoy: The Ethnohistory of the Military Labour Market in Hindustan, 1450–1850*. Cambridge: Cambridge University Press.

Kopytoff, Igor, ed. 1987. *The African Frontier: The Reproduction of Traditional African Societies*. Bloomington: Indiana University Press.

Kothari, Komal. 1991. "Introduction: A View on Castes of Marwar." In *The Castes of Marwar: Being a Census Report of 1891*, ed. M. Hardyal Singh. Jodhpur: Books Treasure, i–xiii.

———. 1994. "Musicians for the People: The Manganiyars of Western Rajasthan." In *The Idea of Rajasthan: Explorations in Regional Identity, Vol. 1: Constructions*, ed. Karine Schomer et al. Delhi: Monohar & AIIS, 205–37.

Krishna, Anirudh. 2002. *Active Social Capital: Tracing the Roots of Development and Democracy*. New York: Columbia University Press.

Krishnamurthy, Mekhala. 2018. "Reconceiving the Grain Heap: Margins and Movements on the Market Floor." *Contributions to Indian Sociology* 52/1: 28–52.

Kulke, Hermann. 1976. "Kshatriyaization and Social Change." In *Aspects of Changing India: Studies in Honour of Prof. G. S. Ghurye*, ed. S. D. Pallai and Govind S. Ghurye. Bombay: Popular Prakashan, 398–409.

Kymlicka, Will. 2002. *Contemporary Political Philosophy: An Introduction*. Oxford: Clarendon Press.

LaFontaine, Jean. 1985. "Person and Individual: Some Anthropological Reflections." In *The Category of the Person*, ed. Michael Carrithers, S. Collins, and S. Lukes. Cambridge: Cambridge University Press, 123–42.

Laidlaw, James. 2000. "A Free Gift Makes No Friends." *Journal of the Royal Anthropological Institute* 6/4: 617–34.

———. 2013. *The Subject of Virtue: An Anthropology of Ethics and Freedom*. Cambridge: Cambridge University Press.

Lambek, Michael, ed. 2010. *Ordinary Ethics: Anthropology, Language, and Action*. New York: Fordham University Press.

Latour, Bruno. 2005. *Reassembling the Social: An Introduction to Actor-Network-Theory*. Oxford: Oxford University Press.

Law, John. 1986. *Power, Action, and Belief: A New Sociology of Knowledge?* London: Routledge.

Leach, Edmund. 1957. "The Epistemological Background to Malinowski's Empiricism." In *Man and Culture*, ed. Raymond Firth. New York: Harper Torchbooks, 119–38.

Lee, Richard B. 2012 [1984]. *The Dobe Ju/'Hoansi*. 4th ed. Belmont, CA: Wadsworth.

Lerche, Jens. 1993. "Dominant Castes, Rajas, Brahmins and Inter-Caste Exchange Relations in Coastal Orissa: Behind the Facade of the '*Jajmani* System.'" *Contributions to Indian Sociology* 27/2: 237–66.

Levi, Scott C. 1994. *The Banjaras: Medieval Indian Peddlers and Military Commissariat*. Madison: University of Wisconsin Press.

Lévi-Strauss, Claude. 1969 [1949]. *The Elementary Structures of Kinship*. Trans. J. H. Bell, J. R. Sturmer, and R. Needham. Boston: Beacon Press.

Lewis, Herbert. 1998. "The Misrepresentations of Anthropology and Its Consequences." *American Anthropologist* 100/3: 716–31.

Lincoln, Bruce. 1991. *Death, War, and Sacrifice: Studies in Ideology and Practice*. Chicago: University of Chicago Press.

Lorenzen, David N. 1978. "Warrior Ascetics in Indian History." *Journal of the American Oriental Society* 98/1: 61–75.

Lovejoy, Arthur O. 1936. *The Great Chain of Being: A Study of the History of an Idea*. Cambridge, MA: Harvard University Press.

Lukes, Steven. 1973. *Individualism*. Oxford: Basil Blackwell.

Macfarlane, Alan. 1978. *The Origins of English Individualism: The Family, Property and Social Transition*. Oxford: Basil Blackwell.

———. 1993. "Louis Dumont and the Origins of Individualism." *Cambridge Anthropology* 16/1: 1–28.

Mahmood, Saba. 2011. *Politics of Piety: The Islamic Revival and the Feminist Subject.* 2d ed. Princeton, NJ: Princeton University Press.

Maine, Henry J. S. 1861. *Ancient Law: Its Connection with the Early History of Society, and Its Relation to Modern Ideas.* London: John Murray.

Majumdar, D. N., et al. 1955. "Inter-Caste Relations in Gohanakallan, a Village near Lucknow." *Eastern Anthropologist* 8/3: 191–215.

Malamoud, Charles. 1982. "On the Rhetoric and Semantics of *Purusartha.*" In *Way of Life: King, Householder, Renouncer,* ed. T. N. Madan. New Delhi: Vikas, 33–54.

Malara, Diego M., and Tom Boylston. 2016. "Vertical Love: Forms of Submission and Top-Down Power in Orthodox Ethiopia." *Social Analysis* 61/4: 40–57.

Malcolm, John. 1832. *A Memoir of Central India.* 2 vols. London: Parbury, Allen & Co.

Malinowski, Bronislaw. 1922. *Argonauts of the Western Pacific.* London: Routledge.

Mandal, Debabrata. 1998. *Social Structure and Cultural Change in the Saharia Tribe.* New Delhi: V. K. Gupta.

Mandawari Village Crime Notebook (VCNB). 1973–present. Begun police station.

Mandelbaum, David G. 1970. *Society in India.* 2 vols. Berkeley: University of California Press.

Manor, James. 1997. "Karnataka: Caste, Class, Dominance and Politics in a Cohesive Society." In *Politics in India,* ed. Sudipta Kaviraj. Delhi: Oxford University Press, 322–61.

———. 2010. "Prologue: Caste and Politics in Recent Times." In *Caste in Indian Politics,* ed. Rajni Kothari. 2d ed., rev. James Manor. Delhi: Orient Blackswan, xi–lxi.

Manu. 1886. *The Laws of Manu: Translated, with Extracts from Seven Commentaries.* Trans. and ed. Georg Bühler. Oxford: Clarendon Press.

Manucci, Niccolao. 1907 [1708]. *Storia do Mogor, or Mogul India, 1653–1708.* Trans. and ed. William Irvine. 3 vols. London: John Murray.

Marriott, McKim. 1959. "Interactional and Attributional Theory of Caste Ranking." *Man in India* 39/12: 92–107.

———. 1960. *Caste Ranking and Community Structure in Five Regions of India and Pakistan.* Poona: Deccan College Postgraduate Research Institute.

———. 1968. "Caste Ranking and Food Transactions: A Matrix Analysis." In *Structure and Change in Indian Society,* ed. Milton B. Singer and Bernard S. Cohn. New York: Current Anthropology for the Wenner-Gren Foundation for Anthropological Research, 133–71.

———. 1969. Review of *Homo Hierarchicus* by L. Dumont. *American Anthropologist* 71/1: 155–75.

———. 1976. "Hindu Transactions: Diversity without Dualism." In *Transaction and Meaning: Directions in the Anthropology of Exchange and Symbolic Behavior,* ed. Bruce Kapferer. Philadelphia: Institute for the Study of Human Issues, 109–42.

———. 1978. "Intimacy and Rank in Food." Paper delivered at 10th International

Congress of Anthropological and Ethnological Sciences, New Delhi, 10–18 December.

Marriott, McKim, and Ronald Inden. 1973. "Caste Systems." In *Encyclopaedia Britannica, Vol. 3*. Chicago: Encyclopaedia Britannica, Inc., 982–91.

———. 1977. "Toward an Ethnosociology of South Asian Caste Systems." In *The New Wind: Changing Identities in South Asia*, ed. Kenneth A. David. The Hague: Mouton, 227–38.

Masters, Brian. 1990. *Maharana: The Story of the Rulers of Udaipur*. Ahmedabad: Grantha.

Matras, Yaron. 2004. "The Role of Language in Mystifying and Demystifying Gypsy Culture." In *The Role of the Romanies: Images and Counter-Images of "Gypsies"/Romanies in European Cultures*, ed. Nicholas Saul and Susan Tebutt. Liverpool: University of Liverpool Press, 53–78.

Matthai, John. 1915. *Village Government in British India*. London: T. Fisher Unwin.

Mauss, Marcel. 2002 [1925]. *The Gift*. Trans. I. Cunnison. New York: W. W. Norton.

Mayaram, Shail. 1991. "Criminality or Community? Alternative Constructions of the Mev Narrative of Darya Khan." *Contributions to Indian Sociology* (n.s.) 25/1: 57–84.

———. 2003. *Against History, Against State: Counterperspectives from the Margins*. New York: Columbia University Press.

Mayer, Adrian C. 1960. *Caste and Kinship in Central India*. London: Routledge & Kegan Paul.

Mehrotra, Raja R. 1977. *Sociology of Secret Languages*. Simla: Indian Institute of Advanced Study.

Metcalf, Barbara, and Thomas Metcalf. 2006. *A Concise History of Modern India*. 2d ed. Cambridge: Cambridge University Press.

Michelutti, Lucia. 2008. *The Vernacularisation of Democracy: Politics, Caste, and Religion in India*. New Delhi: Routledge.

Mines, Diane P. 2005. *Fierce Gods: Inequality, Ritual and the Politics of Dignity in a South Indian Village*. Bloomington: Indiana University Press.

———. 2014. "Remnants of Patronage and the Making of Tamil Valaiyar Pasts." In *Patronage as Politics in South Asia*, ed. Anastasia Piliavsky. Cambridge: Cambridge University Press, 80–103.

Mines, Mattison. 1988. "Conceptualizing the Person: Hierarchical Society and Individual Autonomy in India." *American Anthropologist* 90/3: 568–79.

———. 1992. "Individuality and Achievement in South Indian Social History." *Modern Asian Studies* 26/1: 129–56.

———. 1994. *Public Faces, Private Voices: Community and Individuality in South India*. Berkeley: University of California Press.

Mines, Mattison, and Vijayalakshmi Gourishankar. 1990. "Leadership and Individuality in South Asia." *Journal of Asian Studies* 49/4: 761–86.

Moffatt, Michael. 1979. *An Untouchable Community in South India: Structure and Consensus.* Princeton, NJ: Princeton University Press.

Monier-Williams, Monier. 1876. *A Sanskrit-English Dictionary Etymologically and Philologically Arranged, with Special Reference to Greek, Latin, Gothic, German, Anglo-Saxon, and Other Cognate Indo-European Languages.* Oxford: Clarendon Press.

Moodie, Megan. 2015. *We Were Adivasis: Aspiration in an Indian Scheduled Tribe.* Chicago: University of Chicago Press.

Morgan, Lewis Henry. 1881. *Houses and House-life of the American Aborigines.* Chicago: University of Chicago Press.

Mosko, Mark. 2010. "Partible Penitents: Dividual Personhood and Christian Practice in Melanesia and the West." *Journal of the Royal Anthropological Institute* 16/2: 215–40.

Mosko, Mark, and Margaret Jolly, eds. 1994. *Transformations of Hierarchy: Structure, History and Horizon in the Austronesian World.* London: Routledge. Special issue of *History and Anthropology* 7/1–4.

Munn, Nancy. 1992. *The Fame of Gawa: A Symbolic Study of Value Tansformation in a Massim (Papua New Guinea) Society.* Durham, NC: Duke University Press.

Nesfield, John C. 1883. "The Kanjars of Upper India." *Calcutta Review* 77: 368–98.

De Neve, Geert. 2000. "Patronage and 'Community': The Role of a Tamil 'Village' Festival in the Integration of a Town." *Journal of the Royal Anthropological Institute* 6/3: 501–19.

Nigam, Sanjay. 1990a. "Disciplining and Policing the 'Criminals by Birth,' Part 1: The Making of a Colonial Stereotype—The Criminal Tribes and Castes of North India." *Indian Economic and Social History Review* 27/2: 131–64.

———. 1990b. "Disciplining and Policing the 'Criminals by Birth,' Part 2: The Development of a Disciplinary System, 1871–1900." *Indian Economic and Social History Review* 27/3: 257–87.

Olivelle, Patrick, ed. 2009. *Dharma: Studies in Its Semantic, Cultural and Religious History.* Delhi: Motilal Banarsidas.

O'Malley, Lewis S. S. 1925. *History of Bengal, Bihar and Orissa under British Rule.* Calcutta: Bengal Secretariat Book Depot.

Ortner, Sherry. 1984. "Theory in Anthropology since the Sixties." *Comparative Studies in Society and History* 26/1: 126–66.

Osella, Filippo. 2014. "The (Im)morality of Mediation and Patronage in South India and the Gulf." In *Patronage as Politics in South Asia,* ed. Anastasia Piliavsky. Cambridge: Cambridge University Press, 365–94.

Ovington, John. 1928 [1689]. *A Voyage to Surat in the Year 1689*. London: Jacob Tonson.

Oxford English Dictionary. 2004. 2d ed. Oxford: Oxford University Press.

Pande, Ram. 1974. *Agrarian Movement in Rajasthan*. Delhi: University Publishers India.

Pandian, Anand, and Daud Ali. 2010. *Ethical Life in South Asia*. Bloomington: Indiana University Press.

Parry, Jonathan P. 1979. *Caste and Kinship in Kangra*. London: Routledge & Kegan Paul.

———. 1986. "*The Gift*, the Indian Gift and the 'Indian Gift.'" *Man* (n.s.) 21/3: 453–73.

———. 1989. "On the Moral Perils of Exchange." In *Money and the Morality of Exchange*, ed. Jonathan Parry and Maurice Bloch. Cambridge: Cambridge University Press, 64–93.

———. 1991. "The Hindu Lexicographer? A Note on Auspiciousness and Purity." *Contributions to Indian Sociology* (n.s.) 25/2: 267–85.

———. 1994. *Death in Banaras*. Cambridge: Cambridge University Press.

———. 1998. "Mauss, Dumont and the Distinction between Status and Power." In *Marcel Mauss: A Centenary Tribute*, ed. Wendy James and Nicholas J. Allen. Oxford: Berghahn Books, 151–74.

Parsons, Talcott. 1970. "Equality and Inequality in Modern Society, or Social Stratification Revisited." *Sociological Inquiry* 40/2: 13–72.

Passi, Alessandro. 2001. *Dharmacauryarasāyana* (*L'Elisir del furto secondo il dharma*). Milan: Edizioni Ariele.

———. 2005. "Perverted *Dharma*? Ethics of Thievery in the *Dharmacauryarasāyana*." *Journal of Indian Philosophy* 33/4: 513–28.

Peabody, Norbert. 1991a. "In Whose Turban Does the Lord Reside? The Objectification of Charisma and the Fetishism of Objects in the Hindu Kingdom of Kota." *Comparative Studies in Society and History* 33/4: 726–54.

———. 1991b. "*Koṭā Mahājagat*, or the Great Universe of Kota: Sovereignty and Territory in 18th century Rajasthan." *Contributions to Indian Sociology* 25/1: 29–56.

———. 2003. *Hindu Kingship and Polity in Pre-colonial India*. Cambridge: Cambridge University Press.

Peacock, Vita. 2013. "Agency and the *Anstoß*: Max Planck Directors as Fichtean Subjects." *Anthropology in Action* 20/2: 6–16.

———. 2015. "The Negation of Hierarchy and Its Consequences." *Anthropological Theory* 15/1: 3–21.

———. 2016. "Academic Precarity as Hierarchical Dependence in the Max Planck Society." *HAU: Journal of Ethnographic Theory* 6/1: 95–119.

Piliavsky, Anastasia. 2011. "A Secret in the Oxford Sense: Thieves and the Rhetoric of Mystification in Rural India." *Comparative Studies in Society and History* 53/2: 290–313.

———. 2013a. "Borders without Borderlands: On the Social Reproduction of State Demarcation in Western India." In *Borderland Lives in Northern South Asia*, ed. David N. Gellner, 24–45. Durham, NC: Duke University Press.

———. 2013b. "The Moghia Menace, or the Watch over Watchmen in British India." *Modern Asian Studies* 47/3: 751–79.

———, ed. 2014a. *Patronage as Politics in South Asia*. Cambridge: Cambridge University Press.

———. 2014b. Introduction to *Patronage as Politics in South Asia*, ed. Anastasia Piliavsky. Cambridge: Cambridge University Press, 1–35.

———. 2014c. "India's Demotic Democracy and Its 'Depravities' in the Ethnographic *Longue Durée*." In *Patronage as Politics in South Asia*, ed. Anastasia Piliavsky. Cambridge: Cambridge University Press, 154–75.

———. 2015a. "The 'Criminal Tribe' in India before the British." *Comparative Studies in Society and History* 57/2: 323–54.

———. 2015b. "India's Human Democracy." *Anthropology Today* 31/4: 22–25.

———. 2015c. "Patronage and Community in a Society of Thieves." *Contributions to Indian Sociology* 49/2: 135–61.

Pinch, William R. 2006. *Warrior Ascetics and Indian Empires*. New York: Cambridge University Press.

Pirie, Fernanda, and Judith Scheele. 2014. "Justice, Community, and Law." In *Legalism: Community and Justice*, ed. Fernanda Pirie and Judith Scheele. Oxford: Oxford University Press, 1–24.

Pitt-Rivers, Julian A. 1968. "The Stranger, the Guest and the Hostile Host: Introduction to the Study of the Laws of Hospitality." In *Contributions to Mediterranean Sociology*, ed. John G. Peristiany. The Hague: Mouton, 13–30.

Platts, John T. 1884. *A Dictionary of Urdu, Classical Hindi, and English*. London: W. H. Allen & Co.

Plowden, Chichele W. 1883. *Report on the Census of British India Taken on the 17th February 1881*. London: Eyre & Spottiswoode.

Pocock, David F. 1955. "The Movement of Castes." *Man* 55: 71–72.

———. 1973. *Mind, Body and Wealth: A Study in Belief and Practice in an Indian Village*. Oxford: Basil Blackwell.

———. 1988. "Persons, Texts and Morality." *International Journal of Moral and Social Studies* 3/3: 201–16.

Price, Pamela. 1989. "Kingly Models in Indian Political Behavior: Culture as a Medium of History." *Asian Survey* 29/6: 559–72.

Price, Pamela, and Arild E. Ruud. 2010. *Power and Influence in South Asia: Bosses, Lords, and Captains*. London: Routledge.

Qanungo, Kalika R. 1960. *Studies in Rajput History*. Delhi: S. Chand & Co.

Quigley, Declan. 1993. *The Interpretation of Caste*. Oxford: Clarendon Press.

———. 2005. *The Character of Kingship*. Oxford: Berg.

Radcliffe-Brown, A. R. 1965. "On Social Structure." In *Structure and Function in Primitive Society*. New York: Free Press, 188–204.

Radhakrishna, Meena. 1989. "The Criminal Tribes Act in Madras Presidency: Implications for Itinerant Trading Communities." *Indian Economic and Social History Review* 26/3: 269–95.

———. 1992. "Surveillance and Settlements under the Criminal Tribes Act in Madras." *Indian Economic and Social History Review* 29/2: 171–98.

———. 2001. *Dishonoured by History: "Criminal Tribes" and British Colonial Policy*. Hyderabad: Orient Longman.

Raheja, Gloria G. 1988a. "India: Caste, Kingship and Dominance Reconsidered." *Annual Review of Anthropology* 17: 497–522.

———. 1988b. *The Poison in the Gift: Ritual, Prestation, and the Dominant Caste in a North Indian Village*. Chicago: University of Chicago Press.

———. 1989. "Centrality, Mutuality, and Hierarchy: Shifting Aspects of Inter-Caste Relationship in North India." *Contributions to Indian Sociology* (n.s.) 23/1: 79–101.

Rajasthan Kesari. 29 May 1921.

Raheja, Gloria G., and Ann G. Gold. 1994. *Listen to the Heron's Words: Reimagining Gender and Kinship in North India*. Berkeley: University of California Press.

Rana, Mahendra S. 2006. *India Votes: Lok Sabha and Vidhan Sabha Elections 2001– 2005*. New Delhi: Sarup & Sons.

Rathore, Aakash S., and Rimina Mohapatra, eds. 2017. *Hegel's India: A Reinterpretation, with Texts*. Delhi: Oxford University Press.

Rawat, Ramnarayan S. 2011. *Reconsidering Untouchability: Chamars and Dalit History in North India*. Bloomington: Indiana University Press.

Rawat, Ramnarayan S., and K. Satyanarayana, eds. 2016. *Dalit Studies*. Durham, NC: Duke University Press.

Richards, John F. 1978. *Kingship and Authority in South Asia*. Madison: University of Wisconsin Press.

———. 1995. *The Mughal Empire*. Cambridge: Cambridge University Press.

Richards, John F., and V. N. Rao. 1980. "Banditry in Mughal India: Historical and Folk Perceptions." *Indian Economic and Social History Review* 27/1: 95–120.

Richardson, David. 1803. "An Account of Bazeegars, a Sect Commonly Denominated Nuts." *Asiatic Researches* 7: 451–79.

Rio, Knut. 2014. "Melanesian Egalitarianism: The Containment of Hierarchy." *Anthropological Theory* 14/2: 169–90.

Rio, Knut, and Olaf Smedal. 2009. *Hierarchy: Persistence and Transformation in Social Formations*. London: Berghahn Books.

Risley, Herbert H. 1908. *The People of India*. Calcutta: Thacker, Spink & Co.

Robbins, Joel. 1994. "Equality as a Value: Ideology in Dumont, Melanesia and the West." *Social Analysis* 36 (October): 21–70.

———. 2004. *Becoming Sinners: Christianity and Moral Torment in a Papua New Guinea Society*. Berkeley: University of California Press.

———. 2013a. "Beyond the Suffering Subject: Toward an Anthropology of the Good." *Journal of the Royal Anthropological Institute* 19/3: 447–62.

———. 2013b. "Monism, Pluralism and the Structure of Value Relations: A Dumontian Contribution to the Contemporary Study of Value." *HAU: Journal of Ethnographic Theory* 3/1: 99–115.

———. 2015. "Dumont's Hierarchical Dynamism: Christianity and Individualism Revisited." *Hau: Journal of Ethnographic Theory* 5/1: 173–95.

Robbins, Joel, and Jukka Siikala. 2014. "Hierarchy and Hybridity: Toward a Dumontian Approach to Contemporary Cultural Change." *Anthropological Theory* 14/2: 121–32.

Rose, Horace A. 1908. "Hindu Betrothal Observances in the Punjab." *Journal of the Royal Anthropological Institute of Great Britain and Ireland* 38: 409–18.

Rose, Horace A., et al. 1911. *A Glossary of the Tribes and Castes of the Punjab and North-West Frontier Province: Based on the Census Report for the Punjab, 1883. 3 vols*. Lahore: Superintendent Government Printing, Punjab.

Rosen, Lawrence. 2006. *Law as Culture: An Invitation*. Princeton, NJ: Princeton University Press.

Rüdinger, Johann C. C. 1990 [1782]. "Von der Sprache und Herkunft der Zigeuner aus Inden." In *Neuester Zuwachs der teuutschen, fremden und allgemeinen Sprachkunde in eigen Aufsätzen*. Hamburg: Buske, 37–84.

Russell, Robert V. 1916. *The Tribes and Castes of the Central Provinces of India*. 4 vols. London: Macmillan.

Saeed, Fouzia. 2001. *Taboo! The Hidden Culture of a Red-Light Area*. New Delhi: Oxford University Press.

Sahlins, Marshall. 1958. *Social Stratification in Polynesia*. Seattle: University of Washington Press.

———. 1972. "The Original Affluent Society." In *Stone Age Economics*. London: Tavistock, 1–39.

———. 1981. "The Stranger-King or Dumézil among the Fijians." *Journal of Pacific History* 16/3: 107–32.

———. 1983. "Other Times, Other Customs: The Anthropology of History." *American Anthropologist* 85/3: 517–44.

———. 1985. *Islands of History*. Chicago: University of Chicago Press.

———. 1999a. "Two or Three Things I Know About Culture." *Journal of the Royal Anthropological Institute* 5: 399–421.

———. 1999b. "What Is Anthropological Enlightenment? Some Lessons of the Twentieth Century." *Annual Review of Anthropology* 28/1: i–xxiii.

———. 2008. "The Stranger-king, or Elementary Forms of the Politics of Life." *Indonesia and the Malay World* 36/105:177–99.

———. 2010. "The Whole Is a Part: Intercultural Politics of Order and Change." In *Experiments with Holism: Theory and Practice in Contemporary Anthropology*, ed. Ton Otto and Nils Bubandt. London: Wiley-Blackwell, 102–26.

———. 2015. "An Anthropological Manifesto: Or the Origin of the State." *Anthropology Today* 31/2: 8–11.

———. 2017. "The Original Political Society." In David Graeber and Marshall Sahlins, *On Kings*. Chicago: University of Chicago Press, 23–64.

Saller, Richard P. 1984. "*Familia, Domus*, and the Roman Conception of the Family." *Phoenix* 38/4: 336–55.

Sather, Clifford. 2006. "'All Threads Are White': Iban Egalitarianism Reconsidered." In *Origins, Ancestors and Alliance: Explorations in Austronesian Ethnography*, ed. James J. Fox and Clifford Sather. Canberra: Australian National University Press, 73–105.

Saul, Nicholas, and Susan Tebutt, eds. 2004. *The Role of the Romanies: Images and Counter-Images of "Gypsies"/Romanies in European Cultures*. Liverpool: University of Liverpool Press.

Saussure, Ferdinand de. 2011 [1916]. *Course in General Linguistics*. Trans. W. Baskin. London: Duckworth.

Saxena, S. S, and Padmaja Sharma. 1972. *Bijoliyā Kisān Āndolan kā Itihās.* Bikaner: Rajasthan State Archives.

Sbriccoli, Tommaso. 2016. "Land, Labour and Power: A Malwa Village, 1954–2012." *Economic and Political Weekly* 51/26–27: 8–16.

Scheffler, Samuel. 2010. *Equality and Tradition: Questions of Value in Moral and Political Theory*. Oxford: Oxford University Press.

Sen, Amritopura. 2017. "Caste, Networks and Work in West Bengal." PhD diss., National University of Singapore.

Servan-Schreiber, Catherine. 2003. "Tellers of Tales, Sellers of Tales: Bhojpuri Peddlers in Northern India." In *Society and Circulation: Mobile People and Itinerant Cultures in South Asia, 1750–1950*, ed. Claude Markovitz et al. Delhi: Permanent Black, 275–305.

Shah, A. M., and R. G. Shroff. 1958. "The Vahīvanca Bāroṭs of Gujarat: A Caste of Genealogists and Mythographers." *Journal of American Folklore* 71/281: 246–76.

Shah, Popatlal G. 1967. *Vimukta Jatis: Denotified Communities in Western India*. Bombay: Gujarat Research Society.

Shāh, Vāris. 1966 [1766]. *The Adventures of Hir and Ranjha*. Ed. M. Hasan. Trans. C. F. Usborne. Karachi: Lion Art Press.

Sharma, Girija S. 2005. *Sources on Social and Economic History of Rajasthan, 17th–20th century AD*. Bikaner: Vikas Prakashan.

Sharma, Gopi N. 1970. *Rajasthan Studies*. Agra: Lakshmi Narayan Agrawal Educational Publishers.

Sharma, Ursula. 1978. "Women and Their Affines: The Veil as a Symbol of Separation." *Man* (n.s.) 13: 218–33.

Sherring, Matthew A. 1872. *Hindu Tribes and Castes as Represented in Benares*. London: Trubner.

Shryock, Andrew. 1997. "Bedouin in Suburbia: Redrawing the Boundaries of Urbanity and Tribalism in Amman, Jordan." *Arab Studies Journal* 1: 40–56.

———. 2004. "The New Jordanian Hospitality: House, Host, and Guest in the Culture of Public Display." *Comparative Studies in Society and History* 46/1: 35–62.

———. 2013. "It's This, Not That: How Marshall Sahlins Solves Kinship." *HAU: Journal of Ethnographic Theory* 3/2: 271–79.

Shulman, David. 1980. "On South Indian Bandits and Kings." *Indian Economic and Social History Review* 17/3: 283–306.

———. 1985. *The King and the Clown in South Indian Myth and Poetry*. Princeton, NJ: Princeton University Press.

Singer, Milton. 1964. "The Social Organization of Indian Civilization." *Diogenes* 12/45: 84–119.

———. 1972. "Industrial Leadership, the Hindu Ethic, and the Spirit of Socialism." In *When a Great Tradition Modernizes: An Anthropological Approach to Indian Civilization*, ed. Milton Singer. New York: Praeger, 272–380.

Singh, Bhrigupati. 2015. *Poverty and the Quest for Life: Spiritual and Material Striving in Rural India*. Chicago: University of Chicago Press.

Singh, R. C. P. 1996. *Kingship in Northern India*. Delhi: Motilal Banarsidas.

Singh, B. P. 2004. "Kanjars." In *The People of Punjab*. Delhi: Manoharlal.

Singha, Radhika. 1993. "'Providential Circumstances': The Thuggee Campaign of the 1830s and Legal Innovation." *Modern Asian Studies* 27/1: 83–146.

———. 1998. *A Despotism of Law: Crime and Justice in Early Colonial India*. Delhi: Oxford University Press.

Singhji, Virbhadra. 1994. *The Rajputs of Saurashtra*. Bombay: Popular Prakashan.

Sinha, R. K. 1992. "The Extent of Rajputization among the Bhilala of Malwa." *Journal of the Indian Anthropological Society* 27: 239–46.

Sinha, Surajit. 1962. "State Formation and Rajput Myth in Central India." *Man in India* 42/1: 35–80.

Skaria, Ajay. 1998. "Being *Jangli*: The Politics of Wilderness." *Studies in History* 14/2: 193–215.

———. 1999. *Hybrid Histories: Forests, Frontiers and Wildness in Western India.* Delhi: Oxford University Press.

Sleeman, William H. 1836. *Ramaseeana, or a Vocabulary of the Particular Language Used by the Thugs.* Calcutta: G. H. Gutman, Military Orphan Press.

———. 1839. *The Thugs or Phansigars of India.* 2 vols. Philadelphia: Carey & Hart.

———. 1840. *Report on the Depredations Committed by the Thug Gangs of Upper and Central India, from the Cold Season of 1836–37, Down to Their Gradual Suppression, under the Operation of the Measures Adopted against Them by the Supreme Government, in the Year 1839.* Calcutta: G. H. Huttmann, Bengal Military Orphan Press.

———. 1844. *Rambles and Recollections of an Indian Official.* 2 vols. London: J. Hatchard & Son.

———. 1849. *Report on the Budhuk Alias Bagree Decoits and Other Gang Robbers by Hereditary Profession and on the Measures Adopted by the Government of India, for Their Suppression.* Calcutta: J. C. Sherriff, Bengal Military Orphan Press.

Sneath, David. 2018. "The Savage Noble: Alternity and Aristocracy in Anthropology." In *Who Are "We": Reimagining Affinity and Alternity in Anthropology*, ed. Liana Chua and Nayanika Mathur. London: Berghahn Books, 60–94.

Snodgrass, Jeffrey G. 2004. "The Centre Cannot Hold: Tales of Hierarchy and Poetic Composition from Modern Rajasthan." *Journal of the Royal Anthropological Institute* 10/2: 261–85.

———. 2006. *Casting Kings: Bards and Indian Modernity.* Oxford: Oxford University Press.

Srinivas, Mysore N. 1952a. *Religion and Society among the Coorgs of Southern India.* Oxford: Clarendon Press.

———. 1952b. "Social Anthropology and Sociology." *Sociological Bulletin* 1/1: 28–37.

———. 1956. "A Note on Sanskritization and Westernization." *Journal of Asian Studies* 15/4: 481–96.

———. 1959. "The Dominant Caste in Rampura." *American Anthropologist* 61/1: 1–16.

———. 1968. *Social Change in Modern India.* Berkeley: University of California Press.

Srivastava, Gursharan L. 1957. *Indian Elections and Election Petitions: A Book of Complete and Up-to-Date Information on Fact, Law and Procedure in Regard to All Elections, Meant for Everybody, Whether Trained in Law or Not.* Delhi: Eastern Book Co.

Srivastava, Piyush. 2005. "Forget Tigers, Peacocks Are Going Extinct Too." *Indian Express*. Lucknow, 17 August.

Stasch, Rupert. 2009. *Society of Others: Kinship and Mourning in a West Papuan Place*. Berkeley: University of California Press.

Stein, Burton. 1980. *Peasant, State and Society in Medieval South India*. Delhi: Oxford University Press.

Steinhoff, Uwe. 2015. *Do All Persons Have Equal Moral Worth? On "Basic Equality" and Equal Respect and Concern*. New York: Oxford University Press.

Strathern, Marilyn. 1988. *The Gender of the Gift: Problems with Women and Problems with Society in Melanesia*. Berkeley: University of California Press.

———. 1992. "Parts and Wholes." In *Conceptualizing Society*, ed. Adam Kuper. London: Routledge, 75–104.

Subha, K. 1997. *Karnataka Panchayat Elections 1995: Process, Issues, and Membership Profile*. New Delhi: Concept Publishing House.

Surana, Pushpendra. 1983. *Social Movements and Social Structure: A Study in the Princely State of Mewar*. New Delhi: Manohar.

Suri, Pushpa. 1977. *Social Conditions in Eighteenth Century Northern India*. Delhi: Delhi University Press.

Tambs-Lyche, Harald. 1997. *Power, Profit, and Poetry: Traditional Society in Kathiawar, Western India*. New Delhi: Manohar.

Tapper, Nancy. 1991. *Bartered Brides: Politics, Gender and Marriage in an Afghan Tribal Society*. Cambridge: Cambridge University Press.

Tarlo, Emma. 1996. *Clothing Matters: Dress and Identity in India*. London: Hurst.

Tawney, C. H., trans. and ed. 1901. *The Prabandhacintāmaṇi, or Wishingstone of Narratives*. Calcutta: Asiatic Society.

The Telegraph. 1998. "Gang of Pardhis Busted." Calcutta, 31 July.

Tessitori, Luigi P. 1917. *Bardic and Historical Survey of Rajputana: A Descriptive Catalogue*. Calcutta: Asiatic Society of Bengal.

Tilche, Alice, and Edward Simpson. 2017. "On Trusting Ethnography: Serendipity and the Reflexive Return to the Fields of Gujarat." *Journal of the Royal Anthropological Institute* 23/4: 690–708.

The Times Higher Education Supplement. 26 March 2007. (https://www.timeshighereducation.com/news/most-cited-authors-of-books-in-the-humanities-2007/405956.article?storyCode=405956&sectioncode=26).

Tocqueville, Alexis de. 2000 [1835]. *Democracy in America*. Trans. and ed. Delba Winthrop and Harvey C. Mansfield. Chicago: University of Chicago Press.

Tod, James. 1920 [1829–32]. *Annals and Antiquities of Rajasthan, or the Central and Western Rajput States of India*, ed. William Crooke. 3 vols. London: Oxford University Press.

Tolen, Rachel J. 1991. "Colonizing and Transforming the Criminal Tribesman: The Salvation Army in British India." *American Ethnologist* 18/1: 106–25.

Tönnies, Ferdinand. 1957 [1887]. *Community and Society.* Trans. C. Loomis. East Lansing: Michigan State University Press.

Trawick, Margaret. 1990. *Notes on Love in a Tamil Family.* Berkeley: University of California Press.

Trivedi, Madhu. 1999. "Tradition and Transition: The Performing Arts in Medieval North India." *Medieval History Journal* 2/1: 73–110.

———. 2002. "Female Performing Artists in North India: A Survey." In *Art and Culture: Painting and Perspective, Vol. 2*, ed. Ahsan J. Qaisar and Som P. Verma. New Delhi: Abhinav Publications, 153–71.

Turner, Ralph L. 1926. "The Position of Romani in Indo-Aryan." *Journal of the Gypsy Lore Society* (3d s.) 5: 145–89.

Ujwal, K. D. S. n.d. *Bhagawatī Śrī Karṇī Māhārāj.* Ujlan (Marwar): self-published.

Unnithan-Kumar, Maya. 1997. *Identity, Gender and Poverty: New Perspectives on Caste and Tribe in Rajasthan.* Oxford: Berghahn Books.

Urban Dictionary. www.urbandictionary.com.

Vaid, Divya. 2014. "Caste in Contemporary India: Flexibility and Persistence." *Annual Review of Sociology* 40: 391–410.

Vashishta, V. K. 1982. "Abolition of Chandi in the Rajputana States." *Rajasthan History Congress, Proceedings of the Sirohi Session, Vol. 13.* Jaipur: Rajasthan History Congress.

———. 1985. "Transition in the Position of Charan Community in the Princely States of Rajputana during the Colonial Period." *Journal of the University of Baroda.*

Vaudeville, Charlotte. 1996. *Myths, Saints and Legends in Medieval India.* Delhi: Oxford University Press.

Vidal, Denis. 1997. *Violence and Truth: A Rajasthani Kingdom Confronts Colonial Authority.* Delhi: Oxford University Press.

Vij, Shivam. 2010. "An Election in Matsura." *The Caravan: A Journal of Politics and Culture* 2/8.

Vilaça, Aparecida. 2010. *Strange Enemies: Indigenous Agency and Scenes of Encounters in Amazonia.* Durham, NC: Duke University Press.

Village Survey Monographs: Ramnagar Kanjar Colony. 1967. Census of India 1961 Series, Vol. 37. New Delhi: Indian Registrar General, Manager of Publications.

Vischer, Michael P., ed. 2009. *Precedence: Social Differentiation in the Austronesian World.* Canberra: Australian National University Press.

Vitebsky, Piers. 2005. *Reindeer People: Living with Animals and Spirits in Siberia.* London: Harper Collins.

———. 2017. *Living without the Dead: Loss and Redemption in a Jungle Cosmos*. Chicago: University of Chicago Press.

Viveiros de Castro, Eduardo. 1992. *From the Enemy's Point of View: Humanity and Divinity in an Amazonian Society*. Chicago: University of Chicago Press.

———. 2001. "GUT Feelings about Amazonia: Potential Affinity and the Construction of Sociality." In *Beyond the Visible and the Material: The Amerindianization of Society in the Work of Peter Rivière*, ed. Peter Rivière et al. Oxford: Oxford University Press, 19–43.

Wade, Bonnie C. 1998. *Imaging Music: An Ethnomusicological Study of Music, Art, and Culture in Mughal India*. Chicago: University of Chicago Press.

Waghorne, Joanne P. 1985. *Images of Dharma: The Epic World of C. Rajagopalachari*. Delhi: Chanakya Publications.

Wagner, Kim A. 2007. *Thuggee: Banditry and the British in Early Nineteenth-Century India*. Basingstoke, UK: Palgrave Macmillan.

Wagner, Roy. 1991. "The Fractal Person." In *Big Men and Great Men: The Personifications of Power in Melanesia*, ed. Maurice Godelier and Marilyn Strathern. Cambridge: Cambridge University Press, 159–73.

Waldron, Jeremy. 2002. *God, Locke, and Equality: Christian Foundations in Locke's Political Thought*. Cambridge: Cambridge University Press.

———. 2007. "Dignity and Rank." *European Journal of Sociology* 48/2: 201–37.

———. 2008. "The Dignity of Groups." *Acta Juridica* 1: 66–90.

———. 2012. *Dignity, Rank, and Rights*. Oxford: Oxford University Press.

Walker, Benjamin. 1968. *Hindu World: An Encyclopedic Survey of Hinduism*. 2 vols. London: George Allen & Unwin Ltd.

Walker, Harry. 2020. "Equality without Equivalence: An Anthropology of the Common," *Journal of the Royal Anthropological Institute* (n.s.) 26: 146–66.

Walpole, Spencer. 1890. *A History of England from the Conclusion of the Great War in 1815*. London: Longmans, Green.

Washbrook, David. 1991. "'To Each a Language of His Own': Language, Culture, and Society in Colonial India." In *Language, History, and Class*, ed. by Penelope J. Corfield. London: Basil Blackwell, 179–203.

Waterfield, Henry. 1875. *Memorandum on the Census of British India 1871–72*. London: Eyre & Spottiswoode.

Waugh, Linda R. 1982. "Marked and Unmarked: A Choice between Unequals in Semiotic Structure." *Semiotica* 38/3–4: 299–318.

Weisgrau, Maxine. 1997. *Interpreting Development: Local Histories, Local Strategies*. Lanham, MD: University Press of America.

West Bengal State Archives, Foreign (Internal-A), May 1925, proceedings 118–22. Samuel G. Pinhey, Letter (No. 35), 28 May 1925.

Westphal-Hellbusch, Sigrid. 1975. "Changes in the Meaning of Ethnic Names as Exemplified by the Jat, Rabari, Bharvad, and Charan in Northwestern India." In *Pastoralists and Nomads in South Asia*, ed. Lawrence S. Leshnik and Gunther-D. Sontheimer. Wiesbaden: Otto Harrassowitz, 117–38.

Wheeler, J. Talboys. 1867–81. *The History of India, from the Earliest Ages.* 4 vols. London: Trübner.

Whitehead, Henry. 1921. *The Village Gods of South India.* Calcutta: Association Press.

Willerslev, Rane. 2007. *Soul Hunters: Hunting, Animism, and Personhood among the Siberian Yukaghirs.* Berkeley: University of California Press.

Williams, H. L. 1889. "The Criminal and Wandering Tribes of India." *Journal of the Gypsy Lore Society* 6/1: 34–58, 110–35.

Williamson, Thomas. 1810. *The East India Vade-Mecum.* 2 vols. London: Black, Parry & Kingsbury.

Wilson, Horace H., ed. 1855. *A Glossary of Judicial and Revenue Terms, and of Useful Words Occurring in Official Documents Relating to the Administration of the Government of British India.* London: William H. Allen.

Wilson, James. 2007. "Nietzsche and Equality." In *Nietzsche and Ethics*, ed. G. von Tevenar. Oxford: Peter Lang, 221–40.

Wise, James. 1883. *Notes on the Races, Castes and Trades of Eastern Bengal.* London: Harrison & Sons.

Wiser, William H. 1936. *The Hindu Jajmani System: A Socio-Economic System Interrelating Members of a Hindu Village Community in Services.* Lucknow: Lucknow Publishing House.

Witsoe, Jeffrey. 2013. *Democracy against Development: Lower-caste Politics and Political Modernity in Postcolonial India.* Chicago: University of Chicago Press.

Wolf, Eric R. 1966. *Peasants.* Englewood Cliffs, NJ: Prentice-Hall.

Woodburn, James. 1982. "Egalitarian Societies." *Man* 17: 431–51.

Wouters, Jelle. 2015. "Feasts of Merit, Election Feasts or No Feasts? On the Politics of Wining and Dining in Nagaland, Northeast India." *South Asianist* 3/2: 5–23.

Yule, Henry, et al. 1903. *Hobson-Jobson: A Glossary of Colloquial Anglo-Indian Words and Phrases, Etymological, Historical, Geographical and Discursive.* London: John Murray.

Ziegler, Norman P. 1976a. "Marvari Historical Chronicles: Sources for the Social and Cultural History of Rajasthan. *Indian Economic and Social History Review* 13:219–50.

The authorized representative in the EU for product safety and compliance is:
Mare Nostrum Group
B.V Doelen 72
4831 GR Breda
The Netherlands

www.ingramcontent.com/pod-product-compliance
Lightning Source LLC
Chambersburg PA
CBHW031412270326
41929CB00010BA/1425